Enriching the Brain

Published by Jossey-Bass
A Wiley Imprint
989 Market Street, San Francisco, CA 94103-1741   www.josseybass.com

Jossey-Bass books and products are available through most bookstores. To contact Jossey-Bass directly call our Customer Care Department within the U.S. at 800-956-7739, outside the U.S. at 317-572-3986, or fax 317-572-4002.

Jossey-Bass also publishes its books in a variety of electronic formats. Some content that appears in print may not be available in electronic books.

Library of Congress Cataloging-in-Publication Data

Jensen, Eric.
  Enriching the brain: how to maximize every learner's potential / Eric Jensen.
     p. cm.—The Jossey-Bass education series.
  Includes bibliographical references and index.
  ISBN-13: 978-0-7879-7547-0 (cloth)
  ISBN-10: 0-7879-7547-8 (cloth)
  ISBN: 978-0-4702-2389-5 (paper)
  1. Learning, Psychology of. 2. Learning—Physiological aspects. 3. Learning. 4. Brain.
5. Teaching. 6. Educational psychology. I. Title. II. Series.
  LB1057.J46 2006
  370.15'23—dc22   2006014169

Printed in the United States of America
FIRST EDITION
HB Printing   10 9 8 7 6 5 4 3 2
PB Printing   10 9 8 7 6 5 4 3 2 1

More Praise for *Enriching the Brain*

"*Enriching the Brain* effectively reveals the limitations of the traditional 'fixed brain theory' and offers a vivid picture of the human brain as a dynamic and changing organ. It convincingly demonstrates how an enriching environment improves brain functioning and enhances intelligence for all learners."

—Robert Kuklis, professional development associate,
Center for Performance Assessment
and adjunct professor, Sacred Heart University

"This book fills an incredible need. It is time for educators to become familiar with the latest research on learning and the positive message that the neurosciences have for all of us."

—Renate Nummela Caine, professor emeritus of education,
California State University, San Bernadino,
and executive director, The Caine Learning Institute

Dedicated to my wife, Diane. No one has enriched my life more than she has. Thank you.

CONTENTS

FIGURES AND EXHIBITS

EXHIBITS

PREFACE

For most of the past two hundred years, the prevailing view in the scientific and medical world was dominated by Mendelian genetics. That meant, "You are what your parents gave you" and "Things won't get much better—at least not in the brains department." In fact, for most of scientific history, the prevailing paradigm was that humans have a brain of fixed capacity, which simply fills up with experiences and memories during the course of a lifetime. Of course, this brain would grow some in size from birth—but it was believed it reached adult size by the age of ten.

Conventional wisdom also said that intelligence was a fixed number (IQ) and that it stayed that way. This idea of an immutable brain was adopted by many early educators who, once some learners were identified as slow and some as gifted, kept them sequestered with peers as if each had a communicable disease. We now have "special ed," "regular ed," and "gifted ed," almost as if we were sorting laundry or nuts, bolts, and washers. The prevailing view—still found in many schools today—is that students will continue to be the way they are right now. This belief is so widespread that it's the dominant model for most public and private schooling. Indeed, it permeates our society and reaches far beyond our schools, defining the approach of institutions from juvenile detention facilities and adult prisons to nursing homes and senior care residences. Such institutions are beyond my scope in this book, but the insights herein about how the brain changes will be equally useful wherever one looks.

It turns out that the "fixed brain" theory is not just dead wrong, but—embarrassingly—it may be doing a great deal of harm. The human brain is so malleable that it can *be* fixed at artificially low levels by giving it a constant diet of status quo. Millions of students young and old begin to believe that their intellectual destiny is stuck at entry-level testing scores. As a result, millions live lives far below their biological capacity. It's not just a case of an unknown number of Mozarts, Louis Armstrongs, or Einsteins being left as undeveloped seedlings; more commonly, it's a case of many potentially productive members of society becoming low-functioning or dependent on others for everyday living. In addition, there have been countless kids that either dropped out or graduated with no sense of competence, direction, or joy of wonder about learning.

Nonetheless, in spite of a steady diet of revolutionary discoveries about the brain, most policymakers have kept the outdated "fixed brain" paradigm in place. Why? Is it that we collectively want to believe that we are all stuck with the intellectual capital we have? Would that make some people feel superior to others? Would it make some feel comfortable as victims who can blame their troubles on their unalterable inheritance? Or is it simply that the public case for the flexible-brain paradigm has not been made with sufficient power? I see that explanation as the major factor, and *Enriching the Brain* is the latest contribution to my ongoing effort to inform public policy.

A Sketch of the Basic Science

The thesis of this book is that the human brain is a dynamic and changing organ—and that the way we teach, parent, or run our schools can *and does* dramatically change the brains of over 90 percent of all learners. Experience does change brains, and I can provide plenty of evidence to support that assertion. I firmly believe that unless we as educators and parents grasp the significance of this paradigm shift and act on it, we are committing malpractice.

Researchers have learned much about the brain in the past forty years. It changes drastically—as an example, from birth through the teens, the volume of the human brain increases fourfold.[1] And it's not just growth: learning literally changes the brain's *structure*.[2] Even the fully adult human brain can and does generate brand new neurons every day, and certain variables reliably foster this amazing neurogenesis.[3] We can purposefully alter our brain structures and processing by the behaviors we choose.

This suggests an extraordinary capacity to reshape the brain well into our senior years. Most brains can be enriched, and it turns out that so-called slow learners actually benefit from enriched environments just as much or more as the so-called regular or gifted learners. In fact, every brain can become enriched. It's all a matter of degree of enrichment and in what areas. Another way to think of enrichment is that for some it's a more lateral (a wider range) response, and for others it's a more vertical (a deeper, stronger intelligence) response. In either case, all parties win.

Indeed, if you offer the impoverished brain a rich enough environment for a long enough period, the effects can last for years, right through adulthood.[4] Many of the discoveries from animal studies on behavior and development hold true for humans.[5] The massive amounts of data are compelling. Collectively, all of this suggests that the time has come to pause and reexamine our basic thinking about what constitutes learning and enrichment.

Losses and Gains

We all know that the brain is not indestructible. Accidents, trauma, neglect, aging, and drugs of abuse are just some of the potential risk factors. Even the most confirmed advocates of the fixed-brain paradigm will accept that physical and chemical damage do reduce mental capacity. If the human brain is so able to absorb toxins and chaos, wouldn't it make sense that this same brain could absorb positive influences? The research makes it clear that it does.

It takes very little more observation to see that improvement is also constantly occurring. What are the positive factors? They can include smart parenting, nutrition, emotional support, hope, and learning. But one factor stands out: enrichment. Following is the definition of enrichment as it applies to the subject of this book:

> **Enrichment is a positive biological response to a contrasting environment, in which measurable, synergistic, and global changes have occurred.**

Thus enrichment efforts encourage appropriate brain activity at every turn and provide a unique opportunity to positively alter the course of an entire life. Creating enrichment takes less time than applying other learning tools, and it can last longer. It is relatively cheap and can positively influence and even ameliorate some neurological and functional deficits.

Today you probably hear of enrichment all the time. But what does anyone really know about enrichment? What does the relevant research really say about what one can and cannot do? In these days of "doing more with less" and getting the "most bang for the buck," creating enrichment is starting to look more and more practical as a real-world solution to helping students succeed. How, why, and who says so is my subject here. And, as this book will show, it can and should help every learner, whatever his or her starting point, not just the gifted learners that current practice typically includes. The purpose of this book is to explore those questions and discover some relevant answers.

Who Should Read This Book?

If you have any interest in the quality and direction of education, you will find *Enriching the Brain* valuable. And if you are in a position to take action—as a teacher, a school or district leader, a policymaker, or a concerned parent or citizen—this is for you. For the first time ever, you'll find the evidence and support for how you can maximize every learner's potential. The book in your hands can change lives.

Structure of the Book

I begin in Chapter One with a more detailed look at the fixed-brain myth and the reality that actually surrounds us, then explore in Chapter Two the concept of intelligence. These first chapters lay the foundation for the rest of the book by exposing some of the dangerous myths that can actually hold back students eager to learn and develop capacity. Chapter Three provides the core science needed to understand the what, why, and how of enrichment. You'll learn who the pioneers were as well as discover the key studies that influenced our views of what can and cannot be changed in our brains. Chapter Four details the growing brain, from birth through school age. You'll find out what enrichment means at each age and how you can maximize the potential of your child—or any growing child. Brains have different vulnerabilities and different opportunities at each age, and you'll discover the risks and strategies for intervention.

The next chapter looks at particular children with extraordinary opportunities for enrichment. Those from poverty and those with special needs (often these groups overlap) create exceptional opportunities for positive change in the brain. In fact, after reading these chapters, you might rethink your own treatment of those from disadvantaged circumstances. Chapter Six explores the brains at the other end of the spectrum, those labeled as gifted. Here we ask critical questions such as, "Are the brains of gifted children really any different?" You'll get a hard look at what the behavioral and biological evidence tells us about this small subset of the population. The next chapter takes what we've explored so far and broadens the scope. What would policy decisions look like in a school or district in which creating enrichment is the norm, not the exception? The practical issues are dealt with in simple, doable steps. We can make schooling enriching for over 90 percent of all students, and this chapter tells how. Teachers are fairly practical by nature, so

Chapter Eight is packed with specific examples of what an enriched classroom would look, sound, and feel like. You'll get realistic examples from other schools that have made the commitment to enrich every child possible. As you might guess, parents can play a crucial role in this process too. Chapter Nine explores the nuts and bolts of what parenting can contribute to the enrichment formula, especially in early childhood. Parents will get specific, practical, and free or nearly free strategies that will work on almost any child to maximize potential. The final chapter brings theory and practice together and makes a strong call for changing from a "deficit-based model" to an "enrichment-based model" in which schools and their staff commit to the principles of nurturing, growing, and maximizing human potential. Finally, we'll tie up any loose ends, summarize what's next, and make recommendations for the immediate future.

Looking Forward

It's safe to say that few words are as loaded in the educational world as *enrichment*. For many it isn't clear exactly what it is—but it's got to be better than no enrichment. Others may have negative feelings, falsely believing that it's only for the children of some mysterious elite. This book clears up the myths and provides a clear road map for what to do and how to do it. Also, by making a distinction between basic learning, other positive factors, and enrichment, it helps the whole educational community—from parents through policymakers—decide what each and every special population needs to succeed.

Enriching the Brain is about changing the brain for the better. In that sense, it is a book about hope. In a busy, stressful world, often full of bad news, this is also all about genuine, scientifically grounded hope. I trust you're excited about the journey, and I'm glad you've decided to come aboard!

Del Mar, California   Eric Jensen
June 2006

Enriching the Brain

The Fixed-Brain Myth

ARE WE SHORTCHANGING OUR STUDENTS' BRAINS? HAVE WE INSTITUTIONALIZED mediocrity? Is the basic belief system in education to sort, then maintain status quo? That's quite possible. Why? The whole basis of U.S. education—everything we think we know about learning and education and all the resulting policies that affect millions of children and eventually all of us as adults—is based on the pernicious myth that each child has a fixed allotment of brainpower. This allotment was supposedly determined by our genetic inheritance, and just as supposedly cannot be changed over the course of a lifetime. I think of this as the "genes run your life" myth.

The theory seems obvious enough. After all, two tall parents will have tall kids, two white parents will have white kids, and two black parents will have black kids. How hard is that to understand? Genes run the world, and we can't influence them, right?

Not so fast. Not only is this myth dead wrong, it has led great numbers of people to give up because they think they are stuck with the brains they have. Yet it's become clear that actually we change our brains and our brains change us every day. Imagine that: our life experience changes our brains, and the changed brains change our life! As an analogy, if you recently remodeled your house, in many cases the remodeling changed your lifestyle. Your brain said, "Remodel!" and the result of the remodel was a changed house, which changed your lifestyle, which changed your brain. For this chapter to lay the groundwork for the rest of the book, let's begin with four core brain principles.

Principle 1. All human processes are a function of the complex interplay of mind, emotions, body, and spirit. Everything we put into and see emerging from our students, from the simplest to the most complex cognitive expression, is a product of the unique and dynamic brain state that each of us is in at any moment. This includes all actions, thinking, speaking, literature, music, and art. Principle 1 reminds us that there is a basis, an engine and platform, from which all behaviors emerge. It's our body-brain systems!

Principle 2. The body-brain system is governed by a wide range of factors. Some of the factors are hardwired into our DNA. Genes and their protein products are significant players in the equation. Their contribution is often called the "nature" or genetic part of the human equation. The prevailing doctrines claim that the balance between the effects of nature and nurture on our behavior is about fifty-fifty, meaning that half of what makes us who we are is genetic and half is the result of the environment. We now know that it is far more complex than that.

Principle 3. A genetic basis does not by itself explain the wide variances of a human being. Social, environmental, or developmental factors also contribute to cognition and behavior, both directly and indirectly. Directly, we can observe a command to a child or stimulus-response learning event. But indirectly, many factors exert actions on the brain by feeding back upon it to modify the expression of genes and thus the function of nerve cells. Our brains "learn" not just new content in school, but to alter key life processes, which is known as gene expression. In this way, genes continue to play a part in our lives, not by what was inherited, but by what has been "learned" by life. Thus "nurture" is eventually expressed as "nature."

Principle 4. There is a host of factors known to influence brain function. Each operates on different levels, with different outcomes. These include exercise, stress, and new learning. By understanding the factors that regulate the student's brain, we can orchestrate more positive outcomes. As a by-product, this opportunity to influence the brain's poten-

tial by the managing of school factors brings with it a moral and ethical responsibility to maximize potential in all students. Now let's make
some sense of these concepts.

Our New Understanding of Genes and the Environment

It's worth examining genes and their role because the idea that genes
are what your parents passed on to you and you're stuck with what you
have is one of the main tenets of the fixed-brain myth. If you're past high
school and college, you can throw out much of what you learned in high
school biology about genes. Gene expression, gene splicing, and genetic
engineering used to be the realm of science fiction, but today they are
science fact. Yet how did we go from the old nature-nurture debate to a
new understanding?

In 1953, Watson and Crick cracked the genetic code, showing the elegant double helix structure of the DNA molecule that governs it. For
years, many biologists assumed that it is our DNA that controls who we
are. After all, it was believed that genes held the information needed to
guide the growth and development of all our cells. But that's not the
whole story. The old paradigm was that our genes are the blueprints
that make copies called RNA (ribonucleic acid, which is a "messenger
and translator" molecule) involved in cell replication. Those copies activate transcription factors that in turn activate proteins, which influence
our behaviors (Figure 1.1).

The way that happens is extraordinarily complex, but a simple example would be the process of aging. As we get older, certain genes activate
signals that decrease the amount of hormones such as estrogen and
testosterone that are released into our bodies. Those changes in turn
influence our immune systems, cognition, and behaviors. This is clearly
one of the functions of genes, to guide and replicate cell development.
But what if genes had more flexibility than that? What if genes could be
"read" or "not read"? What if genes could even change? If these asser-
tions were true, it might seriously damage the old "fixed brain" myth.

- Humans have about 25,000 genes.
- Genes are a unit of hereditary information carried on our chromosomes as DNA.
- Genes have two functions: (1) to serve as a reliable template for making copies, and (2) to serve as a transcription factor, influencing proteins as gene expression.
- The second function is highly susceptible to environmental influences.

Figure 1.1. What Are Genes?

The Real Source of Human Complexity

Only a few short years ago, scientists thought humans had about two hundred thousand genes. The expensive, complex Human Genome Project was undertaken to discover, label, and code all of the human genes for the scientific good. Imagine the surprise of scientists in 1999, when they discovered that humans have closer to thirty thousand genes. Since then, the number was revised downward again to twenty to twenty-five thousand genes. This discovery was surprising, for many scientists had automatically assumed that people *must* have many more genes than a frog or a fish. Just for comparison, a chicken and a spotted puffer fish also have about twenty-five thousand genes. Wow! Are we at the same genetic level as a seemingly simple organism? If so, where on earth does all the human complexity come from?

Complexity cannot come *only* from genes; we share 70 percent of the same genes as a pumpkin! Even chimpanzees share 98 percent of the same genes as humans! Understanding the genetic code is not yet helpful for understanding human behavior.[1] If you think of the individual genome as a book, the difference between a high school dropout and a Nobel Laureate is little more than 1 percent of DNA. That's the equivalent of about two to three words per page. It must be that genes do not supply all of our complexity or our destiny!

The Discovery of Gene Expression

We have fifty trillion cells in our bodies, and every cell has tulip-shaped structures called *receptors* that receive information. Different cells have different receptor sites for different molecules. Things such as light or heat activate some receptors. Other receptors are receptive to and activated by histamines, stress hormones, nutrition, or androgens. Amazingly, receptor sites don't just process this information, they begin an electrochemical cascade of activity that eventually can affect our genes.[2] So although there is a core of genes that maintain your basic functions, often called "housekeeping genes," there are thousands of others that are responsive to environmental signals.

If genes are not the sole force shaping our lives, what does shape it? It's the environment! That's why genes are often grouped into their "types" of responsiveness to environmental stimuli:

- Early activated
- Intermediate activated
- Late activated
- State dependent
- Activity dependent

Genes generate interplay among themselves because of the complexity of environmental signals. How they respond to the environment depends on the type of signal. In short, if you're exposed to a trauma, you'll activate the expression of multiple genetic factors. Your brain becomes highly mobilized to make changes based on the negative life experience. There's a name for this process; it's called *gene expression* (Figure 1.2).

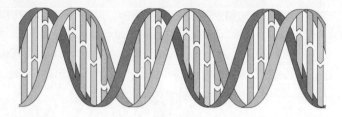

- Gene expression is the process by which genetic information is translated into action.
- Genes provide blueprints and transcription factors for proteins—both influence cell structure and function.
- Cell functions can influence our behaviors.
- The old paradigm was that information flow only moved outward from genes to proteins.
- The new paradigm is that genes can be activated by everyday environmental signals.

Figure 1.2. What Is Gene Expression?

For decades, we thought of the human body and brain as being a one-way street, unfolding from our genes outward. The new science tells us otherwise. It's actually a two-way street, in which genes influence our lives and our lives influence our genes (Figure 1.3). The meaning of this is profound. The fact that the process goes *both* ways is a revolution in biology, and it has implications for us in education. We now know that it is possible to influence gene expression purposefully, and it's done in laboratories every day.[3]

The critical understanding is that genes have two core functions; one is well-known to laypersons, the other is not. First, the more well-known function of genes is to serve as highly reliable templates, similar to a blueprint, that can replicate perfectly. Every gene, in every cell of the body, provides you and me with high-quality copies of its information. The fidelity of this template is impeccable, and everyday experience won't typically change it. Only rare, random mutations can influence the quality of our genetic blueprints.

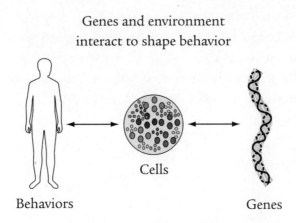

Genes and environment
interact to shape behavior

Cells

Behaviors   Genes

Figure 1.3. A Two-Way Street.

The second function, which is less well-known to the general pub-lic, is that genes have what is known as a transcriptional function. This means that they can influence the structure, function, and other bio-logical characteristics of the cell in which each is transcribed (or expressed). And while every cell has all the genes of your whole body, a particular cell will only express or activate a small portion (estimates are 10 to 20 percent) of its genes. Why? A kidney cell will remain a kidney cell partly because the portion of the genes that are unique and intrin-sic to that cell type (a kidney, for example) will get expressed, and the other "non-kidney" genes are effectively repressed. When genes are expressed in a cell, that activation changes the phenotype (characteris-tics) of that cell. In fact, it directs the manufacture of specific proteins that, in a typical human, characterize that cell.

This is where it gets interesting. Although the first function of genes, the blueprint function that was mentioned earlier, is impervious to the outside environment, the *other* function, the transcription function, is susceptible to the environment. Alterations in what the organism con-siders "status quo" will influence the expression of genes by altering their messages to proteins. Factors such as stress, nutrition, exercise, social factors, trauma, and even extended emotional states can each influence gene expression. This information is new and highly relevant, not just to scientists, but to those interested in education and parenting.

In 2000, the Nobel Prize for physiology went to Eric Kandel, whose lifelong work on memory has now turned to the genes and environment interactions. Kandel explodes the idea of fixed genes. Here's how he summarizes his findings. First, he says, "The subjective experiences of human consciousness, our perception of free will, behavior, and social dynamics can modulate gene expression, and vice versa." That's astonishing enough by itself. But he continues, "The regulation of gene expression by social factors makes bodily functions, including all functions of the brain, susceptible to social influences." And finally—read this next sentence twice—he maintains, "These social influences will be biologically incorporated in the altered expressions of specific genes in specific nerve cells of specific regions of the brain."[4] By social factors, Kandel means a host of possibilities: (1) being alone, or being happily married, (2) being in a group or team or partnership, (3) being in a crowd, or (4) living in crowded conditions or in wide-open spaces. Each social condition might be seen in a typical school, so there's clear relevance to educators. The environments affect our cells.

What Genes Can and Cannot Do

Twins, who have identical genes, often grow up with a great deal of similarities. But remember, environment is not powerless, even with twins. It's possible for them to develop differences in their bodies and, amazingly, different metabolic rates. One study tested twins who lived apart, one staying at sea level and the other going to live in the mountains.[5] Their metabolic rates adapted to the different climates. Even with twins, one can grow very different if one works in a much colder climate or at a much higher altitude than the other. Thus, gene expression is powerful enough even to influence what used to be sacred between identical twins, metabolism.

This tells us that genes alone do not determine outcomes. Yes, genes have a great deal of influence on many things. But anytime someone tells you there's a "spelling gene," a single "IQ gene," a "math gene," a "depression gene," or even a "cancer gene," you can have a good laugh.

Why? Genes may play a part in some of those things, but they are not the whole story.

Very few of your genes create inevitability (eye color and skin color are visually obvious, exceptional examples). If both your parents are African American, it is inevitable; you will be born with dark skin. If both your parents were over six feet tall, you might not play for the Bulls or Lakers, but you will be tall for your culture (that's assuming a positive state of nutrition; in cases of extreme neglect, even a child from tall parents would be much shorter than predicted).

Now we see that the environment can influence gene expression. And the result of alterations in a gene's activity can change height, weight, response to stressors, the immune system, and a host of other outcomes. Amazingly, we have some influence over this complex process. And, if orchestrated well, it is possible to tip the genetic-environment equation in favor of the environment. Here are some examples of everyday environmental activators for gene expression:

- Stress
- Trauma
- Nutrition
- Exercise

To summarize, all cells in your body have sensors that read their environment, assess the incoming data, and act to maintain their survival. The signals travel from the environment to the genes and from the genes to proteins, going both ways. On a larger scale, it's the interaction between the genes and the environment that determines the life of the organism. But what if the environment was so bad that your genetic material wasn't cutting it? What if the environment was so toxic, you had to mutate to survive? Could you mutate?

The Fixed-Genes Myth Debunked

The very idea that any gene would ever change used to elicit laughter (or outrage) from most biologists. But pioneering scientist John Cairns showed that an organism could actively rewrite its own genes to adapt to new stressful environments. This seminal experiment with bacteria showed that not all mutations were random.[6] Instead, the bacteria he looked at were able to change their own genetic make-up. Cairns put bacteria in a test tube and subjected them to highly stressful conditions—they were stuck with no available food sources. Well, more accurately, the test tube contained food that the bacteria were not designed to eat, process, or metabolize. Yet the bacteria survived—by mutating into forms that could use the available resources. This amazing biological event was reinforced in another experiment in which genes in a parasite actively changed to accommodate a new environment.[7] Now, more and more scientists are questioning the rigidity of the theory of genetic control.[8] Instead of the more stringent explanation by Richard Dawkins in *The Selfish Gene,* a newer understanding is Ridley's *The Cooperative Gene.*[9]

It is now established that contrasting, persistent, or traumatic environments can and do change the actions of genes. The new field is called epigenetic ("outside of genes") control of an organism. And if you look up the word *epigenetic* on the Internet, every reference is from within the past few years—it's a completely new understanding of biology. One scientific paper showed how change could happen prenatally.[10] Exposure to prenatal distress influenced the genetic material in the newborn *after* conception. In another study, researchers showed that the actual genes do not even have to change, but instead, heritable changes in gene expression can occur without a change in DNA sequence.[11] This is a revolutionary new insight because it suggests that the environment has even more to do with outcomes in behavior than we ever thought. Charles Mann writes that although the developing insight has not eliminated genetic influences on behavior, it has tilted the table a bit more in favor of environment.[12]

Can You Program Your Future?

Genes are the coding for brain and body processes in much the same way that blueprints define, but don't make a house. And just as in the process of building a house, modifications can and do happen. We remodel our houses, too. Every day, genes influence proteins, which influence molecular activity. But it goes the other way as well. The stunning news is that your lifestyle, the environment you live in, can also influence your perception of stress, and that can influence the release of cortisol, which can influence protein messaging, which, in turn, can influence genetic material. The way you perceive life (as either stressful or not) can alter your body's reaction to events, thus influencing whether your body produces stress hormones. You can influence your brain and the expression of your own genes. Thus, a genetic blueprint is not a mandate. It's just a part of the big picture.

The son or daughter of an Olympic athlete such as Marion Jones, Michele Kwan, or Mia Hamm may have a good heritage—and parents who care about fitness and athletic perfection—but that does not guarantee becoming a famous athlete. Not even genetic engineering can put a lock on that (yet). Unfortunately, you'd still need to work your tail off to become a top athlete or musician, even if you hit the genetic lottery. For example, Jack Nicklaus will probably keep his legend intact. He's one of the greatest golfers of all time, and his son Gary is a pro too, but Gary Nicklaus is simply a very good golfer. He played for years on the lower-tier before making the PGA Tour. He just qualified for it after nine years of trying. There are no "golf genes"—and there are no genes for any other discipline, either. There's no doubt genes play a role, but it is our varied experiences that create the greatest complexity and widest variation in brains.

Changing Brains Through Experience

It's also very clear that the human brain is highly experience-dependent. That means that the life you lead influences your brain—sometimes for the worse, sometimes for the better. The research on this is over thirty years old; it's become institutionalized in neuroscience by now.[13] You don't just start with a small brain at birth that simply gets bigger and fills up with information as you grow. Every infant's brain is a highly malleable, highly complex structure with more than a trillion connections (known as synapses) already in place at birth. These connections ensure that the infant can eat, breathe, and respond to the environment. But they are not fixed; some will die from disuse and others will flourish with constant usage.[14] Our one hundred billion cells are awaiting the wonders of life experience to decide whether to live, grow, or die. Brains will produce new neurons, lose neurons, make connections, and lose other connections, all based on our experience.

For example, going to college and taking hard classes changes the brain more than taking easy classes.[15] In short, the human brain is designed to interact with the world and make changes, depending on the quality of interaction. If the interactions are positive and sustained, you'll get one set of changes. If the interactions are negative and intense, you'll get a different set of changes. We change based on our life experiences. This makes the "fixed brain" myth dead in the water and simply outdated and incorrect science.

Negative Experiences Can Change the Brain

Infants are often glamorized on television or in magazines as having amazing, fast-learning, soak-up-the-world brains. But it works both ways: a brain that soaks in a brand-new language is the same one that soaks in trauma, abuse, and negative environments, too. Children are not resilient; they need time to develop resiliency. If you give a child an interesting, loving, and safe environment, you can expect healthy brain development. But expose a child to abuse, neglect, injury, poor nutrition, or other environmental risk factors, and what you can expect—and what you will almost certainly get—is far different.

One way to measure brain changes is with a soft tissue scan of the brain, a process called magnetic resonance imaging, or MRI. Studies of the normally developing brain in childhood and again in adolescence show constant changes. White matter volume (myelin) increases with age. The volume or mass (gray matter) increases during childhood, then slowly decreases before adulthood. Yet these changes are both genetic *and* environmental. Prenatal exposure to drugs can cause massive brain cell death.[16] Figure 1.4 shows what neglect looks like by comparing a healthy brain with a neglected one. Under conditions of severe neglect,

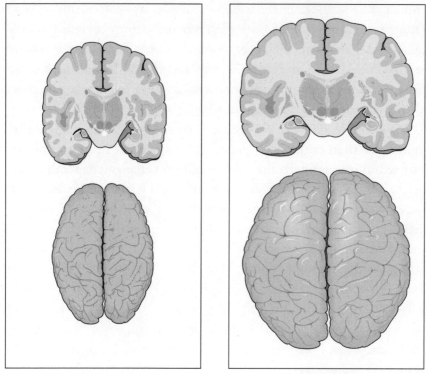

Extreme neglect   Normal

Figure 1.4. Brain Comparison of Three-Year-Old Children.

the genes that code for growth are disrupted. The message to the body's cells is to "conserve" and not grow. The results are often dramatic. These two brains are both three years old. The smaller brain shows the response to neglect; when resources are scarce, the brain grows less, so there will be less to maintain. The smaller brain can recover to full healthy size only if given immediate, comprehensive, and long-term enrichment.

A child who has been severely neglected may have a brain weight of 25 percent less than that of a typical healthy child. Expose a child to early stressors such as abandonment, threats, or violence, and you may get a brain with a dysregulated stress response system and lower IQ.[17] This child will be statistically more likely to suffer from stress and anxiety disorders and even depression. Expose a brain to toxins, chemicals, alcohol, or other environmental contaminants, and you increase the risk for mental retardation and, later, even Parkinson's disease. The brain changes, sometimes for the better, sometimes for the worse, and genes are only a small part of the equation.

CATASTROPHIC BRAIN CHANGES.   Exposure to catastrophe can lead to very dramatic change indeed—but the response can vary according to the age of the sufferer. For example, the loss of the left hemisphere through injury can be devastating in a sixty-year-old human, including loss of language capacity and a large portion of memory. In a three-year-old child, however, the exact same loss would likely have a very different outcome. With proper rehabilitation, the child's right hemisphere may take over the lost functions from the left brain and allow the child to lead a full life. The *plasticity* or ability of the brain to remap itself wholesale is markedly stronger in earlier years. The speculation and theory for why the young brain can make greater changes across the board goes like this:

- The young brain has many areas (mainly in the cortex of the temporal, parietal, and frontal lobes) that are not yet committed to any function.
- The young brain also has an overproduction of synapses (brain cell connections) that are not all in use—many are uncommitted to any specific function.
- The young brain also has high levels of androgens, nerve growth factors, and neurotransmitters, all of which help support brain function and the capacity of the brain to rewire itself.

Two famous cases in brain research history illustrate the extent of the changes people can suffer—and live through. The first involves a patient known as "H. M.," who went for treatment of seizure disorders in August 1953. These seizures were dominantly found in his temporal lobes (located on the sides of the head, around the ears), as is common. In those days, before effective anti-seizure drugs such as Tegretol, surgery was used in the hope that it would alleviate recalcitrant seizures. Dr. William Scoville performed a bilateral resection of the patient's medial temporal lobe, including the hippocampus, and the seizures decreased significantly. That was the good news. The bad news was that there were quite severe side effects.

At the time, the surgeons didn't know all of what the hippocampus did. They surely know now: it's the part of the brain that helps form, store, and retrieve explicit daily memories. H. M. remembers things that happened before the surgery, but he cannot form any new verbal or picture memories. If you were to meet him and introduce yourself, he would be gracious and be able to repeat your name. But if you left the room and came back five minutes later, he'd have no idea who you were. Decades later, his brain has shown little improvement. He can, however, show some priming effect. If you repeat a first and last name often, he can sometimes come up with the last name if prompted with the first.[18] But this is a far cry from the typical memory for someone of his age. By the way, H. M. has repeatedly taken intelligence tests—and usually measures in the "above average" range.

Fortunately, H. M. remembers how to do physical tasks, and can even learn new ones—though he won't remember doing so, or exercising them, even though his performance keeps improving. Any experiments given to him involving word-based explicit learning tasks are tricky since they require memory. He can even recall events from his childhood, remembers the names of all of his relatives, and can remember the jobs he had had from his youth all the way up to the surgery in his late twenties. He clearly understands what's said to him. In H. M.'s case, his memory is devastated because of the surgery. Unfortunately, what was removed was both important and irreplaceable.

FROM GAGE TO RAGE.   Here's another, more dramatic example of a changed brain. In September of 1848, Phineas Gage entered neuroscience history. Picture in your mind a James Cagney-type man; tough and street smart. Gage, a twenty-five-year-old railway foreman, was among the best workers; skilled, intelligent, and a good people-person. To blast rock areas and make for straighter rail lines, dynamite was used. The process was to drill a bore into the rock, place a charge and then the fuse, then fill the hole with sand. To make the explosion blow the rock apart, the sand must be tamped down solid. Gage was good at this process and used a forty-two-inch long metal tamping rod, over an inch in diameter. After tamping, the fuse is lit and the rocks fly apart (it is hoped).

According to local records, Gage prepped a rock, waited for the sand to get placed in it by another, looked away, and assumed the sand was in place. He then pounded down the tamping rod, and the dynamite exploded—sending the rod back into his face like a long bullet. It entered under his left cheek, went up and through his left eye, streaked through the frontal lobe of his brain and blasted out the top of his skull. The deadly projectile landed some 150 feet away. As would be expected, Phineas Gage staggered and fell to the ground. But soon he got up, in shock and bleeding. He actually talked to others as they took him to a doctor for help. He survived the accident, and the next day's headlines proclaimed a miracle. Most amazingly, Gage lived, the wound healed, and he survived twelve more years.[19]

But what really happened to Gage? He had been bright, kind, smart, and a responsible worker. Because of the accident, he'd lost an eye yet amazingly, his intelligence and memory were intact. But after the accident, he was very different. This formerly kind man suddenly used profanity, had fits of anger or rage, and became an unreliable worker. He often confabulated stories and was morally corrupt. In his final dozen years, Gage appeared in a circus and held two other jobs, both of them driving stagecoaches.

The thirteen-pound tamping iron caused considerable damage to Gage's orbito-frontal cortex.[20] That's the area right behind the eye socket, and it's the area responsible for integrating emotions into everyday life. This brain area helps us feel guilt, empathy, and shame. It helps us in decision making. The area right above it helps us make more socially responsible decisions. In Gage's brain, nothing inhibited the impulsive, crazy, careless, and irresponsible thoughts that stir in any

human being. Whatever entered his mind, came out. He became a nuisance to everyone including his family. His final years on earth, by all
accounts, were not happy or productive ones. Yes, the brain can change
for the worse.

Positive Experiences Can Change the Brain

It's much more obvious when one is exposed to trauma, disease, or long-
term adversity that the brain changes and becomes different. But what
about the opposite effect? Can we alter and improve the trajectory of
the developing brain? The answer, thankfully, is yes. The same brain that
is receptive to damage is also receptive to positive effects. Amazingly,
even changes in social contact can alter genetic expression, suggesting
that the choice of our friends, our workplace, and our children's classroom conditions are changing the brain.[21]

    This regulation of gene expression by environmental factors makes
people susceptible to social influences for good as well as ill. The effects
of these social influences become incorporated in the altered expressions
of specific genes. In other words, our subjective experiences, our behavior, and social dynamics can and do modulate gene expression and vice
versa. This conclusion would have been considered laughable a generation ago. Today, we know all bets are off and there is far greater potential for change in the human brain. A good deal of this book will be
dedicated to showing how it happens and what the evidence is for making positive changes. Even more of the book will be showing you exactly
what you can do and how you can take advantage of this revolution
both in neuroscience and potentially in education.

Summary

This chapter has provided the groundwork for the rest of the book.
We've explored how the fixed-genes myth is outdated. In addition to the
high-tech side of gene changing through harmless retroviruses, there
are much lower-tech avenues for change. Environmental influences, from

stress to nutrition, social contact, and trauma, can alter genes in freshly discovered ways. And while this is not household knowledge today, it will be in just a few years. Genes have two functions, one fixed and the other modifiable by environmental input, and your son or daughter could be the beneficiary of this new understanding. In the next chapter, we'll explore how this new understanding of human possibility plays out in the myths about intelligence.

Rethinking Intelligence

ONE OF THE GREAT MYTHS OF EDUCATION IS THAT WE KNOW WHAT INTELLIGENCE is, how to increase it, and how to assess it properly. A host of related myths follow from this familiar but failed belief. For example, it is a myth that higher IQ always equals greater success in life. Remember that Theodore Kacynzski (the Unabomber) was a very bright man and Harvard graduate. It's a myth that students who score the highest grades wind up doing more good for the country or the planet. It's a myth that schools make wise use of IQ data once they get it. It's a myth that we can collectively define and measure IQ in ways that most agree upon. And, finally, it is one big myth that intelligence is a "thing" at all; that it is something you have or take with you when you travel. It's actually highly dependent on circumstances.

One part of this debate concerns the definition of intelligence. Although original IQ researchers such as Alfred Binet believed that it was a fixed entity within any one individual, others such as Robert Sternberg regard it as multifaceted and somewhat contextual.[1] Sternberg's studies and others confirm that the general human experience of "being smart" or not depends a great deal on the social and physical environment.

Conditions matter; culture, language, and background circumstances all can put anyone at either an advantage or a disadvantage. How intelligent would a Wall Street broker be in the rainforests of Tasmania? How long might that broker survive? How long would an Aborigine from the arid Australian outback survive in an urban environment such as Hong Kong? Some of what we call intelligence is so culture- and context-dependent that it's hard to say we *are* intelligent. It makes more sense to say we can *show* intelligence in certain circumstances.

The myth of fixed intelligence means that school kids get labeled and put in programs in which many will never reach their real potential. Why? If they can't develop and show their intelligence in a certain environment, they get labeled as slow or unmotivated. if someone is waiting for them to *have* intelligence instead of fostering it, it may never surface. The research is clear: there's simply no excuse to impoverish any child's life anymore. In this chapter, I explore both traditional IQ and other ways of being smart, such as emotional intelligence. The argument in this book for enrichment comes from broad definitions of enrichment and intelligence that include cognitive, emotional, physical, and even social factors.

Intelligence and Context

Back in the 1980s a group of American psychologists were alerted to an interesting phenomenon. Brazilian youngsters with no formal schooling were doing fast math as part of business transactions as street vendors. This is a classic example of context-dependent intelligence. Typically, the daily use of math by adolescent street vendors in Brazil is in the 98 to 99 percent accuracy range. But in a laboratory, their accuracy drops by half, even on tasks that require the exact same skills (Figure 2.1).[2] This confirms that the skills are highly context-dependent, not that the learners lack any general cognitive capacity.[3] Unfortunately, most schools seem to have missed this concept.

The evidence of abysmal failure of students to transfer learning from school subjects to real life is legendary and cuts across age, IQ, and social status.[4] The "street math" researchers conclude, "The performance of an individual in an experiment is *inherently grounded* in the social situation of their performance" [italics added].[5] One study at the University of Arizona showed that even students with backgrounds in statistics, math, and science *do not transfer that learning* to novel contexts.[6] Students

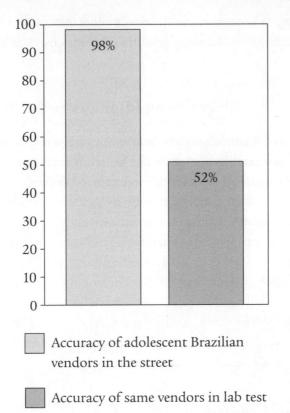

Figure 2.1. *Intelligence Is Contextual.*

Source: T. Carraher, D. Carraher, and A. Schliemann (1985), "Mathematics in the Streets and in the Schools," *British Journal of Developmental Psychology, 3,* 21–29.

in this study had at least six years of science and still demonstrated a considerable lack of acceptable scientific reasoning skills in areas out-side school.[7] These data suggest that schools would do well to focus on much more real-world learning. Field trips, simulations, role plays, apprenticeships, community service work, and away-from-school activities that use school knowledge and skills make much more sense than a focus on field-independent classroom learning. The bottom line is that what people know is very highly embedded in the context of the task they're doing. It takes years to create enough experience to have highly transferable, highly mobile skill sets that map onto many other contexts.

Researching Intelligence

Another part of the intelligence debate springs from two widely differing ways to do research and analyze the research findings. All research attempts to produce a substantially warranted position or assertion: a statement about what is true that reflects conditions in the real world. One type of research is known as quantitative, the other is qualitative. Quantitative research is associated with studies in which one group is compared with another and addresses questions of "what" or "how much" of a difference there might be. The findings are presented as figures or data. Qualitative research involves studies addressing such questions as to "why" or "how" a difference might occur. The findings are presented in descriptive form. Both methods are subject to bias in how the studies are designed, conducted, and analyzed.

Quantitative Research

Quantitative research is characterized by the framing of the data-gathering process as objective, resulting in a static, fixed body of research. The work is characterized by a self-defined paradigm of *hard,* that is, generalizable data. Quantitative researchers treat data as objective, fixed entities with factual and statistical boundaries. For example, I've often seen statements along these lines: "Dustin has a below-average IQ of 90 and has been suspended three times. His reading scores rank him in the 45th percentile, and his math scores are in the 32nd percentile. He's below normal for his grade level."

Quantitative researchers assume that the information is gathered reliably and free of context. They also assume that their gathering and analysis is free of bias and focused on provable cause and effect. Their writing style is impersonal and passive, and their hypotheses are stated empirically. These are the researchers that would accept, for example, the widely used Wechsler Intelligence Scale for Children-Revised (WISC-R) as *the* measure of intelligence. Unfortunately, although the WISC-R and similar scales can have strong diagnostic value, they generate only a small part of the potentially available information about their subjects. The big myth is that this is the right or the only way to measure intelligence.

Supporters of IQ testing have typically been quantitative researchers who have seen great opportunity in the ability of tests to sort children. When IQ tests made their way into schools, some educational practitioners found them to be useful tools for quantifying notions of merit and aptitude, sorting children, and disbursing educational resources accordingly. Tests became more popular as did society's reliance on tests to hold schools accountable. This position is exemplified by books such as *The Bell Curve*.[8] The book is very clear about whom it considers more intelligent. It says that it's all in the numbers; supposedly whites and Asians are smarter than Hispanics and blacks. But this is only one point of view, the quantitative one. What if you gathered different information and analyzed it differently?

Qualitative Research

Qualitative research is a very different matter. Researchers who take this approach see multiple ways of understanding things. They argue that no analysis can be value-free, bias-free, or context-free, so it is always essential to understand how the circumstances affect one's data. Qualitative researchers would posit that it is sometimes impossible to fully differentiate cause and effect and that logic does not always flow from specific to general. Their research culture embraces a deep, rich source of data, partly from observation, surveys, and personal interviews. They might analyze the intelligence paradigm in the student described earlier very differently, using terms like these:

"While his grades are low, Dustin shows strong skills in science and has some interest in literature. His behavior is often unsocial, but he feels that he has been unfairly singled out for his three suspensions. His father moved out when he was two, and his mother died of lung cancer last year. His grandmother has raised him since then. All things considered, Dustin is actually doing remarkably well."

In analyzing Dustin's test scores, here are questions a qualitative researcher might consider:

What if he experienced significant distress from being in an "out group"? *Stereotype threats over time are known to reduce working memory capacity.*[9]

What about Dustin's prenatal experiences? Did his mother experience extreme stress? *Prenatal stress can be a significant factor in reduced brain development, memory, and cognition.*[10]

What if he was subjected to severe racism? *Racial-based stress can be a contributor to cognitive problems.*[11]

What if he lived in a chaotic neighborhood and received substandard health care? *Chronic noise and stress can impair long-term memory and reading ability in children.*[12]

And could he have been intimidated by his test experience? *People administering an exam can nonconsciously influence results among test takers by their demeanor or culture.*[13]

If you look at the data about minorities and IQ through the eyes of a qualitative researcher, the conclusion may be different from that of a quantitative researcher. Now, lower IQ scores among African Americans or Hispanics may seem tainted or suspect. In fact, it would suggest that a whole new set of studies ought to be done. Not surprisingly, those studies in fact have been done. If you equalize your population sample for income, birth order, home environment, family structure, and family resources—compare apples with apples rather than with pineapples or pears—a different and more accurate set of numbers appears. The studies show that no significant IQ difference between whites and blacks remains.[14] But the point here is not who's smarter. The point is that there are many different ways to come up with conclusions about the same topic. A better way to understand the data about students is to mix methods with both qualitative and quantitative research.[15] Such a system embraces the best research from each domain. Then it formulates a single position, which has at least a chance of being fairer than either side would come up with independently.

Here's an example to consider: Marla was one of the brightest students at Washington High. Her grades were more A's than B's, and she made the honor roll every semester. In her senior year, she was voted "Most Likely to Succeed." She met her French boyfriend on a trip to New York during her junior year. Her parents thought of her as being very smart and expected her to go to college. As you might imagine, they were stunned when she wanted to take a year off after high school and travel overseas with her boyfriend. That was twenty years ago. Marla has been living in France with Henri, is happily married, and has two children. Her IQ was 144, well above average.

We all have our opinions about what constitutes "being smart," and they're likely to be different from one another. Was Marla a smart girl? Marla is happy and enjoying life. Her parents might think she was foolish for leaving the country. Naturally, what parents really want is . . . everything! It's a child who is emotionally healthy, financially sound, socially popular, academically successful, with a purpose and passion in life. And, of course, one who marries the right person *and* who lives nearby *and* who provides grandchildren. Maybe intelligence comes in so many expressions that our old model of it has to be put in a larger real-life context than a test administered in an exam room.

What Is Intelligence?

Just about everyone has an opinion on what intelligence is. Some believe it's your grades; others believe its how you do in life. Most believe it is how you do on IQ tests. Still others say it's the applied use of acquired knowledge, skills, or values in ways that appropriately move your life forward. Cognitive psychologist Howard Gardner of Harvard sees many intelligences, not just one, and explains that intelligence is the knowledge or ability to fashion a product or use a skill in a way that's valued by the culture in which you live.[16] In other words, intelligence is something that is used; it's a process that shows up differently in different cultures. If you read up on the topic, what you'll soon discover is that the quality called *intelligence* has more to do with the point of view each would-be expert brings to it and what stands out as worth measuring as a result of that point of view. Collectively, compared to even a generation ago, we now know a great deal more about what intelligence is and how it manifests—but it's far from simple.

One of the prevailing issues is how to distinguish among innate ability, learned intelligence, applied intelligence or ability, general talent, and domain-specific talent. These are not just an alphabet soup; each choice will determine a great deal. For example, if intelligence can be described as a domain-specific talent, you may favor the multiple intelligences view. In this model, an Olympic athlete could have a strong intelligence without being able to add single-digit numbers, because what the sport requires is a bodily kinesthetic intelligence that has nothing to do with abstract math—even though it involves the most exquisite computation of mass, trajectory, and velocity so as to get the athlete to the right place at the right time on the field. As you might be able to guess, the issues are exceedingly complex—and in most cases quite unresolved. Two researchers look at the same data and often come up with different conclusions. It can drive anyone crazy!

In the end, very few people agree on exactly what intelligence is. Does it mean memory; perception; or spatial, problem-solving, and analytic capacity? Or does it also require judgment, sensitivity, and motivation? These are not easy questions. Each of the following models of thinking about intelligence has its supporters and detractors:

- The "*g* factor" theory
- The standard IQ theory
- The theory of multiple intelligences
- The triarchic intelligence model
- The emotional intelligence theory
- The idea of street smarts
- The life quotient (LQ) concept

The "*g* Factor" Theory

This theory was first introduced by Charles Spearman almost a hundred years ago.[17] It says that intelligence is a very general (hence, *g*) mental capability. It is not memorizing, book learning, mastering a narrow academic skill, or test-taking smarts. It is the overall ability set that includes the ability to reason and plan—conceptual thinking, problem solving, and quick and efficient learning. It's also thinking abstractly, comprehending complex ideas, learning quickly, and learning from experience. Another way to put it is that it's an in-depth capability for comprehending one's surroundings—catching on, making sense of things, or figuring out what to do. The *g* factor shows up in so many tests it may be the underlying backbone of all human mental abilities.

Factor analyses of broad test batteries administered to different races, sexes, ages, and national groups have yielded essentially identical *g* factors.[18] Most ardent believers in the theory say that the *g* factor is almost all nature and little or no nurture. But the heritability is well below 1.00; therefore IQ must be subject to some environmental influences. Obviously any heritability studies apply only within the known range of environments represented in the present population.

No one knows all the possible environmental factors that could influence intelligence. The odd thing about it is that worldwide it's been rising over the past fifty years. In the Netherlands, the average scores of nineteen-year-olds rose eight points in one decade—that's half a standard deviation.[19] Amazingly, the gains came on Raven's Progressive Matrices, an instrument with an untimed nonverbal test (free of cultural bias) that many psychometricians regard as a good measure of *g*.

The global IQ gains may be a result of a host of environmental factors. We've seen greater exposure to television, changed nutrition levels, cultural changes, greater experience with the testing process, major shifts in schooling and child-rearing practices. But one could argue that many of those changes are not necessarily good. Yet more gifted people are showing up, somehow. Strangely, in 1952 only 0.38 percent of Dutch test takers had IQs over 140. But thirty years later, when scored by the same norms, more than 9 percent exceeded this figure! If these gains were genuine (nearly a 2500 percent increase) shouldn't there be some grand scientific, academic, or cultural effect?[20] Is there a secret to IQ building the world should know about?

Critics argue that *g* is more of an academic ability, and that there are other co-equal intelligences that are not only independent of *g* but also more important outside of school settings.[21] Other critics find much more scope to intelligence research than the more restricted perspective offered by proponents of the *g* factor. It's clear that we have many more questions to answer.

The Standard IQ Theory

The original intelligence tests were designed by Alfred Binet to measure children's likelihood of school success. Their success rate at doing so is decent—the correlation is about .50. (A correlation of 1.00 would indicate that what the test measures is 100 percent causal, but .50 indicates that something real is happening.) It's good to keep in mind that Binet designed the tests to discriminate and spread the field. The IQ questions were designed not for function in the real world but for the purpose of selecting the more successful students.

They do that really well. All IQ tests ask subjects to show specific information previously learned and to apply prior learning of rules, principles, or knowledge to a novel problem. It's not an accident that nearly 95 percent of the population has scores within two standard deviations of the mean, that is, between 70 and 130. The test design ensures that some questions simply won't be gotten by 99 percent of the test takers. But as noted in the preceding section, the standard-deviation range is a moving target, with almost 10 percent of Dutch test subjects in 1982 scoring close to the cutoff originally used by Lewis Terman in his famous longitudinal study of "genius."[22]

The Stanford-Binet test and the WISC-R are common IQ tests for children. Both have good predictability on school achievement tests, at about 25 percent of the overall variance. In the bigger picture, across all occupations, intelligence test performance accounts for about 29 percent of the variance in job performance. Critics complain that this test favors logical-mathematical, verbal, and spatial intelligences. Others argue that there's a trade-off: gaining processing speed, at least in infants, means giving up affect, which some say is part of emotional intelligence.[23] Critics also argue that testing is used improperly to label students and is not grounded in the real world. At the University of Pittsburgh, Robert McCall has shown that IQ varies 15 to 25 percent before infants reach maturity.[24] Another study asked, If it (the IQ) is a real, true test, why does it vary as much as 10 to 20 points?[25] Intelligence test results change; the average change between ages twelve and seventeen was 7.1 points. Conventional infant intelligence test scores have shown low predictive validity in children under six. The correlation between IQ test scores and grades in school is about 0.50, but this means that 75 percent of the variance in grades is attributable to factors other than "intelligence," such as drive, parental influences, and peer pressure. One thing very few parents and teachers know is that IQ scores vary as much as a standard deviation (15 points) or more within an individual (Figure 2.2).

The Theory of Multiple Intelligences

Gardner's theory of multiple intelligences describes eight different ways to be smart.[26] (Later he added three more, so there may be eleven.) The original list specified logical mathematical, verbal linguistic, bodily kinesthetic, interpersonal, spatial, musical-rhythmic, naturalistic, and intrapersonal intelligences, while the three added later are naturalist, spiritualist, and existentialist. His definition of intelligence is the ability to solve problems or use an idea, product, or skill in a way that is valued by one or more cultures. In a way, his model defines the output or end product of thinking. He adds that the type of intelligence must be represented in the brain, have populations that are especially good or bad at it, and show a prehuman evolutionary history for its development.

Many educators have accepted alternative theories of intelligence. Gardner's seminal contribution to sociology, psychology, and education is the notion of "many ways to be smart." Critics of Gardner's theories take one of two approaches. Some complain that the science doesn't match up; no distinct brain areas support any given intelligence, and domain-specific intelligences are widely distributed. Others believe that

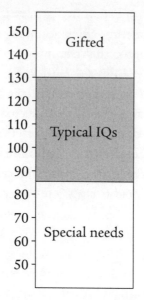

Typical IQ range is 85 to 130
15 percent variance within individuals

Figure 2.2. IQ Can Vary.

Source: R. B. McCall (1983), "Environmental Effects on Intelligence: The Forgotten Realm of Discontinuous Nonshared Within-Family Factors," *Child Development,* April, 54(2), 408–415.

when people are actually tested for these intelligences, it's no different from a talent; they just don't test out in those intelligences. Gardner would reply that the critics' definition is too narrow; talents and intelligences may be interchangeable.

The Triarchic Intelligence Model

Robert Sternberg's triarchic theory proposes three fundamental aspects of intelligence: analytic, creative, and practical.[27] He argues that only the first of the three, analytic, is typically measured by mainstream tests. Sternberg emphasizes the need for a balance between analytic intelligence on one hand and creative and especially practical intelligence on the other.

Sternberg also postulates four "intelligent abilities," and he believes that everyone's intelligence embodies various degrees of each of them. As an example, in science, you could memorize an experimental formula (memory), solve a word problem (analysis), create your own science hypothesis (creativity), and, finally, apply this to a hands-on experiment (practical). Sternberg's triarchic intelligence theory has been around for more than twenty years and has many supporters as well as critics. The supporters point to the fact that it includes the balance of logic, creativity, and real-world applications. Those who criticize it are typically those more wedded to the traditional IQ test or the *g* factor theory.

The Emotional Intelligence Theory

In 1995, Daniel Goleman's blockbuster book *Emotional Intelligence* invited us all to rethink what it means to be smart. His hypothesis is a twofold approach to IQ. He says that traditional IQ (logical-mathematical or verbal-linguistic intelligence) contributes only about 20 percent of life success, while emotional intelligence (EI) contributes the other 80 percent. Goleman also suggests that emotional and social skills are important ways to be smart. They are the tools, the processes for being smart in this world, not necessarily the end product. They include being able to understand yourself and others, having empathy for others, being able to lead or persuade others, knowing how to motivate yourself, and managing your own impulses. Goleman's contribution is the emphasis that emotional intelligence may be much more important than traditional IQ.[28]

He cites many types of evidence, but the "marshmallow test" is one of the most compelling. At Stanford, a group of preschool kids were brought into a room and given a choice. They could either have one marshmallow immediately or two if they waited fifteen minutes. About one-third took the marshmallow as immediate gratification and one-third were able to wait the full fifteen minutes, and the others fell in between. The subjects were tracked down fourteen years later. The ones in the first, most impulsive group had far more academic and social difficulties than those in the other two groups. The group who waited the longest scored an average of 210 points higher on the SAT.[29]

Several researchers worked with pairs of adolescent males to determine the effects of emotional intelligence. The authors concluded that emotional intelligence has a significant impact not only on the qualitative level of intelligence actualization but also on the quantitative level of intelligence measurement and scholastic achievement.[30] Another group of researchers found that they could use EI as a standard intelligence. They contend that when measuring EI as an ability or intelligence there are correct (rather than vague) answers on the testing instruments. They summarized other recent data and showed that such measures are reliable.[31] Another study found that the emotional intelligence dimensions were able to predict both academic and social success above traditional indicators of academic intelligence and personality.[32]

But EI is not the perfect indicator. Some critics such as Zeidner and others claim that empirical studies have not yet established that the Multi-Factor Emotional Intelligence Scale assesses a broad EI factor of real-world significance.[33] Zeidner's group asserted that EI is not reliable enough and the tests lack significance. Since then, many studies have been done. For example, EI tests successfully measured attributes that indicate desirable personal and interpersonal skills in medical school applicants. But they were no better than traditional tests on the academic side.[34] A college study of several hundred freshmen found that academic success was strongly associated with several dimensions of emotional intelligence but not with all students.[35] In another sample, EI was significantly associated with linking maladjustment and negative behaviors for college-aged males, but not for females.[36] In addition, one critic agrees that emotion-related abilities do exist but claims that developmental and clinical research show that these emotion-related abilities and competence stem more from the direct effects of emotions than from a whole new form of intelligence.[37]

The Idea of Street Smarts

Many people lack a college degree—or even a high school education—yet continually find ways to thrive in life. They might be good at problem solving, making money, finding a mate, or getting the best deals. If you were to give them a traditional IQ test, chances are they'd do poorly—but nonetheless, it's not unreasonable to view them as intelligent. Why? Many researchers believe that intelligence is not something you have as much as something you do. It means you don't get taken by scam artists, you know the safest way to get home, you have found an honest mechanic, and you know where to turn when you need help. In other words, street-smart intelligence is having the ability to survive in the real world. An example of street smarts would be the way many homeless people survive in a city, on zero benefits, in bad weather, and with no salary for year after year. Another example could be a political adviser who has the uncanny ability to find an opponent's weak spot and exploit it.

The young Brazilian street vendors described earlier provide a good model of street-smart intelligence at work. Similarly, shoppers in California who had no difficulty at all in comparing product values at the supermarket couldn't do the same mathematical operations later in paper-and-pencil tests.[38] These examples may seem like oddities, but in every occupation—in every talent—you will find people who are just good enough to do it on the spot in the real world, but not on a written test. They believe in themselves, and their personal or professional lives seem to run just fine. One study added that optimism might also be an important key to the puzzle.[39]

In another example, a good handicapper wagering on harness races must know plenty of probabilities.[40] Researchers found that the sharp handicappers used a highly complex interactive model, without having been taught it, that had as many as seven variables. Yet their real-world ability to do this successfully was unrelated to scores on intelligence tests. From examples like these, it seems reasonable to conclude that intelligence or talents may be context-specific, and that knowing where and how to use the ability is the big payoff.

The Life Quotient (LQ) Concept

You'd think six different ways to understand or measure intelligence would be enough. But I have one more to add to the mix. What I call the "life quotient" (LQ) is a balanced aggregate of the six measures just discussed. Having a high LQ means having the cognitive ability, domain-specific talents, and real-word motivation to succeed in the world you live in. The LQ needed for survival in central Afghanistan would be very different from the LQ needed for living in downtown New York City. LQ means you have what it takes to succeed—which is not necessarily a high test score or a specific talent. In this model, the one greatest asset is the ability to juggle life. Can you go to school, work out, take care of your kids, be sure to get health insurance, not let your driver's license expire, and still have a relationship? Everything requires an investment of money, emotions, social capital, or time. Juggling everything so that the eventual outcome is positive is an extraordinary feat. It takes both true problem-solving intelligence and real-world volition to carry it out.

Volition, mental force, or motivation is another powerful indicator of LQ. You can go a long way in life if you simply won't quit. In fact, many people become world-class experts on something just by working harder at it than anyone else has been willing to work. At the pro level, all the golfers have the skill to win a tournament. Tiger Woods became the number one golfer in the world by being willing to work more than his peers. His rival Vijay Singh toppled Tiger from the number one spot by simply working harder for two years straight. When you look close at what superior students do, a big part of it is sheer practice time. A strong body of research on expertise indicates that domain-specific knowledge (simply working harder at acquiring it) is the most important single component in effective learning. The students with the highest grades at school study an average of twenty-four hours a week, much more than their underperforming peers.

Psychology pioneer Martin Seligman did a study with 140 eighth-grade students. He measured old-fashioned self-discipline to find out how it influenced academic achievement. The researcher used an array of self-reports, parent reports, teacher reports, and monetary choice questionnaires to assess the level of self-discipline to find out how well it predicted final grades, school attendance, and standardized achievement-test scores. These students entered competitive high school programs and were also given a questionnaire on study habits and a group-administered IQ test.

The results are reassuring to parents who stress character and study habits over "innate" smarts. Self-discipline accounted for more than twice as much variance as IQ in final grades, high school selection, school attendance, hours spent doing homework, hours spent watching television (inversely), and the time of day students began their homework. In short, it's the sheer effort and self-discipline that matters more than raw "talent."[41]

The value of self-discipline thoroughly outstrips intelligence and other components.[42] One of the few researchers who has studied expert success, Ericsson says that it does take time, often five to ten years of work, to produce "true expert" status. Becoming an expert is not based on how smart you are, but how hard you practice at getting better. This requires enormous self-discipline. Again, LQ is three things. First, it is the aggregate of the other measures. Second, it is the ability to juggle life so that you constantly optimize your outcomes. And finally, it is highly motivated, hard work.

How Do We Measure Intelligence?

Every method of thinking about intelligence that I've described has its supporters and critics. Advocates of every definition of intelligence can show statistics to support their views. At UCLA, Albert Mehrabian used statistics to get a handle on the many forms of intelligence and finally concluded that when success measures were regressed against intelligence and personality scales or factors, intelligence did not account for variance beyond that explained by personality.[43] In other words, he's saying that some personality types are more likely to succeed than others. For example, in Hollywood, a fit body, white teeth, and a great smile with a likable personality do go a long way. Like others, Mehrabian invites us to consider a broad-based measurement of individual success potential.

Assessing intelligence is a smorgasbord of possibilities. You may or may not be sold on one or another of these, but they all have their advocates. My attitude is that it's always a good idea to read works that are contrary to your point of view. It does the mind some good. Interesting

books include Stephen Jay Gould's *The Mismeasure of Man,* Robert Sternberg's *Encyclopedia of Human Intelligence,* Stephen Ceci's *On Intelligence:
More or Less,* Daniel Goleman's *Emotional Intelligence,* and Howard Gardner's *Frames of Mind.*[44] The point is to understand that many of the best
minds from the past fifty years disagree on what intelligence is. This suggests that we should be a bit skeptical when schools tell us that our son
or daughter is or is not smart. We might all want to keep a very open
mind about what we mean when we say "smart."

Is Intelligence Fixed or Variable?

We can all agree that humans (using their brains, one hopes) change the
world; now we're going to say, our brains change, and here's how we
change our brains—and that means intelligence, too. Yet countless studies attest to IQ as inborn—all nature—and others say it's mostly all nurture. Some say IQ is fixed and that's what makes it reliable. These
viewpoints differ because each is using a different definition for intelligence. Here's how they line up:

Intelligence Model	More Fixed or More Variable?
g factor	Fixed
Standard IQ	Fixed
Multiple intelligence	Variable
Triarchic intelligence	Variable
Emotional intelligence	Variable
Street smarts	Variable
Life quotient	Variable

It's easy to see that the traditional models (*g* and IQ) consider intelligence to be fixed, and the newer, less traditional ones consider it more
mutable. Although many cultures believe that the primary determinant
of success in life is effort, the prevailing American view is that talent
means more than hard work.

This makes the traditional fixed view of IQ measurement appealing
here. So if the tested IQ of a child is 85 but rises to 100 as the child

becomes a teenager (because of whatever improvement in the child's circumstances), the fixed-IQ advocates would claim that the real IQ was 100, and the 85 score was a suppressed IQ based on abuse, neglect, or impoverished conditions.

In other words, the fixed-IQ advocates argue that everyone has a *set* IQ, and all the enhancement and enrichment in the world will only bring someone up to their personal genetic capacity—which is not necessarily to be a star performer, honor roll student, or Mensa member. With the cards you've been dealt at birth, what you can do with your intelligence is accept it. The claim says that if you get a healthy upbringing, your IQ will be stable and it won't change regardless of any efforts to create enrichment. Could intelligence really have a settling point in each of us? And how high is that point? No one is sure, but it's worth exploring. Visionary scientist Ray Kurzweil says that we may be able to raise intelligence dramatically with artificial means, including nanotechnology. His book *The Singularity Is Near* studies many new exciting and frightening options that are based on brand-new technologies.[45] The human engineering side may be fraught with political, social, economic, and ethical considerations. But on a more practical level, in *Outsmarting IQ,* Harvard professor David Perkins has elegantly shown how IQ is not fixed.[46]

The best way to convey this idea is that the greater the existing level of intelligence, the less that can be done for it. The lower the baseline of intelligence, the greater the capacity for positive change. This eliminates the "either or" or "black and white" thinking. In addition, we might think of intelligence as having breadth (lateral in scope) or depth (more specialized in one area, like IQ). In short, there is always room to grow.

Can Intelligence Be Lowered?

To understand how intelligence can be changed, it's important to know that it actually can be lowered. In the very worst schools, children learn so little that they actually drop back from the national IQ norms for every year of attendance. For every year in school, they do worse! This sounds crazy, but it really is possible to be going to school and losing ground. This pattern of scores appeared in at least one rural Georgia school system in the 1970s.[47] And it's certainly possible for schools to suppress IQ development. E. S. Lee studied a group of black students for several years, comparing those who stayed in their original southern school with those who moved to Philadelphia at various ages.[48] For the students who moved, IQ scores went up reliably more than half a point for each year that they were enrolled in the Philadelphia system, compared with their southern counterparts who stayed in Georgia. Those who stayed retained their initial IQ scores.

Lack of school can be even worse. When the schools in one Virginia county closed for several years in the 1960s to avoid integration, most black children were left with no formal education at all. Compared to controls, the intelligence-test scores of these children dropped by about 0.4 standard deviations (6 points) per missed year of school.[49] In fact, older siblings were predicted to have lower scores than their younger counterparts.

Operational IQ can be lowered in other ways, as well. For example, one study of college students showed how prejudice hurts cognitive capacity. These all-white subjects were first administered a commonly used test to assess the degree of racial bias in their thinking. Then the fifty-nine students were interviewed by either a black person or a white person, after which they were tested on their ability to concentrate on a challenging mental task. The results showed that, for participants who had been interviewed by a black person, the more bias they appeared to demonstrate in the first test, the worse they performed on the second, cognitive test. In contrast, highly biased participants who were interviewed by a white person, even about racially sensitive issues, suffered no subsequent loss of mental function.[50] This suggests that being racist uses up mental capacity!

Environmental factors and diseases apparently unrelated to intelligence can hurt IQ. Children exposed to high levels of domestic violence had IQs that were, on average, eight points lower than those of unexposed children.[51] Children with attention deficit/hyperactivity disorder (AD/HD) have a lower overall cognitive ability as evidenced by a Full

Scale IQ test in comparison with non-AD/HD children. Effect sizes were significant on all measures across the board.[52] Drug abuse can lower scores, as can brain injuries.[53] Malnutrition or consistent subpar nutrition can lower IQ scores. Exposure to violence and trauma-related distress is associated with substantial (seven to ten point) decrements in IQ in young urban children.[54] To recap, many factors can reduce IQ scores as compared with those of children in a healthy, well-educated environment:

- Poor schooling
- Prejudice
- Domestic violence
- Disorders
- Drug abuse
- Poor nutrition
- Trauma

You'll notice that each of those is a negative factor. We could add to the list other factors that have been found to reduce a child's intelligence. Marian Diamond, who has researched enrichment extensively, suggests we avoid the following negative factors in raising children, too:

- A vacillating or negative emotional climate
- Sensory deprivation
- High levels of stress and pressure
- Unchanging conditions lacking in novelty
- Long periods of isolation from caregivers and peers
- A heavy, dull atmosphere lacking in fun or in a sense of exploration and the joy of learning
- A passive rather than active involvement in some or all activities
- Little personal choice of activities
- Little chance to evaluate results or effects and change to different activities
- Development in a narrow, not panoramic, range of interests[55]

Can Intelligence Be Raised?

If intelligence can be lowered in such predictable ways, it seems reasonable to consider whether and how far it can be enhanced. For starters, it seems likely that simply reversing each of the listed negative factors might do some good.

The theory that intelligence can be raised is testable in many ways. Following are some of the more vivid examples.

The French Adoption Study

One way to assess the possibility of changing intelligence is to locate adopted children who had tested with low IQ before placement, measure their IQ later, and look for correlations with environment. In France, researchers reviewed 5,003 files of adopted children and identified sixty-five deprived children who were between four and six years of age and had an IQ less than 86 (mean = 77, SD = 6.3) before adoption, then retested them after they lived in their new homes for eight to ten years. The results showed a significant gain in IQ. But the change proved to be dependent on the difference in socioeconomic status (SES) between the original and adoptive families. The lower the initial IQ, the greater the gain, up to 19.5 IQ points in the lowest-SES families.[56] The gain was measurable but less notable in the children who were less deprived initially. One question about this study was whether the children would maintain their gains into adulthood. That is uncertain for now.

Preschool Enrichment

The Perry Preschool in Ypsilanti, Michigan, ran a study that combined child development specialists and social workers. The team worked with fifty-eight preschool children four hours a day for two years. These children came to school with higher IQs and better reading and writing scores than similar children entering first grade. By third grade, however, their gains were no better than the control students' scores.[57] Yet the story is far from over. When the researchers followed up on these children years later, they discovered that those in the experimental enrichment program were different. They were more likely to graduate, more likely to go to college, and less likely to need social services or get arrested. They earned more money and stayed married longer, too. It was clearly a case of results over the long haul and lifelong success, not just the quick fix.

Long-Lasting Study

At the University of North Carolina at Chapel Hill, a group of researchers began the Abecedarian Project, a carefully controlled study in which fifty-seven infants from low-income families were randomly assigned to receive early intervention in a high-quality child care setting and fifty-four were in a nontreated control group.

Early treatment was full-time, high-quality educational child care from infancy to age five. Both control and experimental groups received nutritional support and medical care. In addition, the experimental group was given developmentally appropriate activities, games, enriching learning, and social-emotional support. This group achieved strongly positive results across the board (Figure 2.3 and Figure 2.4).

Cognitive test scores were collected between the ages of three and twenty-one years and academic test scores from eight to twenty-one years were analyzed. The first phase of the project intervention was ended after five years. Sixteen years later, 104 of the 111 original subjects were located. Treated children, on average, attained higher scores on both cognitive and academic tests, with moderate to large treatment effect sizes observed through age twenty-one.[58] Compared with the untreated controls, those receiving the experimental treatment-enriched condition showed the following differences:

- Higher mental test scores through age twenty-one
- Enhanced language skills
- Consistently higher reading achievement scores

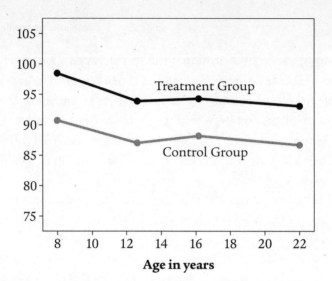

Figure 2.3. Abecedarian Enrichment Project: III Infants in First Five Years: Math Scale Scores.

Source: Ramey, C. T., Campbell, F. A., Burchinal, M., Skinner, M. L., Gardner, D. M., and Ramey, S. L. (2000). "Persistent Effects of Early Childhood Education on High-Risk Children and Their Mothers," *Applied Developmental Science, 4,* 2–14.

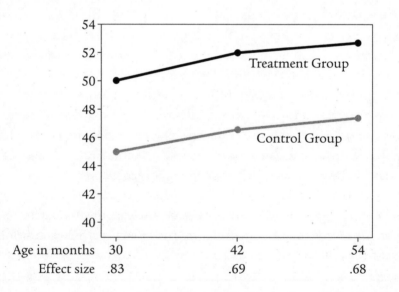

Figure 2.4. Abecedarian Enrichment Project: III Infants in First Five Years: Verbal Scale Scores.

Source: Ramey, C. T., Campbell, F. A., Burchinal, M., Skinner, M. L., Gardner, D. M., and Ramey, S. L. (2000). "Persistent Effects of Early Childhood Education on High-Risk Children and Their Mothers," *Applied Developmental Science, 4,* 2–14.

- Moderately higher mathematics achievement scores
- More likely still to be in school at age twenty-one (40 percent versus 20 percent)
- More likely to attend a four-year college (35 percent versus 14 percent)
- Less likely to have trouble with the legal system

Some critics charge that the IQ gains seen in the experimental group had risen, then leveled off during childhood. This is true; they did rise, then level off. But that's because they began as impoverished and moved up to find their healthy baseline, or "natural" zone. If all you care about is IQ, you could be cynical. However, in the area of life skill intelligences, the area of practical value where it matters most, the Abecedarian students did very well. In fact, the enrichment response continued for years. It could be argued that the enrichment response actually unfolded over time, given that the more different ways the subjects were measured, the more the differences were found.

Enrichment as Rehabilitation

One program was designed to modify the intelligence of mentally retarded, disadvantaged adolescents. The study was based on 57 matched pairs drawn from the total research sample of 218 adolescents. Enrichment programs extended over two years, and the subjects were pre- and post-tested on a battery of criterion measures: general and specific cognitive tests, scholastic achievement, classroom interaction, and self-concept. The students were placed in one of four groups to receive either specific, instrumental enrichment or general enrichment in a residential or day care setting. Those receiving the most intense (residential), specific (instrumental), and lasting care performed best on all measures.[59] This again strengthened the position that the worse off the subjects, the more they get from enrichment. But it also suggests that we might want to broaden our measurement to find out what *other gains* have occurred.

School Enrichment Study

To test the sample population hypothesis that disadvantaged kids could benefit from enrichment, another program was done with school-age children. Craig and Sharon Ramey's Project CARE had lower-, middle-, and upper-middle-class kids in the educational enrichment program. The middle- and upper-income kids thrived, as did the lower-income kids in the program. But the carefully matched, random sample of comparison kids not in the program also improved. Children in both the middle and upper middle class had IQs above average, and none of them showed any extra boost in IQ from the program. There were other benefits later in life, but so far, no IQ boost.[60] This study had the same kinds of results as the one mentioned before it. If there was an initial deficit, the children improved. Otherwise, there was little measurable IQ benefit. This leads us to our thesis once again: how we measure changes is important. If the children's IQ levels were the only thing that mattered, this study does not sound very compelling. After all, enrichment requires contrast from the prevailing environment, so those from more contrasting environments benefited the most. But there's much more to this.

The Ramey program was interesting because it showed other benefits of enrichment besides cognition. At the University of Chicago, two other investigators decided to assess whether or not skills acquired during specialized "school enrichment programs" contributed to students' later academic success in medical school. These researchers were not looking for IQ changes but for anything that might show changes years later. Three criteria were used for medical school success: lack of delaying events (teenage pregnancy, arrest, failure to graduate, and so on), student status (suspended, active, graduated, employed, and so on), and Licensing Examination—Step I scores (these are a crucial stepping-stone for a job). Of the three, one had a positive result. Participants from the enrichment programs experienced significantly fewer delaying events.[61] For students who are more at risk, participation in these research-based enrichment programs may develop critical thinking and problem-solving skills that help improve graduation chances. Similarly, a predental-school enrichment program to enhance skills of minorities proved successful.[62]

Behavioral Enrichment Program

At UCLA, psychologist Adrian Raine's group studied subjects who participated in an enrichment program from ages three to five. He was interested in the behavioral side of enrichment. Over a decade later, the follow-up was done. Compared with the control subjects, all the participants had lower scores for schizotypal personality and antisocial behavior at age seventeen and for criminal behavior at age twenty-three.[63] Those enriched who had shown some signs of malnutrition at age three years showed greatest resistance to schizotypy at ages seventeen and twenty-three and to antisocial behavior at age seventeen.

The results are consistent with an increasing body of knowledge that implicates an enriched, stimulating environment in improving outcomes. This was one of the first studies to show a prevention effect for schizophrenia and criminal behavior.

Summary

In this chapter, we've explored two critical concepts. The first is the thesis that IQ is not so easily quantified. There are many ways to measure intelligence, and ultimately, many ways to be smart. The second thesis is that regardless of what measure one uses of intelligence, it is not fixed. Not only does our IQ vary within our own lives, but it varies depending on our life experiences. Many programs were introduced, each of which showed clearly that the brain can and does change. Now that we see that our brains are quite malleable, how exactly is it that they do change over time? That's the subject for the next chapter.

The Science Behind
Enrichment

IN CHAPTER ONE WE INTRODUCED THE IMPORTANT CONCEPT OF TWO-WAY changes in our brains. Our genes can affect us, but most of the changes we experience are either a gene-environment interplay or just flat-out environmental effects. The expression "changing brains" would have been laughable one or two generations ago. Today, we think of not "if" the brain can be changed, but "how much" it can be changed.

Much of what we've learned about the brain's plasticity and potential for enhancement has been derived from laboratory-based enrichment studies. The qualities that drive enrichment are relevant to educators who are looking at ways of improving the quality or quantity of learning not only for special populations but for all learners. This chapter will take a closer look at these studies, how the brain benefits, the factors that contribute to enrichment, and what this might mean for the educational realm.

First, a reminder of our definition of enrichment, as mentioned in the Preface:

Enrichment is a positive biological response to a contrasting environment, in which measurable, synergistic, and global changes have occurred.

In other words, *enrichment is the response from a measure of difference.* You can measure enrichment or track it *only* in comparison with something else. In a laboratory setting, the experimental condition is superior *only when contrasted* to lesser (control) conditions.[1] Even laboratory enrichment, with all the bells and whistles, may still be far inferior to what the experimental subjects would experience in a different environment. That is, when assessing the impact of various conditions on the brains of the subjects, it's *the difference* that counts. Nothing matters more in the field of enrichment research except the law of contrast. Without it, you have nothing. Keep this in mind when considering both the animal and human studies described in this chapter because it's more than important—it is everything. Without a measurable difference from a baseline, no enrichment response occurs. This critical definition implies the following:

> The purpose is to maximize the individual's potential.
> The actions that are taken are to enhance the environment.
> The result (when done properly) is the "enrichment response."

The enrichment response is universally positive and can modify the brain at any age. Whenever the word *enrichment* is being used, it is describing something that affects the subject differently, and is more encompassing, more effective, and longer lasting than basic, everyday learning.[2] However, because of the brain's structural and safety limitations, it cannot "take in" an unlimited amount of new learning per day; to do so would create massive cognitive instability by overloading networks, meaning that the new learning would overwhelm the old. In addition, it would likely be very stressful. Remember that trauma is an example of overwhelming input. As a rule, the older the brain, the more it protects past knowledge—it's a survival function. But over time, our brains *can* take in a massive amount of new learning.

All of this takes time. But since most of us are so far short of that limit, there's plenty of room for enrichment! There is some evidence that suggests that the enrichment response may be closer to the "top end" of learning, in terms of how much can be learned in a given period, but we don't know for sure.[3]

Much of what I present in this chapter will be research from animal models (for ethical reasons). The rat (or mouse) models are used for several reasons. First, rats are cheap, easy to work with, and reproduce fast. They rarely live longer than thirty months and won't eat you out of your lab. In addition, the rat brain has many similarities to a human brain, although it is smaller, less folded, and less variable from individual to individual compared with human brains.

Obviously, there are limits to animal research. Two researchers who have studied the dilemma of animal versus human models have found that we can at times generalize, advising that in many cases, the procedures of some selected animal testing can be applied to children.[4] Examples of safe and appropriate testing might include simple behavioral tasks, learning, memory, or studies on nutrition. These work well in both human and animal models. What doesn't work, of course, would be tasks involving language, complex learning, or specific latency-dependent studies.

No one is suggesting that everything shown in animal studies has a one-to-one correlation with human studies. There are simply some methodologically transferable models. These include doing an experiment and measuring new learning, spatial memory, and other brain changes. Having said that, no one knows exactly *how much* we can interpret from animal data. Nonetheless, it is reasonable to review the work and speculate on its implications for human growth and development. We'll begin with the first pioneer in enrichment studies.

The Early Brain Detectives

Many consider the Canadian psychologist Donald Hebb the original trailblazer in the world of changing brains. Sitting at home and watching as his pets roamed the house, he got an idea. Why not test which was better for an animal—free roving or being cage raised? It didn't take long for him to test his hypothesis. Naturally the free-roving rats did better on maze running. Hebb early on realized that the brain changes as a result of the environment. His 1947 book *Organization of Behavior* remains a classic to this day.[5] But better research was needed. Fortunately, some other human "lab rats" were sniffing around the same topic.

Mark Rosenzweig began as a biological psychologist with colleagues Edward Bennett and David Krech at UC Berkeley. In one of the first experiments of its kind, their lab showed a difference in brain chemicals between "maze-smart" and "maze-dull" rats.[6] The rats in the more complex environment increased levels of the chemical acetylcholine, which is strongly correlated with memory formation. When this first study on the differences between the brains was published, it made hardly a ripple in the scientific press. After all the question remained: Was this nature or nurture? What if the "maze-smart" rats were already that way at birth? This called for new research and a new approach.

Enter an enthusiastic young scientist named Marian Diamond. She had been a professor at Cornell University and had moved to Northern California when her husband, Richard, accepted a teaching post at UC Berkeley. It would be safe to say no one was more excited about studying enrichment in the early 1960s than Marian Diamond. She, alongside colleagues Krech, Bennett, and Rosenzweig, developed many of the enrichment protocols still used today. Their early scientific definition of a laboratory's enriched environment, which became fairly standard, was a combination of complex inanimate and social stimulation. Today, that seems quite stark compared to all the possibilities, but it was *the standard*.

In 1962, two studies, both published with little fanfare, were to change our thinking about learning, environments, and the brain. In the first, the Berkeley team discovered that if you separated rats into three conditions, those in an enriched condition (compared with those in standard or impoverished conditions) developed a heavier cerebral cortex.[7] The enriched condition had a cage full of toys, and the rats had many cagemates. The toys were changed daily and usually consisted of boxes, tubes, wheels, and other objects of curiosity to a rodent. The impoverished environment was smaller and had no toys, and the rats were solitary (Figure 3.1). After several weeks in each environment, the rats were studied. Their brains were chemically fixed and thin slices were made for viewing under a microscope. The enriched rat brains had a statistically significant thicker cortex in 100 percent of the experimental

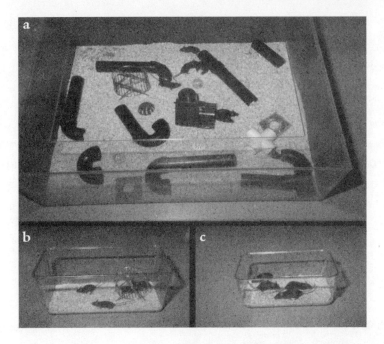

Figure 3.1.   Lab Cages for Enrichment Studies.

Note: a = enriched; b = standard; c = impoverished. *Source:* Photo courtesy of Henriette van Praag.

subjects. They also had more complex dendrites (Figure 3.2). Imagine that—a busier, more complex *outside* environment will physically alter the physical structure *inside* the brain!

In another equally unheralded experiment, Purdue University researcher Joseph Altman discovered what he believed were brand new neurons (neurogenesis) in adult mammals.[8] But many colleagues were uncomfortable with his methodology, and they discounted the startling results. After all, if true, this would have overturned the century of dogma asserting that the adult brain could not grow new cells. It took almost forty years, but researchers did eventually confirm Altman's animal research in humans.[9]

While both of these early studies seem pivotal in retrospect, no one could have predicted the snowballing effect either would have in

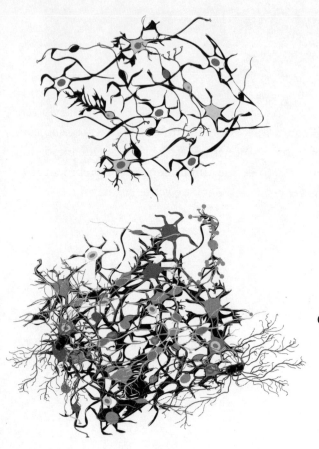

Simple network

Complex network

Figure 3.2. Simple versus Complex Dendrites.

neuroscience. Bill Greenough at the Beckman Lab at the University of Illinois, Champagne-Urbana, campus ran dozens of what are now considered "classic" enrichment studies showing a wide range of positive effects. Environmental enrichment is now a broadly accepted concept. Other studies have uncovered many more of the variables that specifically influence the genesis of new neurons.

How Enrichment Is Studied

Reading the literature on enrichment is both exciting and frustrating. On one hand, the new potential it reveals offers amazing hope. But on the other hand, it's very hard to compare "apples and oranges" all the time. Experimental protocols for animal studies vary wildly, with no general agreement as to conditions, numbers (or even species) of subjects, feeding protocols, or housing. Nonetheless, the specifics are important here because the only way to define and understand enrichment is to understand what the experimental data are actually showing.

Despite the differences among lab studies, it's possible to describe some factors shared by most animal protocols in general terms. They involve either two or three of these conditions:

- The so-called lab norm: a standard wire or glass cage about one cubic foot in volume (30cm x 18cm) containing two to four animals (usually female rats).
- The experimental enrichment condition: a larger cage (86cm x 76cm), with six to twelve animals that have opportunities for frequent social contact and changes in stimulus objects: tunnels, nesting material, housing, toys, and whatever else the experimenters think of. The food locations are changed frequently. In addition, animals are often given the opportunity for voluntary physical activity on running wheels.
- The experimental impoverished condition: a single animal in a smaller cage than the one with the control group. This animal has no social contact and no daily changes in physical environment.

The basics of food and water are provided to all groups. Typically the conditions are maintained for periods ranging from ten to up to ninety days. At the end of the experiment, the animals are removed from the cages and their brains are studied.

The lab norm is regarded as a control condition even though it is common knowledge that rats do not normally live like that. Most rats live in basements, around walls, in fields, behind kitchen areas, and generally close to any food source they can find. My guess is that for a rat, a truly enriched environment would be a four-story apartment building about a half century old. The building would have plenty of cubbyholes, pipes, empty boxes, and holes in the walls. It would have a college fraternity living on the top two of the four floors. The bottom two floors would include a small deli open on weekdays only, with no one around on weekends. The fraternity tenants would have a high tolerance for mess, and would leave food out daily. I suspect the rats would call that setup "heaven."

Lab experiments can get complex, but you might still get good data in simpler ones. In an experiment at the Salk Institute of Biological Studies in La Jolla, California, researcher Henriette van Praag put rodents in three cage groups. The first one was a small Pyrex cage with water, food, and the usual wood chip curls on the base of the cage. The rodent was solo and the cage was changed daily, but no toys or littermates were provided. This is typically referred to as an "impoverished condition." If you or I were in it, we'd call it "solitary confinement" and would not be happy. The second of three cages was more than double in size compared with the first. The biggest difference was that the rodent got some company, two to three littermates, each from the same genetic strain to eliminate genetic variability.

The third cage was the enriched condition with significant environmental complexity. This cage was eight to twelve times the size of the solitary cage. The rodents had four to six littermates, so there was a constant source of social contact. Toys were changed daily; novel objects were moved or new ones were added. Most important, this cage had a running wheel. Mice, especially females, enjoy running. There were counters to measure the amount of running done on the wheel, and mice will sometimes run several miles in a night. This is especially impressive considering it takes thirty rodent steps to match a single human stride. In this case, the mice with the running wheel in their cage developed better brains than those without one. They performed better on search-and-find challenges and memory skill tasks. This suggests the value of voluntary gross motor activity as contrasted with a more sedentary lifestyle.[10]

Because of the friction from animal rights advocates, many studies with animals are done in remote locations, secure buildings, or underground labs. At the Salk Institute, Henriette van Praag designed an interesting experiment deep below street level, featuring five conditions. The first cage was a control, with no toys or littermates. The second allowed the mice to run a simple maze task each day for five minutes. The third put the mouse in a small opaque pool known as a Morris water maze. It had to find a transparent hidden platform just below the surface, and this took some stressful swimming to do that. The fourth condition put the mice in a highly enriched cage full time but with no running wheel. They had social variety and "toys" consisting of pipes, tunnels, and objects to climb on daily. The final condition featured running wheels, but none of the other conditions. Out of the five conditions, the one with the mice that grew the most new neurons was the fifth, the running wheel setup. In fact, the mice in this condition grew 50 percent more than those in any other condition, including the enriched one. But the mice that *kept* the most of the neurons over time, the ones with the greatest cell survival rate (85 percent), were those in a complex, enhanced environment. Running seems to produce more brain cells than being sedentary. But it is the complex, enhanced environment that helps the neurons survive.

One conclusion we might take from this experiment is that maybe running ought to be considered part of an enriched environment; it certainly supports enhanced brain results. Other studies have supported its effect on neurogenesis.[11] Dr. van Praag herself has noted, "Essentially, all measures affected by an enriched environment depend on, and have not been dissociated from, an increase in voluntary motor behaviour or exercise."[12] I asked Dr. van Praag about this and, characteristically, she hesitates to make claims about interpretations of the rodent data to human populations. But I asked her a different question: "Did this experiment change your own habits?" She said she had taken up jogging. And when I pressed her about what kind of education she wanted for her own son, she said she would hope the school would have plenty of "gross motor activities" (recess or physical education?) available. I have found this type of response common among researchers: it's the model

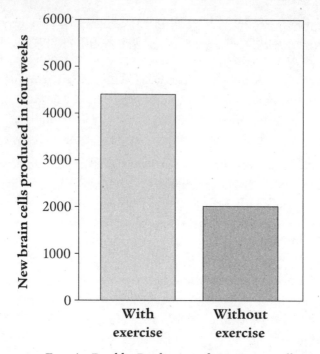

Figure 3.3. Exercise Doubles Production of New Brain Cells in Mice.

Source: From H. van Praag, G. Kempermann, and F. Gage, "Running Increases Cell Proliferation and Neurogenesis in the Adult Mouse Dentate Gyrus," *Nature Neuroscience*, 1999, 2, 266–270.

of, "Don't ask me for practical applications *on the record*, but in my own life, I'm covering my bases just in case." Personally, I think that's pretty smart.

How Enriched Environments Benefit the Brain

Animal studies have found that enriched environments can induce important changes in the brain, including enhanced functioning and development in areas related to cognitive capacity, learning, memory, and resilience. Depending on the design of the study, the results might include more neurons, longer dendrites, more connections, heavier brains, greater brain mass, more intra- and intercortex connectivity, and enlarged capillaries. Changed brains can be contrasted with a control group and measured in many ways.

To understand, measure, and validate these changes, researchers use a variety of both "old school" methods and very smart new ones. These include

- Behavioral tasks such as running a radial arm maze or swimming in a Morris water maze
- Brain scans such as an MRI to measure changes in tissue volume
- Use of marker dyes such as a green fluorescent protein that glows when a cell divides to show increased new cell generation
- Autopsies, which can reveal precise measurements of brain weight, cell-to-cell connectivity, or even the density of synapses

Enhanced environmental stimulation can affect the brain in many ways. To simplify the discussion here, I'll focus on six fundamentally different effects. They are consistent—and for every study I describe, there are many others with similar findings.

- *Metabolic allostasis:* Changes in blood flow, baseline chemical levels, and metabolic functioning
- *Enhanced anatomical structures:* Larger neurons and more developed cell structures
- *Increased connectivity:* Increased circuitry and branching from one neuron to another
- *Responsiveness and learning efficiency:* Enhanced electrical signaling, cell efficiency, and neural processing
- *Increased neurogenesis and growth factors:* Production of new brain cells as well as special proteins important for the brain's survival
- *Recovery from trauma and system disorders:* Protection from stress and greater capacity to heal when damaged

It is true that any of these changes can (and sometimes do) happen without efforts to enhance the environment. But it is *the degree, the rate,* and *the complexity of change* that differentiate efforts at environmental enrichment from other, more basic, learning or maturational processes. The studies reliably show that changes do occur from enhanced environmental efforts.[13] In many cases, they can facilitate what seem like miracles. For the moment, suffice it to say that there are many verifiable and enticing benefits to the enrichment process. When taken as a whole, they really do seem remarkable.

Metabolic Allostasis

The word *allostasis* refers to a resetting or readjustment of baseline brain levels. Environmental stimulation can enhance blood flow in the brain as well as boost levels of chemicals important to learning, mood, and cognition. The first group of relevant studies were by neuroscientist Matti Saari, whose group in Canada has shown changes in regional cerebral metabolism.[14] In addition, his group found that these changes in blood flow are regionally specific to the thalamic, cortical, and hippocampal areas.[15] Those areas play critical roles in learning, consciousness, and memory, and we must pay close attention to the results.

Another area of high interest is the neurotransmitters, a group of chemicals that includes erotonin and dopamine. These are essential for learning, mood, memory, and communication within the brain. Animal studies have found that levels of these chemicals can be altered as a result of enrichment efforts. Acetylcholine, a common neurotransmitter known to help with memory formation, also increases in enrichment studies.[16] Remarkably, enrichment exercise can even enhance activity of opioid (pleasure and analgesic) sites.[17] Enrichment efforts can help regulate serotonin to enhance mood and improve cognitive flexibility.[18] This research is highly relevant because of the relationship to stress and stress disorders.

Studies show that rats getting an enrichment protocol gain some protection from stress disorders. In fact, it can lead to pronounced changes in neuroendocrine regulation compared with those in a more basic control environment.[19] The enrichment protocols decrease the release of stress-responsive hormones.[20] In addition, enrichment studies support the reversal of social isolation, too.[21]

Researchers find, as a result of changes in specific chemicals, a reduction in nonhuman primate aggression from an enrichment effect in the environment.[22] These are all positive effects from essential brain chemicals that can improve mood, memory cognition, or both. Most teachers would be ecstatic to have students with enhancements in these areas.

Enhanced Anatomical Structures

Scientific studies have shown that nearly every indicator of optimal brain functioning improves with successful enrichment. Enrichment involves changes in the physical brain, and these enhanced anatomical structures may provide the scaffolding necessary for increased cognitive tasks. In fact, enrichment pioneer Bill Greenough has shown that enrichment protocol efforts increase the brain's vascular system, which increases oxygen to the neurons.[23] He also confirmed increases in the number of glial cells, which interact closely with neurons.[24]

Neuroscientist Marian Diamond has shown a number of enrichment effects, including a thicker cortex and increases in the size of neurons (Figure 3.4).[25] Besides Diamond's studies showing increases in glial cells and in cortical depth, various researchers have found increased dendritic length, and more complex (higher order) branching on the dendrites, better enabling them to make more future connections.[26] It sounds like all of these changes would add mass to the brain, and they do. Brain weights also increase with enrichment.[27] These effects are robust and have correlated with overall brain weight increases of 7 to 10 percent after 60 days.[28]

Increased Connectivity

Enrichment studies show development of new circuitry in the brain. The evidence for increased connectivity comes from seeing changes as a result of neurons "talking" to each other, creating new synapses (Figure 3.5).

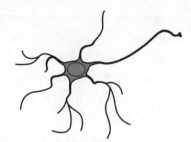

Impoverished neuron

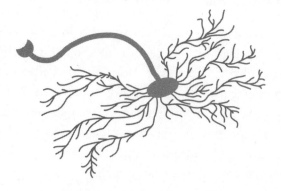

Enriched, complex neuron

Figure 3.4. Impoverished versus Enriched Neurons.

First, there are studies showing changes in the necessary dendritic branching for connectivity in multiple areas of the brain, including the visual area.[29] And more important, there is an increase in synapses from new connections and dendritic spine counts.[30] More dendrites per neuron and more synapses per neuron are correlated with increased connectivity. This result occurs in animals given enrichment protocols compared with those raised in isolation or non-social environments.[31] This increased connectivity and mapping may be important to cognition and processing.

Connectivity is a tricky issue because there are competing models of how this occurs. Bill Greenough and his colleagues at the University of

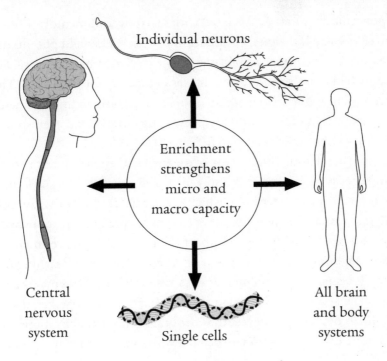

Individual neurons

Enrichment
strengthens
micro and
macro capacity

Central
nervous
system

Single cells

All brain
and body
systems

Figure 3.5. Enrichment Strengthens Neural Capacity.

Illinois, Champagne-Urbana, have shown that motor learning induces the formation of new synapses in mouse models.[32] But seven years later another study showed that associative learning changes the size of existing synapses, possibly facilitating neurotransmission. Yet it *does not* increase the number of synapses in the hippocampus.[33] This contrasting set of data suggests there may be developmental phases in which the same stimulus produces altogether different results. It may also be a case of differences in brain geography; getting the effect in one area of the brain (versus another) may do the job better or in a more timely way.

Responsiveness and Learning Efficiency

On each side of our heads, near our ears, are our temporal lobes. The hippocampus is buried deep within our temporal lobes, and we have two of these C-shaped structures. Studies suggest that the tissue in the hippocampus, an area associated with learning and memory, becomes better at electrical signal conduction points.[34] The field potentials of synapses in the hippocampus increase with enrichment effects.[35] Cells in enriched rats also showed an increased capacity for plasticity.[36] These changes can influence our senses, too. Studies show an improvement in the capabilities of our auditory processing, and we can even spur the development of the visual system.[37]

Another astonishing factor of an enriched environment is that it influences protein synthesis and gene transcription. Rats show higher levels for the messenger RNA, which is essential for memory.[38] After frequent stimulation, neurons change and become more responsive. An enriching environment may support the process of long-term potentiation, meaning it enhances the very processes by which learning takes place. It also improves memory.[39] We see rats that perform mazes better, remember spatial cues better, and learn faster.[40] Taken together, the electrophysiological data suggest that the brain can make activations easier and more often, a function associated with new learning and plasticity.

Increased Neurogenesis and Growth Factors

Recent studies show that adult lab animals (and humans) generate new brain cells (neurogenesis) and that enrichment efforts can accelerate this process. In elderly mice exposed to an environmentally complex housing condition, the quantity of new brain cells generated was not 10, 20, or 50 percent higher, but a whopping 500 percent higher than for the nonenriched control group.[41] As early as 1998, researcher Gerd Kempermann discovered that rats grew brand new brain cells every day. By use of an ingenious staining technique, involving a green fluorescent protein extracted from jellyfish, his team was able to identify and photograph newly dividing neurons. And in a later study, Kempermann, a Swede working with San Diegan Fred Gage at the Salk Institute in La Jolla, California, got permission to inject the same dye into the brains of elderly Swedish patients with inoperable cancer. When the patients eventually died from cancer in the following months, Kempermann and Gage were able to autopsy the brains and verify that humans can and do grow new brain cells.[42] Additional groundbreaking research has shown not only that humans do grow new neurons but that the rate of growth can be increased by enrichment efforts.[43]

Growth factors are critical chemicals that regulate and support the growth and survival of brain cells and have been linked to increased rates of cognition.[44] Research has shown an increase in gene expression for brain-derived neurotrophic factors in songbirds after exposure to an enriching environment, and an increase in an insulin-like growth factor was also found in enriched rats.[45] These growth factors are linked to the proliferation, survival, and functionality of new neurons. Rats in enriching environments had significantly higher survival rates (85 percent) of new neurons compared with the control and other experimental conditions, in which rates ranged from 42 percent to 56 percent.[46] What does all this lead to? It seems to be the daily positive environmental influences on the subject over the long haul that are critical for enrichment, not just the one-time burst of activity.

Figure 3.6 summarizes the current understanding about a key role for neurogenesis. The production of new neurons is partly genetic and partly modifiable by human experience. We not only can alter our behaviors to produce more new neurons (which are correlated with learning, mood, and memory) but can enhance their survival changes with behavioral modifications using enrichment protocols.

Recovery from Trauma and System Disorders

Many animal studies suggest that enrichment effects can influence recovery from genetic disorders, trauma, and brain impairments. Mice bred for slower learning (variety 129/SvJ) are known to do worse on maze tasks, and they have lower neuronal production than do their genetically bred typical counterparts.[47] But they improved dramatically in an enhanced environment in two ways: neurogenesis and learning performance.[48]

In rodents with neonatal binge alcohol exposure, enrichment efforts improved learning dramatically.[49] Early environmental neglect causes profound neural and behavioral effects. Animals reared in isolation show

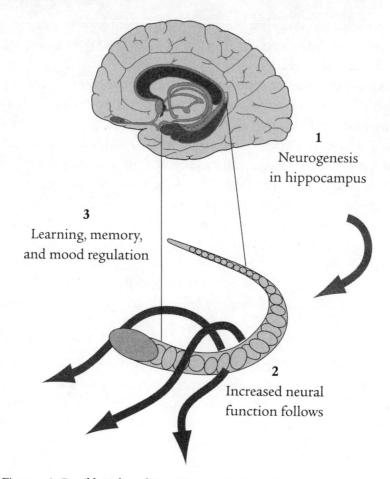

1
Neurogenesis
in hippocampus

3
Learning, memory,
and mood regulation

2
Increased neural
function follows

Figure 3.6. Possible Value of New Neurons Enhanced During Enrichment.

Source: Adapted from T. Shors, "Fresh Memories Need New Cells," *Nature*, 2001, 410, 372–376; and G. Kempermann, "Why Grow New Neurons?" *Journal of Neuroscience*, 2002, 22(3), 635–638.

increased anxiety and poorer performance in learning and spatial memory tasks. But later enrichment efforts reverse some or all of the deficits induced by isolation rearing.[50] In addition, environmental enrichment leads to a functional reversal of the effects of maternal separation through the development of neural compensation.[51] The negative effects of a stressful social experience can affect us even at the micro level of our cells.

At Duke University, experimenters showed that an enriching environment could override even a genetic mutation in mice that caused obesity.[52] One advantage of these types of animal studies is that a disability can be induced, and the animal can be placed in study to determine if an enhanced environment can help in rehabilitation. That's been done quite often. Humans suffer a variety of challenging brain insults. But the good news is that some of these problems have been induced and repaired with enrichment in mice models.

Enrichment benefits have been found when there's exposure to environmental lead, debilitating head injuries, alcoholism, stroke, and toxic exposure.[53] Studies with contrasting environments show that those in an enriched condition have more protective strengths and recover faster from exposure to injury.[54] These results are found in the enriched condition as compared with those in the standard or control condition. These studies collectively suggest that we may be able to facilitate learning-underperforming and special needs learners with an enrichment program.

What Have We Learned?

The results of over forty years of enrichment studies have suggested that *no single experimental variable* can account for all of the effects of an enriching environment. Because of the wide variance of models used to study enrichment, both the variables and the effects create a complex puzzle. There is *no standard protocol* for all enhanced, complex environmental studies, and although mammals have been used extensively, no one at this time can safely extrapolate all studies to all species. When designing a study, the greater the number of factors, the more complex, the more difficult, the more expensive the experiment. As a result, most investigators will focus on only one or two factors at a time. The results are far from final and more studies always need to be done.

Let's do a quick review before we go on. Hopefully you remember the one single essential ingredient necessary. In every single study on maximizing the brain, the dramatic animal or human results come *only* from contrasting the results of the "enhanced conditions" with the "standard cages" or the "impoverished conditions." The contrast concept is essential because it defines the very nature of improving the brain. Enrichment-like programs show no generalized benefit unless contrasted with something worse. The greater the contrast, the more the benefit. More important, the more impoverished the prevailing environment before the experiment, the greater the likely enrichment. The richer the prevailing environment, the more active, complex, and healthy the subject's life before the experiment, the lower the chances for the enrichment effects to be observable.

Having said that, some conclusions can be reliably drawn about the key factors and conditions common to most of the enrichment studies using both animals and humans. As a starter, we should say the single strongest thing to keep in mind is contrast. Let's walk through the essential assumptions for enrichment success.

Factors Contributing to Enrichment

The following factors have been shown to maximize the contrasting effects:

- Physical activity (versus passivity)
- Novel, challenging, and meaningful learning (versus doing what is already known)
- Coherent complexity (versus boredom or chaos)
- Managed stress levels (versus stressful conditions)
- Social support (versus isolation)
- Good nutrition (versus poor-quality food)
- Sufficient time (versus one-shot experiences)

The following sections take a closer look at these seven factors and what they mean.

Physical Activity

The studies show that enrichment results from *doing* rather than *observing others* receive enrichment factors. Studies of "couch potato" rats, those exposed to the sight of others in an environment that produced enrichment for participants, showed that they derived no benefits whatsoever.[55] Meanwhile, voluntary wheel running has been shown to enhance learning, as have other types of mammal exercise.[56] Most but not all environmental complexity or enhancement studies allow voluntary gross motor activity.[57] Some enrichment effects also show up following involuntary motor tasks, but the benefit is apparently greater when the participant does the activity willingly.

For example, mice enjoy running, and when given a running wheel may run up to five miles a night (they're nocturnal). But mice (and rats) dislike swimming, and they find it very stressful. Although one cannot match the amount of time on running wheels with swimming, mice showed far more enrichment effects from the voluntary running activity, whereas involuntary swimming had no effect.[58] It may be that the running releases key chemicals. A team discovered that growth factors may be what support the beneficial effects of exercise on the brain.[59] These factors appear to have a host of positive effects on brain function.

Educational Implications: Students who watch interesting and engaging activities that others do, but are not actively participating, are not likely to show an enrichment response. Students must actually do it! This has to strike K–12 educators as particularly ironic in the current climate of reducing physical education and recess, all the while focusing on "sit and git" test preparation.

Novel, Challenging, and Meaningful Learning

If you already know how to do something, you already have in place the neurons and the connections to support the use of that learning. But to create an enhanced effect called enrichment, the learning and memory must be new, tough, and worthwhile. The evidence is clear that new motor learning creates new synapses in the cerebellum, especially when it's challenging.[60] There is also evidence that the more you learn, the more you *can* learn. Complex, environmental enhancements produce higher levels of proteins associated with learning and memory.[61]

Novel learning is a critical ingredient of enrichment and contributes to synaptic development and survival. Although simple physical activity may enhance the *production* of new cells, it seems that learning may *increase their survival* and *functionality*.[62] Somehow, though, all learning is not treated the same by our brains. Stimulation alone does not drive change in the brain; it has to be behaviorally relevant. When we learn something that is meaningful (scientists call this a "behaviorally relevant" task), something different goes on in our brains.

But any new learning has to be worthwhile, too. Neuroscientists Michael Kilgard and Michael Merzenich have repeatedly shown in nonhuman primate experiments that an area of the brain (*nucleus basalis*) gets activated when we think the task is "worth learning." In other words, stimulation of the nucleus basalis causes a "cortical imprinting" when there is relevant data from environmental stimuli. Without this activation, we don't release the acetylcholine necessary to form the memory to "save" the new learning.[63]

In addition, other studies have shown that the context of the activity changes how the brain responds to it, and more meaning is better. For example, take a lab monkey (such as a Rhesus Macaque) and train it to do a task—say, stacking small rings onto a tall skinny stick. Laboratory monkeys do tasks like these all the time. The interesting thing is that if the task is irrelevant and silly for the animal, nothing changes in the brain; the monkey actually quits doing it. But if the task is behaviorally relevant (it provides new food, mating, or housing opportunities), then measurable changes occur in the monkey's brain.[64]

In humans the same thing happens. If a nonmusician walks up to a piano and pounds out random keys, not much happens in his or her brain except a lot of scattered activity. Now take musically naive participants and scan their brains before teaching them to read music and play the piano. Give them fifteen weeks of lessons and scan their brains again and you'll see physical changes.[65]

Educational Implications: These findings suggest some essential questions: Do the learning experiences activate curiosity, challenge, and imagination? Are they relevant and meaningful to students and appropriately designed for the learner?

Coherent Complexity

Coherent environmental complexity is contrasted with the two extremes of boredom or chaos. The ideal for the brain is the middle ground; not to sleep all day or to have constant panic. Ideally, we avoid distress and confusion. At the University of Illinois, Bill Greenough's lab experimented with complex housing for the rodents. His staff of grad students often found or built cardboard "doll houses" or the equivalent of frontier or apartment buildings with multiple rooms and unusual ramps, doors, and exits. They even modeled cages after a circus, including tightropes to maximize challenge.

Environmental complexity means that it takes thoughtful decision making to navigate the physical terrain, interact with the other life forms, and get to the resources you need for survival. Typically, in rodents or primates, complexity means variety, challenge, and unpredicted changes in the physical environment. The results are better, more complex brains. Today that doesn't sound so amazing, but Greenough's original work was so controversial that when he submitted the results to a prominent scientific journal, they were promptly rejected. Greenough was also rejected for tenure at his University. But eventually his groundbreaking research has been validated again and again.

These environmental events were originally shown eliciting a positive change in the brain over forty years ago.[66] More recently, we know that complexity alters things even at key levels of nerve growth factors needed to maintain brain health.[67] If we investigate the opposite, boredom, it does have negative outcomes on the brain. In fact, a boring environment had a more devastating thinning effect on the brain than an exciting environment had on thickening the cortex.[68] In a human study in this area, UCLA researcher Bob Jacobs found that learners who had more challenge and more complexity in their academic schedules had more dendritic growth and connectivity.[69] For the college-age learners Jacobs studied, the greater the complexity in their lives, the greater the complexity that was found in their brains.

Busy environments are no problem for the brain. In fact, we thrive on them! The problem begins with unintelligible data and continues when the subject cannot sort out the new environment. Brains don't mind complexity, but they do struggle with chaos.[70] The complexity is what offers the contrast for the enriched animal.[71] Alternatively, brains do poorly with boredom; they generally thrive on some level of stimulation. The issue of boredom is big because in animal studies, the negative effects of boredom on the dendrites of brain cells are significant. In fact, there's a greater negative from boredom than there is a positive with enrichment.[72] The good news is that the effects of boredom can be reversed through enrichment.

Educational Implications: Many of these studies suggest there is potentially as much or more downside to boredom than upside to the complexity. Is it possible that kids at school are being harmed if they are in a boring environment? Certainly students' behaviors suggest they are less motivated when school isn't interesting to them. Question: Is the school environment of greater richness and complexity than the one the student is in outside of school hours? Does it offer sufficient variety, challenge, and unpredictability?

Managed Stress Levels

While all the other factors may seem traditional in that they are often described as promoting learning, moderated stress levels may come as a surprise. It turns out that excess stress (more specifically, distress) is a destructive factor in nearly every single life situation—cognition, health, social conditions, neurogenesis, gene expression, and many others. In a moment you'll see how distress can come from a variety of not-so-obvious factors.

A simple understanding of key cellular behavior will make the importance of stress control very obvious: cells *always* are either protecting themselves from danger (in a threat-distress mode) or in a growth mode. You can't run from a forest fire and at the same time take a piano lesson. Cells cannot be under the attack of distress and simultaneously grow and reproduce. They won't communicate properly with

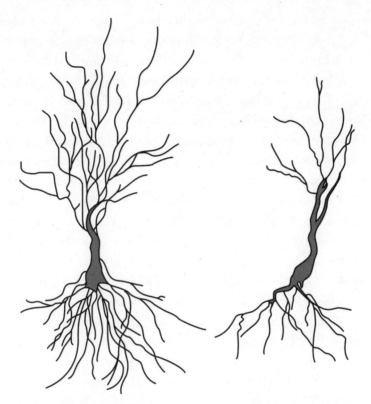

Typical healthy neuron
from mammal in
nonstressed condition

Typical neuron
from mammal in
high-stress condition

Figure 3.7. The Effect of Chronic Stress on Neurons.

other cells under distress, either. The dendrites, the branch-like extensions from neurons mentioned earlier, were reduced by 18 to 32 percent in one study that exposed them to stressors (Figure 3.7).[73] Excess stress impairs the healing of wounds and reduces resistance to further stressors.[74] Stress can also cause long-term damage to the brain's adaptive systems.[75]

Maybe worst of all, distress reduces the number of new neurons that the mammalian brain generates each day.[76] For young students this may seem irrelevant, but it suggests that the body's overall systems are being taxed excessively. Rapid aging clearly does not enhance or support cell growth or maintenance.[77] This is not an issue of vanity (at least at the school age), but it is a question of neurological integrity. Studies clearly link excess distress with lowered cognitive capacity. But what are examples of sources of distress in a school setting?

Excess acoustical noise is one stressful source. To measure this, it is easy to find schools in an airport flight path. Evans and Maxwell examined one hundred random student groups enrolled in two New York City schools, one of which was in a flight path, the other not.[78] The students exposed to the air-traffic noise had scores as much as 20 percent lower on a reading test than those of children in the other school. Yet amazingly, enrichment can positively affect auditory cortex neurons that are more sensitive to quiet sounds, more selective for tone frequency, and with a better response rate. There is solid evidence of physical changes in auditory cortex processing resulting from an overall environment designed to create enrichment.[79] Pekkarinen and Wiljanen reported dramatic improvement in students' speech discrimination after classrooms were refitted with sound-absorbing material that reduced ambient noise.[80]

Poor lighting (flickering fluorescents, too dim, wrong type, and so on) can be very stressful on learners. One study was done with twenty-one thousand students from three districts in Washington, Colorado, and California and another with eight thousand students.[81] After a review of school facilities, using architectural plans, aerial photographs, and maintenance plans, each classroom was assigned a lighting code indicating the amount of sunlight it received during particular times of the day and year. The students in the rooms getting the most natural sunlight or those using skylights scored highest. They were showing an enrichment response! In fact, students with the most sunlight in their classrooms progressed up to 20 percent faster on state standardized math tests and 26 percent faster on reading tests compared with students in classrooms with the least lighting. These gains are astonishing considering how hard school districts try to raise reading and math scores.[82]

For this particular factor, we can see how a new look at stress and distress is warranted.

Educational Implications: Here are the three key questions:

- Is the environment one that would typically inspire and challenge the learner, or is it chaotic, uncomfortable, or overwhelming? Less stress is better!
- Does the physical environment present factors that are stressful to students, such as poor acoustics and bad lighting? If so, the stress from these can reduce or eliminate the positive enhancement from other enrichment factors.
- Do the students have the life skills to deal with stressors in an environment? Stress is about the perception of control, and students need the skills or mind-set to believe they can influence their environment.

Social Support

An important factor in enrichment studies is the social grouping. Multiple studies have shown that social conditions matter.[83] In animal studies, rodents reared in isolation show increased anxiety, neophobia, and poorer performance in learning and spatial memory tasks. But when that isolation is eliminated with enhanced social environments, the problems recede.[84] Those with a more social environment recovered much quicker anatomically from brain lesions and performed better behavioral tests.[85] In addition, they developed better memories with better social conditions than those in solitary.[86]

In most studies on enrichment, social enhancement is paired with physical environment enhancement. But what if you separate the effects? The results show that the long-term effects of the physical and the social enrichment are different. In a study comparing mice in a physically enhanced environment with those that had dual (social and physical) enrichment factors, the mice in the dual environments had enhanced levels of two key growth factors that support brain plasticity.[87] Even after eighty days, when the mice were released into the researcher's "wild" (a large, controlled, fenced-in compound), the socially enhanced mice showed more affiliative and less aggressive social behavior.

There are many examples of the power of social conditions on our brains. There is the possibility that social influence could effect not just genetic expression but also genetic constitution.[88] In genetic studies, Nobel laureate Eric Kandel maintains that social environments, emotions, and belief systems are strong enough to regulate gene expression.[89] Gene expression is the activation of specific signals by genes to proteins that influence cell function and process. This is profound because we now know that the influence of genes goes both ways; from the gene to the outward world *and vice versa.* This tells us that the school environments are possibly having profound effects on our students, many of which we are not even monitoring or understanding.

Educational Implications: School social environments are possibly having profound effects on our students, many of which we are not even monitoring or understanding. Educators should consider approaches that help students achieve positive status in a safe affiliated social group.

Good Nutrition

One of the nice things about doing nutrition studies with rodents is that the compliance rate is pretty high as contrasted with a teenage human population. In animal studies, nutrition has consistently shown to make a positive difference in learning and memory. In fact, there are hundreds of studies showing varied positive effects. On the negative side, we know that poor nutrition post-weaning contributes to behavior changes later on—particularly hyperactivity.[90] We also know that a deficiency in essential fatty acids (omega 3s) can reduce performance on spatial tasks.[91] By contrast, when the correct nutrition is given, there's an improvement on spatial tasks, often a hallmark of rat intelligence.[92] Dietary supplements such as choline can make lifelong enhancements to memory function.[93]

Human studies have also focused on nutrition, showing that it's clearly important to the brain and that nutritional enhancement can help reduce the negative effects of suboptimal factors. Good nutrition is mandatory in the early years of brain development.[94] Food must supply the necessary nutrients, including proteins, unsaturated fats, vegetables, complex carbohydrates, and sugars. The brain also needs a wide range of trace elements such as boron, iron, selenium, vanadium, and potassium.

In a study examining the long-term cognitive impacts of nutritional supplements (given to children from birth to age seven), the findings were significant. Not only were numeracy, reading, and vocabulary test scores higher ten years later, when followed up at ages eleven to twenty-six there was even improved socioeconomic status compared with the control group.[95] In another study done at a preschool, those receiving good nutrition as part of an enrichment program had less antisocial behavior at ages seventeen and twenty-three.[96] This suggests the lasting value (over fourteen years later!) of early nutrition.

Finally, the question about food quantity is essential. While it's clear from both casual observation and controlled studies that hunger and impoverished diets are bad for most health, behavioral, and cognitive outcomes, there's a paradox. Too much food is bad, too. In fact, reducing total food intake—having less, but eating smarter—actually produces more brain cells than having plenty of food all the time.[97] Possibly the quantity of food creates problems. In fact, this study suggests that dietary restriction (not malnutrition) may allow your brain to be more efficient by having either less total food to process or possibly having fewer excitotoxins in the diet. Excitotoxins are known to stimulate the production of free radicals (charged oxygen molecules with an unpaired electron) with potentially adverse health consequences. What are the parents and school doing about kids who eat too much? Surprisingly, this may not be "just" an obesity problem or a worry of early onset diabetes; now there is the possibility that kids who eat smart but eat less may be maximizing their intelligence!

Educational Implications: Certainly, a portion of a child's daily nutrition is outside the reach of educators, but educators can influence student's nutrition through both parent education and school lunches. To make further sense of this factor, here are two critical questions:

- Are students getting a steady dose of highly processed foods with high fructose corn syrup and additives such as preservatives or pesticides? If so, the first thing is to eliminate the negatives.
- Second, are students getting sufficient positive nutrition? This means more than the basics of healthy proteins, fruits, complex carbohydrates, and vegetables. Students need supplements to complement the good basics.

Sufficient Time

The enrichment response means that the system has become stable with the new learning and changes from the environment. One study showed that mice that were exposed to intensive novel learning (about a year in human time) and then isolated without any reinforcement for several weeks (years in human time) still retained the synapses and the learning.[98] A wide range of rat brain changes induced by eighty days of enrichment efforts were more persistent than those induced by thirty days of enrichment efforts.[99] This suggests that although we don't want to rain on the parade of anyone who is doing short bursts of enhancement, the lasting enrichment effects are most likely to happen when the original efforts are sustained over some time.

In human studies, of course, we've learned that the human body is extraordinarily complex, and this very complexity means that any changes must get integrated across an intricate web of systems and subsystems. Although simple one-time learning tasks such as memorizing word definitions or times tables may be internalized fairly quickly, more complex learning is harder for our brains and takes time to integrate and take effect.

On a simple level, learning a new complex task means initially results of high metabolic activity as measured by PET scans. But after the task is learned, overall metabolic activity drops as the whole brain "takes a breather."[100] We become more metabolically efficient because we use less sloppy processing. At the micro level, learning means new connections are made and a memory is formed. But at the macro level, learning is the process by which multiple, new patterns are introduced. Only by using the learning or behavior over time does the new pattern become memorized by the system. At some point this new pattern becomes more attractive to the system than the old one, and it takes over as permanent.[101]

In human studies, many of the benefits of the early enrichment from the subjects' first five years remained sixteen years later when the subjects were assessed at age twenty-one.[102] Enrichment responses have to have been achieved over a long enough period for the changes to become permanent. It is likely that this involves creating allostatic states for neurochemicals, enhancing neurogenesis, and allowing for the new structures to become fully connected and functional. This takes time. In other words, a few days' effort may produce a measurable enrichment effect, but the chances are that this effect would not last unless supported over the long haul. There's no way around this issue; the more time any subject, animal or human, spends in any environment, good or bad, the more the nervous system organizes resources around responding to that specific environment. The enrichment response becomes permanent only over time.

Educational Implications: How much enrichment is enough? If we apply the results from animal models and extrapolate to human studies, we may need to supply an ongoing enriching environment for at least six or more months to ensure a lasting effect in students. Typically, an enriching protocol is more likely to be offered as an event than as a permanent contrasting protocol. A school district that offers "arts enrichment" once a week for an hour would have a tough time convincing a neuroscientist that it was creating long-term enrichment for the students. It should be said, however, that anything may be better than nothing, since even a limited exposure to enriching conditions may offer priming or other less measurable effects.

If a student is in an impoverished environment nine hours at home a day, then gets one hour of enhancement at school, that one hour constitutes only a tiny fragment of the total and is unlikely to produce substantial long-term benefits, although it's certainly better than nothing—and adding more hours can produce more striking benefits relatively easily. If, in contrast, the prevailing environment of students is already fairly enhanced, even five hours a day of positive school enhancement will have to be very targeted to skills and knowledge that the student doesn't already have to be of value.

More Good News About Enrichment Studies

While the seven enriching factors may seem pretty straightforward, an additional set of distinctions or lessons has emerged from the research. The following three things can be said about the enrichment response:

- It has global impact, not specific; it shows widespread effects in the life of the subject.
- It is generally age independent.
- It is usually intelligence independent.

Global and Widespread Impact

Neurons in multiple parts of the brain show changes. Amazingly, if you create enrichment in a pregnant female rat, her newborn pups will show effects of the enriching environment from the mother.[103]

The changes evident in enrichment are not limited to specific anatomical areas. They also can include changes in body chemistry, changes in capacity to learn, and even changes in the brain's capacity to repair itself. We mentioned earlier that we now know that environmental changes can influence gene expression.

Practical Note: One of the best things we can expect from the process of enrichment is the unexpected. When we begin to enrich on a larger scale, we may see changes that no one has yet seen in a lab!

Age Independence

Enrichment is not limited to any known age window. In fact, in rodent and human studies, the elderly were fully capable of growing new brain neurons.[104] However, neurogenesis does decline significantly with aging, and there are, of course, sensitive periods for normal learning opportunities with the visual, motor, emotional, cognitive, and language systems. There has been quite a bit of discussion and debate over the notion of "windows of opportunity," also known as critical periods or sensitive periods. Some believe that there is no neurobiological evidence for the existence of these periods.[105] Bruer says that an everyday, normal upbringing will result in children who grow up just fine. There are two major problems with his thesis.

One is that it's untestable. He argues that you'd have to run studies that show that the enhancing strategies used during the first three years could also work at any other age, say, ages nine through twelve. There will never be a formal study that does that; to do so would be to deny young children the types of healthy upbringings that we are used to during the first three years, which would be abusive. Second, very few will agree on what's a "normal" or "typical" upbringing. For many kids, "typical" means being highly stressed with poor nutrition and three to five hours a day of television. That, in my opinion, may be typical, but it's not healthy. I'd opt for an enriched upbringing anytime. Fortunately, the largest group of learning possibilities remains wide open *for the lifetime of the subject.*[106]

Practical Note: Having said that, keep this in mind. The longer any human remains in a fixed environment, the more committed the neural system becomes to survival in that particular environment. There may not be any "critical period" for enrichment, but practically speaking, earlier is better because of access to resources, environments with fewer distractions, and more motivated caregivers.

Intelligence Independence

One of the most striking findings is that enrichment works for so-called slower learners. In studies with genetically bred slow or "special ed" mice (from a strain identified as 129/SvJ), the Salk Institute in La Jolla, California, showed that environmental enrichment prompted *twice as much* neurogenesis compared with mice genetically bred as having "normal intelligence" that were in standard housing.[107] What is just as important is that the slower mice retained 67 percent of the new cells and improved on the behavioral tasks. Researchers have found that enrichment induces significant recovery from memory deficits in mice with genetically induced brain damage.[108] And in human studies with high-risk infants, we have also seen a long-term payback from enrichment.[109]

Practical Note: This suggests that environment may be able to override some genetic constraints, meaning that enrichment can happen for any kind of learner, including the underperforming population. Students with special needs might benefit, under certain conditions, from certain activities from which they are traditionally excluded, such as field trips, special events, and classes with enhanced content.

Changing the Environment

As we have seen from the studies, enrichment is the response from a *measure of difference.* An enhanced environment is an ongoing situation that is significantly more challenging, novel, and complex, with better nutrition and less stressful than what would be considered typical for that individual on an everyday basis. The result of that experience is what we would call enrichment.

Generally, with environmental enrichment, the changes are less specific to a spot in the brain (though the differences can certainly be located and quantified) and more of a global experience. In a profound way, environmental enrichment is different from all the other forms of experience. As we have noted, the result of positive environmental change is enrichment. The expression "enrichment classes" is commonly used among educators, and people speak of something as an "enriching experience." Such phrases tend to involve social, political, and educational definitions that may differ from the one I tend to use.

It may be useful to contrast an "enriched response" with an "enriching activity." The first is a macro process, taking place over time; typically weeks, months, or years. The second is a micro process taking place over a period of hours or days. But it may be repeated over time, as with music lessons. On a short-term or one-time basis, an enriching experience is an event that has a significant contrast with what would be considered a typical event or situation for that individual on an everyday basis. For example, taking a typical five-year-old to the circus would likely be an enriching event. The same trip would *not be an enriching event* if the child's parents already work in the circus and the child travels with them.

Changing the Brain—On Purpose!

The enrichment-response-generated changes I've described indicate two primary benefits that may interest educators. The first involves learning and memory; the second involves repair and renewal in cases of brain injury, impairment, and other disorders. The first change suggests to us that we may be able to affect the cognition of all learners, from the average to the gifted. The second change suggests to us that we may be able to improve the cognition of those with impaired learning, the disadvantaged, or brain damaged. But there is another option for changing the brain. Anyone, parents, educators, or trainers, should know how the brain changes in order to better implement their learning strategies.

The enrichment response is the result of a positive, contrasting environment. But what if you can't change the subject's environment by addressing most or all of the seven factors? What if you can only change a few "localized" variables? The research suggests that focused types of learning experiences such as skill building can benefit the brain. If the rest of the environment stays the same but the subject acquires a particular skill that's new to the brain, the brain is still likely to change, but the changes will be narrow and less global. The ability to modify the brain on purpose (that is, with the cooperation of the subject) can happen because of *neuroplasticity,* the capacity that allows for region-specific changes in the brain's structure, mapping, or functioning. It's what occurs when the activity is narrow, such as that of playing the piano over time.

Examples of purposeful plasticity appear throughout the research literature. Pioneering neuroscientist Michael Merzenich and colleagues demonstrated that a monkey that repeatedly used a specific digit eventually developed greater mass in the brain area that controlled such movement. Another study found that some musicians have a larger cortical representation for sensory areas involved in making music than do nonmusicians.[110] These studies tell us that when needed, the brain can purposefully change. But key studies have also shown that processing novel, random input patterns alone will not produce cortical changes.[111] In short, the human brain will change for what is deemed to be relevant to its possessor. But the critical discovery is that we know the factors that regulate this process. Any students can become far more successful in any skill, regardless of whether they are gifted or special needs learners. They only need to address the factors noted in the next section.

Enhancing the Brain Through Skill Learning

One way to purposefully change the brain is through the strength of personal will and practice. It sounds very simple and "old school," but it's the absolute scientific truth. From a survey of the studies and books on the brain and how it responds to change, the following variables stick out for success in skill learning:

- *Attentional mind-set to the task:* It's essential to pay fixed attention. The more the student's mind wanders, the less the rate of change. Even software programs and videogame programs require the subject to stay "locked in" to the content and the process.
- *Low to moderate stress:* This variable is quite slippery because what is stressful for one may not be stressful for another. The bottom line is that the subject must perceive some choice or control over the task and the surrounding conditions. Otherwise, the stress from that loss of control may neutralize the positive effects from the learning.
- *Coherent, meaningful task:* The evidence suggests that random, useless tasks will create little or no change in the brain. It only gets the subjects irritated or bored. They have to buy into the task.
- *Massed practice:* The ideal is sixty to ninety minutes a day, three to five times a week. Very young subjects may be unable to focus

for more than twenty to forty minutes, but teens or adults are better at focusing for longer periods. This length of practice is critical or the brain won't change much.

- *Learner-controlled feedback:* Most tasks will involve learners who will make mistakes. If the feedback is too general, too fast, or too irritating, the learner will become distressed and success will drop. Ideally, subjects should be able to adjust the level and type of task feedback, though with great care it can be designed to be appropriate for each subject.
- *Repetition of task:* The brain will create new connections when there's new learning, but these connections must be reinforced and strengthened or they deteriorate. The repetition should be daily, or at least many times per week.
- *Overnight rest between new learning sessions:* Although new connections and corrections are formed during the daytime, it is the nighttime when the learning is consolidated, organized, and distributed to various areas of the brain for long-term storage. Sleep is a critical ingredient for transfer from short-term to long-term memory.

These variables turn out to be well tested, researched, and validated through countless studies. In fact, if you find a highly effective reading program, music lesson, or skill-building program for athletes, you can be sure that it will follow this formula, without exception. Nonetheless, using this near-magic formula for changing the person involves several challenges: the parties have to be informed about the specific strategies (and not everyone knows them), and it takes the permission and buy-in from the subject for the program to be effective. It also takes a long-term approach of management and support to follow through, or the benefits will diminish. Having said that, the good news is that the brain can and will change.

Why is this subject brought up in a book that is generally about the environment and not specifically skill building? The fact is, you can win the battle on many fronts. Skill building by itself is not an overall, enhanced environment. But it's a great option or an addition to the experience of any child. The greater the personal assets that the student has, the less the environment matters. The better the environment, the less the student assets matter. But if you're serious about success, go after every variable you can.

Summary

Physical activity and learning support the enrichment response in both animal and human models. The physical activity promotes a host of positive changes in the brain, with neurogenesis being one of the more powerful changes. But the new brain cells are not sufficient in their initial form. They must survive and become functional, too. It is believed that new learning acts to promote the survival and differentiation of the cells into functional circuits because it gives the new cells a job or role.[112] This kind of growth is certainly a plausible survival-enhancing scenario for any species.

In short, positive change from an individual's prevailing environment activates the change signals. It starts with physical activity that influences the brain to stimulate the production of raw materials (neurons, growth factors, and so on). Then subsequent learning uses those raw materials to further develop the brain by making new connections and eliminating excess synapses. Evidence for this hypothesis comes from several studies that show that in untrained laboratory animals, most of the adult neurogenesis degrades quickly. Without a need or application, the brain allows new neurons to die off.[113] The application of this research to public models is emerging.

Both parents and schools need to hear this clearly: *contrast is the key* to creating the enrichment response. The factors that contribute to this contrast are very straightforward. They include (1) physical activity, (2) novel, challenging, and meaningful learning, (3) coherent complexity, (4) managed stress levels, (5) social support, (6) good nutrition, and (7) sufficient time. In the upcoming chapters, we'll see how these become manifested in classrooms and homes.

4

The Malleable Brain

DEBATE IN THE NEUROSCIENCE COMMUNITY RANGES ACROSS A SLEW OF ISSUES, but one thing is unanimous. The human brain is constantly changing. This chapter describes some of those changes and the opportunities that present themselves for maximizing the brain's potential. We have just been starting to understand the types of change and the mechanisms for change in the past few years. It now seems that humans change far more than ever believed as they grow from birth to maturity. The disadvantage to human infants being born helpless is their vulnerability to harm. Yet the advantage is their enormous receptivity to the new world they're born into. Their relatively delayed rate of brain development makes humans highly susceptible to the longer influence of postnatal experiences. This susceptibility can be described in a couple of ways:

• *Malleability* refers to our brain's broad capacity to change as a result of general long-term experiences that are happening to it. Malleability could explain, for example, the brain changing with exposure to stress, repeated trauma, or even nutrition. We can say our brains are highly malleable; if we expose an infant to abuse or neglect, the child's emotional systems may be changed semipermanently.[1] This malleability means we can either develop our emotional world properly or not develop it and risk serious consequences. Researcher Dr. Stanley Greenspan understands the role of emotions in the developing child's cognitive and social world.[2] Although many treat the growing-up time as a three-part world of motor skills, language, and cognition, Greenspan focuses on the power of the emotional brain. As a generalization, malleability means the ability to change over a longer period of time and with greater passivity than other types of change.

• *Neuroplasticity* refers to use-dependent cortical reorganization—changes that result from what the organism in question does. This process occurs when the brain changes as a response to a specific experience. When we learn to tie our shoe, ride a bike, speak a language, play a sport, build a boat, type, or play an instrument, the brain will change. It is a measurable and often significant remapping of the brain's topological real estate. In a way, it's like suburban sprawl—land once used for farming is sold and now it is used for housing. This is a revolutionary concept; it says not just that the brain changes from experience, but that it "buys, sells, and homesteads neural real estate" based on what you actually do on a daily basis. As a result, people today are being less shocked by ground-breaking books such as *Change Your Brain, Change Your Life,* which shows how lifestyle, nutrition, relationships, and exercise can make significant changes in your emotional and behavioral world.[3] Your three-pound brain is bustling with change at this time (Figure 4.1).

Genetic and Environmental Changes

What's the source of all the brain changes? Is it nature or nurture that defines what an infant will become? The question is irrelevant; it tries to split what cannot in fact be divided. Bill Greenough, one of the modern pioneers of neuropsychology, has been exploring how the brain changes since the 1970s. He says that measuring and contrasting the effects of genetics and environment is a bit like asking if height or width contributes more greatly to the area of a rectangle—they both contribute! His early experiments (using rats to measure enrichment and extending the findings to human development) have become classics.[4] He describes brains as changing in one of the following ways at a time:

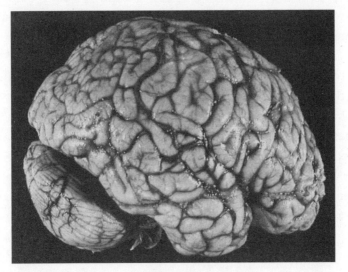

The human brain is malleable, not fixed.
Early years can have a profound effect.
Many negative changes are reversible, others are not.

Figure 4.1. The Human Brain.

- Experience-independent change
- Experience-expectant change
- Experience-dependent change

Experience-Independent Change

Some changes occur more or less regardless of what an individual does or experiences. For example, the human brain grows like crazy in the months following birth, increasing from an average weight of four hundred grams at birth to one thousand grams at one year and continuing to grow for years afterward.[5] That kind of growth is going to happen in over 90 percent of all humans. Only extreme circumstances (such as neglect) would change that developmental trajectory. By the teenage years, the volume of the human brain has quadrupled.[6] Metabolically, from birth to four years of age, the cerebral cortex's use of glucose rises, reaching more than twice the glucose usage of the adult brain and continuing thus until the age of ten years.[7] During adolescence, the levels of andro-gens and estrogens (male and female hormones) increase, susceptibility to drugs increases, the stress response system changes, and the frontal lobes slowly begin to mature. At the other end of life—outside my scope here—chemical processes associated with aging set in.

All of these changes are tendencies of the species—inborn and for the most part controlled by genes. Yet even they are not 100 percent totally predetermined. Life experiences from nutrition to the social envi-ronment can influence the degree to which these changes take place. As an example, an infant who is severely neglected will develop an under-sized brain.

Experience-Expectant Change

The second type of change, experience-expectant, is a more clear, more definite combination of genetics and environment. It means that the brain is ready for and expects something to happen, but it still needs prompting. For example, the human brain is designed for communica-tion. Humans, without any training at all, will use gestures, grunts, shouts, and sign language. You may have had the experience of being in a foreign culture and not knowing the language spoken. Years ago I vis-ited Huahine, one of the outer islands of French Polynesia. At the time, there were no English-speaking persons on the island. Everything (apolo-gies to the Polynesian language) sounded like gibberish to me, so I resorted to hand signals and fractured repetition of phrases spoken to me. The amazing thing was that, after a week, with no formal training, I was actually learning some words and getting along much better. What I have is clearly a brain designed to learn to speak a language. What we hear helps so much that most kids on a summer break lose ground in terms of vocabulary development.

The brain is set up to respond to language exposure, but it will not develop a speaking vocabulary without exposure and prompting. The unfortunate children who survive without language exposure—called "feral children"—or cases of severe deprivation demonstrate this. For example, "Genie" was discovered in Los Angeles in 1970, strapped to a potty-chair at the age of thirteen.[8] She had been neglected for years, received no normal social human interaction, and had never been taught to speak. When found, she communicated at that time only through grunts and groans. Since age thirteen, has Genie learned to speak English fluently? No, in spite of years of intensive support and training by a slew of therapists, psychologists, and linguists, Genie still speaks like a fractured telegram, barking out the broken sentences of a three-year-old. Today, she is middle-aged and living in a sheltered-care home for adults who cannot live alone.

Another example might be susceptibility to stress. If your mother had a stress disorder or depression at age forty-five, will you also have the same problem? Genes may play some role in this equation, but a minor one. If you expose yourself to the same risk factors, you might become depressed, too. But if you lower your risk through lifestyle changes, you just might stay depression-free. Remember, genes are the coding for brain-body processes; they function in much the same way that blueprints provide the structural plans for a house. But they don't guarantee the outcome. Every day, your genes influence proteins, which in turn influence molecular activity. But it goes the other way, too. Your lifestyle, the environment in which you live, can also influence your perception of experience. That influences your bodily reactions (such as stress) and that in turn can influence proteins, which can influence genes. Nutrition is an example of something that can effect our brains.

Experience-Dependent Change

The third type of change is experience-dependent. These changes are 100 percent a result of your life's experiences. Some of these influences are bad (neglect, malnutrition, abuse, and the like), of course, and they can create lasting problems. However, many good influences allow an infant (through primitive sensory biases) to attend to more relevant stimuli (a smiling parent's face) in its busy environment. When I talk about brain change, I am referring to relatively lasting changes, changes that are measurable at least ninety days after the influence in question. There are plenty of ways it can happen. Here are just some of the events that literally change the brain:

Negative	Positive
Trauma	Learning a new language
Drug abuse	A year in a foreign country
Neglect	Sports participation
Separation from parents	Skill building
Traumatic brain injury	Learning to learn
Seizures	Entering a new environment
Physical or emotional abuse	Phonemic awareness training
Malnutrition	Restoration of a sense

In addition, improvements in brain function can be seen after surgery or a stroke—events that damage the brain dramatically are sometimes followed by brilliant recoveries. Areas of the brain retool themselves to deal with different functions, more or less effectively replacing the losses. Even a hemispherectomy—the removal of half the brain—can be followed by nearly normal life, especially if the damage occurs in a young individual.[9] Removing half a brain seems crazy, but it can work. Amazingly, the remaining side of the brain takes over the functions of the removed half. If this operation is done before age two, there are usually no side effects. Between two and four, there are some noticeable losses and learning deficits. At age four to six, there are greater language and learning deficits. The operation is not typically done after age six or seven.

Again, the human brain has enormous capacity for change. For both parents and educators, that's a message of hope.

Infancy and the Developing Brain

Until just a few short years ago, scientists had to make a lot of guesses about what was happening in the brains of young children growing up. Now, using MRIs, researchers are able to take images over a period of years and see year-by-year how the brain changes. Let's take a look at what we know about the brain at its earliest stage of development, even before birth (see Figure 4.5 later in chapter).

The first understanding about our early developing brains is that of vulnerability. Even in the womb, we are highly vulnerable to both good and bad experiences. From birth, the brain is bursting with new, receptive neurons. How receptive? By the age of one, neurons (your largest brain cells) in the prefrontal cortex average around one hundred thousand synapses (connections) apiece. By comparison, neurons in the visual cortex have only twelve thousand synapses apiece.[10] The myelination process (wherein each axon gains a fatty coating of tissue called myelin) is slowest in the frontal lobes as compared with other areas of the brain. Myelination is a process that's both genetic and experience dependent. This process increases your brain's efficiency dramatically, allowing for faster processing, decision making, and acting on those decisions. But it's dependent on which experiences the child has and on maturity levels.

Maturity is a critical matter, because without mature fontal lobes, the child's brain can't understand, rationalize, dismiss, or even reflect on the simplest of life experiences. Young children have billions of neurons and even more synapses making connections out of a chaotic, violent, whimsical, and nonsensical world. Good, bad, or ugly, what comes at the brain at this age is simply taken in and downloaded. You can't have a brain that is fabulous at sponging up new experiences like learning a language and somehow isn't also vulnerable to bad things.

Brain Receptivity

The second condition that makes the brain especially vulnerable at this age is the *brain state* characteristic of very young children. Youngsters are in more highly receptive brain states than are adults. A brain state can be measured several ways: chemically, behaviorally, or electrically. Researchers most commonly talk about brain states in terms of cycles per second (CPS) of brain wave activity (Figure 4.2). The slowest is delta, the 0–4 CPS seen during deep sleep and coma. Theta, half-awake and

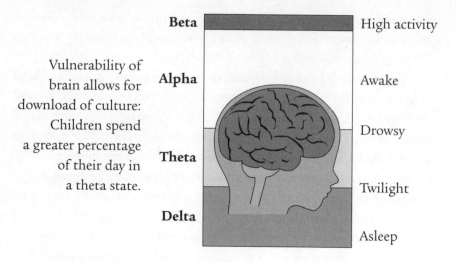

Vulnerability of brain allows for download of culture: Children spend a greater percentage of their day in a theta state.

Beta — High activity

Alpha — Awake

— Drowsy

Theta — Twilight

Delta — Asleep

☐ Range of healthy adult brain states
▨ Range for typical child, ages 2–5

Figure 4.2. Brain Wave Activity.

half-asleep, is 4–7 CPS. Next higher is alpha, the alert but calm state, at 7–12 CPS. Activity or excitement invokes the beta state, 12–25 CPS. There are many other states, but those are the most common.

Of those mentioned, theta is the most passively receptive of the brain states. The delta state is "dead to the world" and too subdued for learning. Both the alpha and beta states are good for learning, but the brain may be analytical, unable to focus or even be critical of the new learning. Interestingly, theta is the state in which we are most receptive. Now, guess in what state children from ages zero to five spend most of their waking hours? You guessed it—it's the most receptive ones, especially theta, the state most conducive for uncritical, undisputed downloading of new information.[11]

It's the same state that hypnotists use for getting the best results with audience members participating in their stage acts. The problem is that kids this age are watching television in this state, too. Children begin watching television early, often by six months of age. The typical

A.C. Nielson viewing pattern shows a steady rise in the number of hours of television watched from early childhood through preadolescence. Does this create a concern for the brain that's downloading culture instead of getting enriched? It should concern you very much, and here's why. More than a third (36 percent) of all children have a TV in their bedrooms. More than one in four (27 percent) have a VCR or DVD player, and 43 percent of four to six-year-olds do.[12] The typical American household has the television set on for more than seven hours each day, and children ages two to eleven spend an average of twenty-eight hours per week viewing. The periods of most violent programming were between 6 A.M. and 9 A.M., with over 165 violent scenes *per hour*.[13]

Does all this have any effect on the young brains? One study compared three large groups of kids (one in a different city). One received typical, violent TV; another group received average or neutral TV; and the third group received no television at all (it's not yet broadcast to that city). In comparing the rates of violence of these kids with those of kids in cities *that already had television,* what do you think was found? Guess which group turned out to be more violent (hurting siblings, misbehavior, bullying, misdemeanor offenses, and so on)? The biggest increase in violence was in the city that went from no television to violent television.[14] Why? The brain is highly receptive to constant streams of images, especially in a receptive, theta state. This was an interesting study because cities were being measured without the "contamination" of having already had television available for decades. In other studies, the starting "baseline" already has the "television effect"; the subjects already may have a higher starting point for violence, since everyone's already been watching it.

Keep this in mind when it comes to choices you make for children. Their brains are going to download the world all day—that's exactly what they're designed to do for survival—brains download the culture. They suck in the images, the sounds, the actions, conversations, neglect, trauma, emotions, and values for every waking hour. The young brain is downloading stress, problems, how to be a mom, how to be a dad, how to deal with life, what humans do all day—both from direct observation and from images in television and movies. This is an undisputed, unedited download that shapes the young child's world in powerful, life-long ways.

If children download an enhanced environment, loaded with positives, the result may be enrichment response. If children download environments full of chaos, distress, or trauma, their brains will also change dramatically but in a negative way. This can reduce the child's ability to regulate emotions later on.[15] The stress response system can become hypervigilant or hyporesponsive. These kids may become very aggressive or very passive and struggle with daily social or emotional decisions. We see such kids in the foster care, juvenile justice, or criminal justice systems.

Brain Maximizer: Avoid all television for children under the age of two. Be highly selective of DVDs for infants and children under five. For children ages two to five, only the television shows *Sesame Street* and *Blue's Clues* have a well-researched, positive track record for social, emotional, and cognitive enhancement. Children's cartoons average about twenty to twenty-five violent acts per hour, which is five times more than typical primetime shows. A typical child's exposure to violent cartoons can lead to increased aggression.[16] This is the time for children to socialize, crawl, explore, talk, try out things, build things, learn games, and be protected from violence and rapid, nonsense brain programming.

Language

The brain areas involved with listening, learning new sounds, and eventually speaking are in the temporal lobes. Although no biological mandate requires language processing in the left brain, certain "soft biases" in information processing are preferential to language skills in the left hemisphere.[17]

The auditory cortex (in the temporal lobes) undergoes dramatic growth and stabilization from the beginning of the last trimester of gestation through the first postnatal year. Infants can discriminate most sounds in their normal environment by six months.[18] Several developmental thresholds occur between birth and six months and again between six months and twenty-four months. These milestones suggest how the infant's auditory system matures toward adult levels in range (decibels), discrimination (in the presence of a masking noise), and temporal resolution (quick word interval changes).

The number of synapses in the language areas reaches its maximum at about one year; about the time children become most interested in receptive and expressive language.[19] This is the time when parents and caregivers should pay special attention. The more the parent's conversations (more words, longer words, complete sentences) between birth and three, the greater the infant's vocabulary. Figure 4.3 shows the relationship between a mother's speech and the vocabulary growth in the infant. When mom talks, infants listen.[20] This suggests the importance

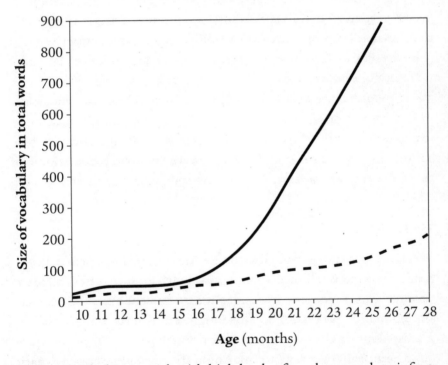

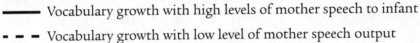

—— Vocabulary growth with high levels of mother speech to infant

- - - Vocabulary growth with low level of mother speech output

Figure 4.3. How Much Does Talking to Your Children Matter?

Source: J. Huttenlocher, W. Haight, A. Bruk, M. Seltzer, and T. Lyons (1991), "Early Vocabulary Growth: Relation to Language Input and Gender," *Developmental Psychology, 27*(2), 236–248.

of eye contact, a gentle touch when speaking, and complete sentences. Short, one-word sentences that simply give a command like "Stop!" will not build a child's vocabulary very much. It's time to lavish the language on the young brain.

Amazingly, the synapses (connecting areas between neurons in the brain) are far more densely packed in the brains of infants and young children than in those of adults. This exuberance of connections may contribute toward greater activity and increased excitability among youngsters that age.[21] High metabolic activity is overdone when you have fever and even convulsions. But it's just right for most children between birth and five years of age, since it is activity and experience that develop the language capacities of the brain. The first big burst in vocabulary occurs between fourteen and twenty-two months. During this spurt, children may learn up to three new words a day, and vocabulary growth will even pick up from there. By first grade, a child may well be learning up to twelve words a day!

Brain Maximizer: This is the time for children to hear real people talk (not television voices). It's the time for full sentences, using real English, in context. Limit the short one- and two-word commands and orders to a minimum. Talk through what you do with children. Expose children to a wide range of conversations with eye contact and gestures or props.

Exploration

The young brain is burning with desire—desire to learn. There is a continuing rise in overall resting brain metabolism (glucose uptake) after the first year of life, with a peak—about 150 percent of adult levels—at around four to five years of age for some cortical areas.[22]

Development of the sensory motor systems occurs through exploration (especially visual, motor, and auditory) during the first two years. The vestibular system in the inner ear is responsible for balance, among other things. It's the system that needs to be activated often to "acclimate and set" itself in the developing brain. The motor cortex is pruning away unused connections very fast at this age. Figure 4.4 shows the number of connections between cells (synapses) in the human motor cortex in two layers of the human brain, graphed as a function of age.

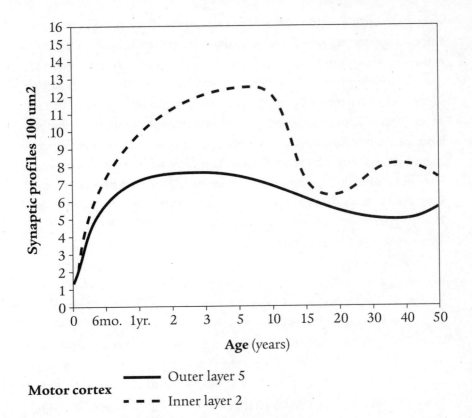

Figure 4.4. Variation of Brain Connections Over a Lifetime.

Source: P. R. Huttenlocher and A. S. Dabholkar, "Regional Differences in Synaptogenesis in Human Cerebral Cortex," *Journal of Comparative Neurology,* October 1997, 387(2), 167–178.

From birth to age two, the human brain has the greatest number of neurons that it will ever have, yet the brain is only one-fourth the size of an adult's. Most of the synapses exist and are available for usage, but not yet functional. We call those silent synapses. Many of these connections do actually form in the first two years of life. By age twelve to twenty-four months, the brain has twice as many synapses as it will have as an adult. Synaptic formation peaks between ages one and five, depending on the area of the brain measured.[23] This is a highly sensitive period, for better and for worse. Why? Because early childhood is a time of intense brain activity, and nature has prepared the newborn with

excess capacity. During the first five years, the human brain overpro-
duces synapses; there are connections between brain cells, but they're
random. One researcher estimated we have about one trillion of them.[24]

The development of the brain relies not so much on having enough
synapses as on having the right ones for the right jobs. Most of today's
researchers support a connectionist viewpoint about brain development.
This model suggests that input to the brain is what alters the "weighting" at the synapses (between the neurons). The altered weights bias and
then help form new, complex neural networks based on life experiences.
Unused synapses disappear and new ones get stronger through usage.
If the experiences are negative, the brain is getting the opposite of
enrichment—it's being impoverished.

The developing brain is especially sensitive to stress. When parents
argue, it's very stressful for little children. Domestic violence is associated with suppression of IQ in young children.[25] That's the last thing
you'd ever want if you care about enrichment. Earlier you read about the
downloading of culture in a child's brain. Early exposure to stress, neglect, abuse, or violence often causes the brain to reorganize itself, increasing receptor sites for alertness and stress chemicals.[26] When the young
brain becomes out of kilter and the chemical responses are abnormal,
it leads to atypical stress responses that can last for a lifetime. There is
no need to "toughen up" a child of five or under. Trust me, they'll get
plenty of exposure to real-word stressors later on.

The young, vulnerable brain is unable to self-regulate exposures to
stress. The frontal lobes are immature, so the child cannot understand,
compartmentalize, or rationalize exposure to violence. That's why it is
so important to keep stress low in the first five years. The research on
early stress is both dramatic and troubling. It suggests that early stressful experiences, before a child is able to handle them, can cause serious
problems later. Distress from maternal separation may cause brain cells
to commit suicide in the infant's brain. The research from laboratory
animal studies showed that distress caused abnormally high numbers
of brain cells to die.[27]

Although the growing brain normally prunes excess synapses and
cells, the neurons in the maternally deprived (highly stressed) animals

died at twice the normal rate! Neglect is bad for any child. This does not mean parents should never leave their children, but it means making sure children are safe and have adults nearby at all times. Scary, abusing, or neglectful circumstances may lead to errant synaptic pruning in the frontal lobes, which impairs emotional development later on. Troubled early relationships cause the child's brain to consume glucose in dealing with stress, rather than using that glucose for early cognitive functions.

Brain Maximizer: Find large, safe, supervised places for your child to play. These can be parks, playgrounds, fields, lawns, the beach, or other open, interesting places. Children will enjoy nature on their own, but with other children, they'll really love it. Sitting indoors watching TV is not enriching.

Primary School Age

What's going on in the world of kids ages five through twelve? There is far more activity observed in these young brains than was originally thought, and it's more diffuse in children relative to adults. Scientists believe that the increasing cognitive capacity during childhood coincides with radical changes. Peak growth rates, the extension of the connecting axons to the memory and language cortex, stretch through and after puberty. A severe, spatially localized loss of gray matter occurs in the lower brain.[28] As the brain gets more streamlined, there is a gradual loss rather than formation of new synapses and presumably a strengthening of remaining synaptic connections.[29] Children have, on average, 60 percent greater brain activation in the prefrontal cortex than that of adults. This highly active brain is sorting out a brand new world, and it takes plenty of glucose to do that. During the educational process, the brain is both losing the unused dendrites and gaining new ones; it's a complex picture.

Children also have significantly more right-hemisphere activity, too. Their brains are not quite as efficient, and they have to work harder, not always using the most efficient areas.[30] As you might guess, this just

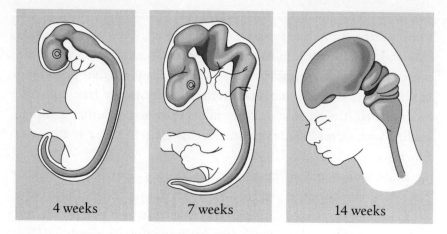

4 weeks   7 weeks   14 weeks

Figure 4.5. The Developing Brain.

about ensures that children end up more susceptible to interference and less able to inhibit inappropriate responses than adults.[31] Adults have more effective interference suppression than children, and they use the opposite (left) hemisphere for the purpose. Interestingly, positive emotions are generated more when we are using our left, not right hemisphere. This suggests that sequential tasks that activate the left hemisphere are more likely to lead to positive thoughts.[32] That also means that youngsters may get a mood lift from analyzing, counting, arranging items in a sequence, following a numeric order, and doing tasks that require a specific order. Brains develop in curious ways, with the sensory and spatial areas first and the frontal lobes being the slowest. This is illustrated in Figure 4.5.

Working memory tasks show a larger degree of immaturity in boys than in girls aged six to ten. Give them just one thing to do at a time. In addition, the visual working memory reaches functional maturity earlier than the corresponding auditory system.[33] This is the time to strengthen social skills and exploratory behaviors in reading, traveling, and imagination. Yet in spite of all the changes going on in the brain at this age, it's almost quiet compared to the firestorm happening from birth to five and in the teen years. Overall, if you're working with these children, enjoy the break. From ages five to twelve, you're in the eye of the storm.

Brain Maximizer: This is a great chance (before they get "too cool" when they're older) to enrich a youngster's life with travel opportunities, exploring nature, visiting museums, participating in plays, taking martial arts, playing soccer, 4H, dance classes, and scouting. Take this golden opportunity—you only get it once!

Unlocking the Teenage Brain

Adolescence is a wild ride for everybody—parents, teachers, and kids. There are fast-moving rapid and dramatic changes in biology, cognition, emotion, and interpersonal relationships. Just about everything that could change, does change. A good metaphor for puberty and the teen years is "starting the engine of a race car with an unskilled driver." The teen brain itself is different, and the teen skill set is different from what the same individuals had as preteens. This has been the recent focus of so many neuroscientific investigators that I can't begin to share all the latest discoveries with you here. We'll focus on just a few of the critical ones.

Many areas of the brain are under major construction during adolescence. In fact, the changes are as dramatic as those happening in an infant's brain. It's safe to call the teen years a "sensitive period" for human brain development. The parietal lobes undergo major changes from ages twelve to seventeen. Certain sub-areas may double or triple in size. The frontal lobes, a big chunk of "gray matter," are the last area to mature, undergoing dramatic changes. Gray matter (brain cells) thickens first (between ages eleven to thirteen) and later thins (reduces 7 to 10 percent) between the ages of thirteen and twenty. In 1999, Jay Giedd and colleagues demonstrated a growth spurt of gray matter in the teen brain.[34] As the child spends more time learning, the brain's dendrites continue to make more connections.

This is followed by massive pruning, in which about 1 percent of gray matter is pared down each year during the teen years, while the total volume of white matter ramps up. Gray matter is overall brain tissue, white matter is the fatty coating on the axons called myelin that speeds up connectivity. It's a bit like the insulating rubber coating on electrical cords that protects raw wires from exposure. MRI results suggest that the thickening of gray matter is due to massive changes in synaptic reorganization, meaning more usage and more connections.[35] These cells become highly receptive to new information. But they're not excited for the long term—the teen brain is not ready for that yet. Larger delayed rewards are valued less than smaller immediate rewards in impulsive individuals. Adolescents' sensitivity to rewards is stronger than that of adults. As a result, kids seek higher levels of novelty and stimulation to achieve the same feeling of pleasure. Risk, rewards, and fun are driving their brains. Keep that in mind with teens; they're terrible at risk management. In fact, their peers make too many decisions ("group think") because, collectively, no one can make up his or her mind except, often, the more impulsive ones. It's almost as if mother nature wanted teens to explore risky things and make babies.

But while this nearly exploding brain has more choices, it is often paralyzed by inefficiency. Just as with infants, it's the thinning back of synapses that creates more efficient decision making. Think of the metaphor of traveling through a dense forest; it's more efficient with a wide, paved road than with a machete, clearing underbrush on foot. Typically, the myelination process pushes back maturing until somewhere between ages sixteen and twenty, and often this extends into the late twenties. Elizabeth Sowell's work at UCLA suggests that the frontal lobes of girls mature faster than those of boys during puberty.[36] But both genders are generally poor at reading and interpreting emotions. Their frontal lobes are still too immature to damp down impulsive responses to the emotions, usually generated from the emotional "smoke detector" we call the amygdala.

Generally, girls "connect the dots" earlier than boys in both emotional and cognitive functions. While most brains become physically mature between the ages of eighteen and thirty, it takes boys until about age twenty-four to catch up to girls' brain development. Using the frontal lobes for self-regulation, teens slowly (way too slowly for most adults who live and work with them) learn about interrupting a risky behavior, thinking before acting, and choosing among different courses of action. Unfortunately, the much-needed maturation of neural networks governing self-regulation hasn't happened in adolescence. These processes suggest that the "under construction brain" areas may be highly unstable, volatile, and unpredictable. The result is that they have a very high risk rate for accidents and injuries.

Playing Catch-Up

The differences are dramatic; all these changes mean that a teen's brain needs more sleep time to learn, organize, and store new learning.[37] One metaphor to consider is that teen brains resemble blueprints and roughly framed buildings more than a finished home. Instead of thinking about a teenage mind as an empty house that needs furnishings, educators and parents would do better to understand it as the rough framing of a house that still needs wiring, plumbing, flooring, and windows. Avoid treating teenagers like adults; they're not. They have the highest accident rate in cars of any age group. Teens are in a developmental fog and often make decisions even a nine-year-old would call stupid. They have sound biological reasons for the following patterns:

- *Susceptibility:* Teens are particularly susceptible to the risky extremes of novelty. Novelty juices up their unstable systems with brain chemicals such as dopamine and noradrenaline. They choose short-lasting, immediate rewards over larger, delayed rewards. Their undeveloped frontal lobes play a significant role in reckless behaviors.
- *Lack of planning:* Teens have trouble anticipating the consequences of their behavior because they rely on their immature frontal lobes. They don't see options very well. They get confused easily under stress and rarely plan more than one move ahead.
- *Emotional stew:* Emotions are essential to learning, and teens are still learning how to understand and manage emotions. They

are poor at reading emotions and weak at selecting the right friends and getting their minds outside their own world of feelings.[38]

- *Crowd morality:* Teenagers will climb the moral ladder only as their frontal lobes develop. To develop a clear moral and ethical compass, one needs real-life experiences, mediated by thoughtful adults. But teens spend an average of twenty-eight hours a week interfacing with digital technology (computers, cell phones, videogames, and television). This time is all unsupervised, most of it alone. To balance this, they often seek friendly (even if it's negative) peer clustering. But they're more likely to engage in risky behaviors when they are in groups than alone.

- *Difficulty in self-regulation:* Teens face a huge risk of chemical imbalances for behavioral and personality disorders such as anxiety, depression, stress, eating disorders, and shifts in sleep habits. Teens are more vulnerable to all of these than adults and have few coping skills.

- *Risk taking:* Teens are extremely vulnerable to addiction, and compared with adults they are less cognizant of the effects of drug use and abuse, and their addictions are harder to break. They see drugs as harmless, for the most part, and tend to believe that they can survive anything.

Does all this chaos and change suggest that the teen brain is too big of a cauldron for positive change? No, in fact, it's quite the opposite. For good or ill, the teen brain is highly vulnerable, and that's both a curse and an opportunity. The bottom line is that they have a tough time predicting the future. Figure 4.6 illustrates how teens struggle in being able to predict the likelihood of relatively straightforward risks.

The brain's wild ride means that multiple systems and structures are undergoing massive changes. That affects the very core of our strongest success strategy in life, predictability. Jeff Hawkins has argued persuasively, in *On Intelligence,* that understanding, developing, and enhancing our capacity to predict is what gives us our intelligence.[39] In general, teens are very poor at prediction skills, and that's one reason

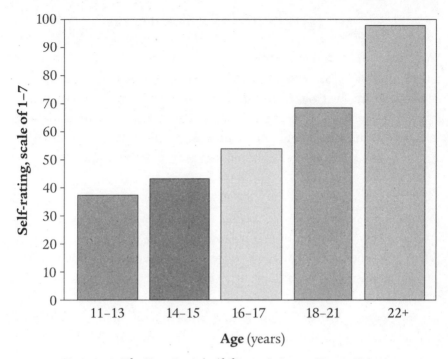

Figure 4.6. The Teen Brain's Ability to Orient to Future Events.

Source: L. Steinberg (2005), "Cognitive and Affective Development in Adolescence." *Trends in Cognitive Science*, 2005, *9*(2), 69–74.

they struggle so much. Their brains are just not done maturing. For more on the importance of prediction to our daily lives, the lay reader might enjoy Hawkins's book. It's a good, upbeat, well-researched primer.

Brain Maximizer: The natural tendency of the teenage brain is to explore, take risks, and socialize. The parent's role is mediation. Manage the risks, stay highly involved in their lives, ask questions, and reduce opportunities for dangerous activities. Ideally, parents will offer safer alternatives to teens for risk taking, such as camping, sports, school theater, wilderness treks, the use of helmets, and padding for activities such as skateboarding. Remember, their brains are *not* adult yet, and they will not make mature, measured decisions. For the teenage brain to be maximized, it should be guided carefully through this dangerous time with focus, love, and involvement.

Are Today's Brains Any Different?

Are the brains of today's young people any different from the brains of those fifty years ago? When we say the brain changes, we of course mean changes from the past, from the expected norm or from a baseline. If the brains were different, and there were changes in the brains, there should be (and is) verifiable empirical evidence in society of the changes in the behaviors of today's children versus those of fifty years ago.

Drivers of Change

What are the examples of factors that can drive change in the brain? Here are some of the changes we have seen in American children growing up as compared with those fifty years ago.

Screen time: Much more sedentary time on computers, games, and TV. Is this bad for the eyes, stress levels, frontal lobes, and learning? Some argue that it means fewer verbal interactions, worse social skills, reduced motor skills, and shorter attention spans. This may have some long-term effects on the brain. Some high school kids are taking online courses at school. This potentially can alter the brain in ways quite different from a school classroom or field trip, or hands-on experiences. How is online work different from a live class, and what are the neural consequences? What are the kids getting exposed to and what are they missing out on? We only know that there will be changes, we just don't know yet whether they will be dangerous or innocuous.[40]

Domestic variances: This may have some long-term effects on the brain. The percentages of children who have been in extended child care prior to starting school went from 25 to 80 percent in just one generation.[41] What are the effects of child care after three months, six months, or even a couple of years? Clearly this is a change in the environment over prior generations. Early evidence of change is cited in the National Institute of Child and Human Development Study. It found (not surprisingly) that children have better cognitive and emotional outcomes when the child care was of higher quality (less than 25 percent of facilities qualify) and if the child spent fewer hours in a facility or the parenting was of higher quality. The study suggests that there are differences in the effects of child care, particularly in the cases of extremes from very good to poor child care.[42] The evidence is clear that the more hours a child is in any day care, the greater the risk for behavioral problems. We know the brain is highly susceptible during these years.[43]

Too much of a good thing: There is currently much greater affluence than for any generation in history. More things are done for kids than ever before. That makes for less practice in delaying gratification, less patience, and less tolerance for a more austere or less resource-consuming lifestyle. Having more is not all good, and there's a price to pay for it.[44] This may have some long-term effects on the brain. We do know that the ability of the frontal lobes to defer gratification is both a function of maturation and the skills that can be learned and strengthened through experience. If children don't get those skills in a hurry-up world without slow board games, puzzles, reading, and other patience-building tasks, how will they get them?

Quantity time: We all hear about "quality time" but what about the quantity of it? It seems like children are getting less infant and pre-K contact with parents, less talking, less touching and caressing. The evidence is that the less maternal time early on, the more the problems later on.[45] This may have some long-term effects on the brain. How does this change in touching affect the brains of young children? Some researchers believe it changes the stress levels for a lifetime. The brain must have enough quality time, but no one knows just how much that actually should be.

Domestic mobility: Families (and of course the children in them) move more than before.[46] There is far more single, mobile parenting than there was two generations ago. Every move uses up resources and increases stress. This does affect schooling, grades, and stress. It may have some long-term effects on the brain.

Smaller families: Could this mean less close family time? There is more child time away from parents, without siblings, in larger houses! Kids have their own rooms now, instead of sharing with a sibling. This may have some long-term social and behavioral effects on the brain.

Does this mean fewer relationship skills modeled and less likelihood of sharing, discussing options, and compromising?

Eating changes: There is a decrease in breast feeding and an increase in formula feeding. This may influence immune systems. More quick, additive-laden, nutrient-deficient foods are eaten. More fast food is consumed, more often. This may have some long-term effects on the brain.

Greater stress: Many believe that children today grow up in a more stressed, nonstop world with little downtime. This means less opportunity for free, creative exploratory play. This may have some long-term effects on the brain. The stress response system can become dysregulated, as in a new negative "set point," by distress, and children are the largest group of those with stress disorders in the country.[47]

Prenatal toxic exposure: There may be greater exposure to prenatal medication, postnatal smoking opportunities, and greater varieties of drugs. Mothers are more stressed than ever. This may have some long-term effects on the brain.

More time on the road: Today's infants and kids spend far more time in cars compared to those of two generations ago. This car time is often spent sleeping or watching DVDs. There used to be more stimulation for kids in cars, and more chances to move around. Now, 100 percent of it takes place with children belted, buckled up in a car seat. It's much safer for children this way, but there may be some long-term effects on brain development from the inactivity.

Less playground time: Concerns about liability have cut back on playground features such as slides, ropes, monkey bars, merry-go-rounds, teeter-totters, and jungle gyms. These reduce the amount of early childhood spinning, rocking, twisting, rolling, and game play that may develop sensory systems. This may have some long-term effects on the brain.

Greater postnatal exposure to toxins: The more polluted the planet, the greater the exposure to risks such as lead, smog, mites, molds, and allergens. There are clear risks from each of these; recent estimates suggest allergies alone cause 1.5 million lost school days each year. These can affect learning and may have some long-term effects on the brain.[48] There are also questions about vaccinations given to children. While they may have an overall positive effect, for some, the assault on the body's immune system, especially through exposure to vaccine preservatives such as mercury or thimerosol (which are still used today), may weaken it.

Violence exposure: Today's children have increased exposure to violence, profanity, and a general disrespect of higher social human culture. This may have some long-term effects on the brain. It has been shown to dysregulate stress responses and lead to greater rudeness and even violence.

How serious are each of the environmental events just described? Would any of them cause lasting changes? Actually, every one of them has the potential for lasting changes. The greatest effect would be, of course, when multiple factors are engaged. In that case, the aggregate of five, seven, or more of the factors I've listed could potentially cause significant disruptive and lasting effects. But any one of them could also cause problems if it was both intense and reinforced by the environment. Most of the changes would not likely be good, either.

Do the Changes Last?

We've shown that the brain changes. We've shown that some of the changes are caused by experiences. They might be for the better or for the worse. Changes can also be subtle or traumatic. Maybe most important, it's refreshing to know that we even have some opportunity to regulate the changes. But will any of those changes last? It's a difficult question to answer. The most accurate answer: "Yes, maybe, and no." Yes to certain changes, maybe to other changes, and no to different changes.

As a generalization, the following things are probably true about the likelihood of changes lasting:

- The longer the exposure to any environmental factor, the more committed the nervous system becomes to coping with that experience. That means more sensory areas adapt, brain and body chemicals re-regulate themselves more completely, and stronger motor memory develops in fine and gross motor muscles as they adapt to the environment.

- The more toxic and intense the changes, the more likely they'll last. For example, lead stays in the human body for years, and it is very difficult to get rid of it.
- The timing of the changes may influence their durability. For changes made during more sensitive times, such as birth to five or the teen years, there may be a greater vulnerability and hence greater effect on the system than the effects of changes at other times.
- The more institutional support there is for the changes, the greater the likelihood of them lasting. For example, if kids own their own Play Stations or Xboxes, visit places with videogames, or can get them online easily, the community culture is supporting and strengthening the habit. The good news is that if the brain is maximized properly and the enrichment response happens, even lifelong problems can be reversed. One rodent study showed that even early stress complications could be reversed with later interventions that may be applicable for humans.[49]

Summary

We've seen in this chapter that the brain is changing very rapidly from birth to age five. It is clearly a "sensitive" time in which certain changes that happen may have a greater effect than during another time. The brain is more vulnerable during this time to both positive and negative factors. The second period we explored was ages five through twelve. For the time being it appears to be a bit calmer and slightly less of a "sensitive" time for brain changes. The third time period, the adolescent and teenage years from ages twelve through nineteen, appears to be another "sensitive" period for brain development and vulnerability to change.

Finally we looked at society as a whole. Although there is no clear anatomical or imaging data to support this hypothesis, these two facts are clear. One, the brain does change as a result of experience, and two, *the experiences* of today's kids are different from those of two generations ago. This suggests to us that their brains are different. In short, it certainly looks as though the changes in our society are likely to create lasting changes in the brains of its members—our children and theirs, and ourselves. Understanding what and how the brain changes is critical for those who want to maximize brain potential.

It is clear that there are countless opportunities to make choices. One choice may enhance or maximize brain development and another may be more neutral or may even impair brain development. Yes, life is full of choices, we all know that. But the point is that certain choices will either maximize a child's brain or contribute to the mediocrity of a "neural wasteland." Take the choices seriously; it's not just a brain we're talking about; it's the life that's either well-lived or frittered away.

Brains at Risk

IN THE PREVIOUS CHAPTER, WE EXPLORED THE DEVELOPMENTAL TRAJECTORY OF brains from birth through age eighteen. But the general tone of the chapter suggested that the children growing up were fairly typical. For them, the results from an enrichment response sound simple if not easy. But in many schools, those identified as gifted are the ones receiving the most enhancement programs for their brains. What's your opinion? Can you get the "enrichment response" from anyone; that is, does enrichment apply to *all* children? This chapter explores that question. The title "Brains at Risk" suggests that there are many brains at risk, and there are. The question is actually guided by neuroscience. Can a brain that has been disadvantaged by adverse genetics or life experience be substantially enriched? The answers may surprise you.

Poverty and the Brain

A child's brain development is threatened by a host of risk factors, some posed by the child's environment, others that are simply natural to any growing child. We'll begin with the issue of poverty and enrichment. Many who have not studied poverty think of it as a problem of no money in the checkbook or bank. Unfortunately, it's not that simple. In fact, if that were the only problem, it would be good news. Broadly, poverty is a condition in which there is a chronic and significant lack of access to resources. It typically leads to an adverse, synergistic effect from multiple risk factors. Only in the past ten years have researchers even begun to understand some of the real ramifications of being poor, which can and do affect children of all ethnicities. This topic is no theoretical discussion; nearly 19 percent of all children in the United States come from low-income families.[1] The effects of poverty on a human being are truly staggering. When compared with their middle- or upper-income classmates, children of poverty are more likely to

- Live on or near toxic waste sites[2]
- Live in areas that did not meet one or more of the Primary National Ambient Air Quality Standards[3]
- Have had more exposure to pesticides and to lead.[4] High levels of lead are dangerous to children because they can cause neurological and developmental impairment (Figure 5.1). Children of poverty also have more exposure to cigarette smoke; the percentage of homes with children under age seven in which someone smokes on a regular basis was 19 percent in 1999.[5]
- Have disabilities. Among children with disabilities aged three to twenty-one in the United States, 28 percent are living in poor families. Yet among the children without disabilities in the same age range, only 16 percent are living in poverty.[6]
- Be from poor families with greater vulnerabilities to budgetary cost fluctuations. Elevated utility bills in a cold winter are inversely related to quality of nutritional intake in low-income infants and toddlers. If families have to spend extra money for heating, it often comes out of their budget for food. Better nutrition often costs more than plain, preservative-laden, packaged food.[7]
- Have parents that are less likely (by a factor of three or four) to initiate conversation just to maintain social contact or build vocabulary.[8] Researchers also point out that children in these homes also hear fewer responsive, supportive, and interactive conversations among others in their homes. Their parents are only half as likely to read to them as compared with high-

*Figure 5.1. Lead and Other Environmental Toxins
Typically Impair Cognitive Development.*

income children.[9] They also use different vocabulary words every day, both fewer and less complex than those heard in families of greater income.[10]

- Live in single-parent households or with no parent.[11] In 1998, for black and Hispanic children living with single mothers, the poverty rates were 54 percent and 64 percent, respectively.[12] Boys in single-parent families were more likely to develop psychiatric disease and narcotics-related disease than were girls, and they also had a raised risk of all-cause mortality.[13] They get less nurturing and emotional support from parents, such as hugs, praise, or supportive statements.[14] The kids get not just less quality time, but less total time from their parents or caregivers.[15]

- Move twice as often, get evicted five times as much, develop fewer social ties, and have more chaos, stress, and disruption in their lives.[16]
- Experience significantly more daily stresses—35 percent more daily hassles and stressors and up (Figure 5.2).[17] For example, at a basic level of traffic risk, children of poverty face 50 percent more street crossings with a six times greater risk in pedestrian accidents.[18] These children also have more contact with aggressive peers.[19]
- Watch far more television than their above-poverty-line peers.[20] Almost 20 percent watch six or more hours a day.
- Have less accessibility to healthier food where they live, are more likely to have higher-priced convenience stores nearby, and, typically, eat a poor diet.[21] Their food is of lower quality, they get fewer nutrients, and they get more additives.[22] Their higher-fat diet is likely to reduce learning by reducing the brain's supply of BDNF, a growth factor involved in neural plasticity.[23]

Each of the listed items acts only as a risk factor. By itself, any one factor would be more likely to be unfortunate or a nuisance. But there is increasing evidence that these factors do not act alone. In fact, if you subtract the positive factors from the environments, these risk factors play off each other with a devastating effect.[24] The negative factors acted in a cumulative and synergistic manner—the more risk children experienced, the more compounding the problem behavior they demonstrated. For more on this topic, see Dr. Ruby Payne's book *Poverty: A Framework for Understanding and Working with Students and Adults from Poverty.*[25]

In addition, duration is an important variable. Chronic early childhood poverty has far more adverse impact on a child than the same experiences at a time later in life.[26] Lower socioeconomic status (SES) affects well-being at multiple levels. We have to look at more than just the individual; it affects the family, the community, the legal system, and school performance.[27] In short, poverty is *not* about how much money flows into the family checkbook. It is a complex array of factors that can have

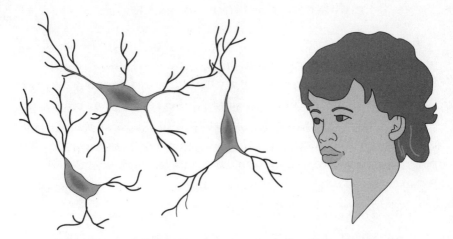

Chronic and overwhelming stress in a child is toxic. Persistent
stress hormones lead to the death of neurons in critical brain
pathways responsible for emotional regulation. Genetics
and experience interact to shape "at-risk" behaviors.

Figure 5.2. Distress and Brain Cells.

devastating overlapping and lasting effects. In a nutshell, poverty is
about chronically limited access to resources with a likely negative, synergistic result. Much of it revolves around the effects of chronic distress.
This leads to a slew of problems, including complications in pregnancy
and miscarriages.

The effects of poverty, however, are reversible. In one interesting
study, moving from high-poverty to middle-class neighborhoods had
positive effects on the achievement scores of eleven- to eighteen-year-old
boys compared with those of their peers remaining in high-poverty
neighborhoods.[28] These male adolescents' scores were comparable to
females' scores, whereas male adolescents in high-poverty neighborhoods scored ten points lower than female peers. This is offered here
not because you and I expect every poor person to move, but because
the premise is that the brains (and behaviors) can change; they're not
stuck that way forever. Naturally, too much moving again becomes a
stress factor.

What Do the Differences Mean?

How do these risk factors play out in a child's brain given the possibility of an enrichment response? For this information, I turn to a different kind of research. Children of poverty become at risk for many reasons. But you may recall that I said earlier that life experiences are brain experiences. What happens to our brains is likely to change them. Unfortunately, one problem creates another (and another). The differences that poverty creates never seem to stop. For example, children of poverty are less likely to get needed medical care for a whole range of problems:

- Falls or head injury (when there's a potential for a head injury causing attention deficit, cognitive deficits, or emotional deficits)
- Mental illness (when denial or shame may prevent the child from getting the needed help)
- Depression (stress increases vulnerability, and the parents may not know the signs or potential treatments)
- Physical impairments (without some baseline of health, children may have vision or hearing impairments and not get the needed tests)
- Behavioral disorders (parents may not know or understand symptoms of AD/HD, reactive attachment disorder, or oppositional personality disorder)

At school, children of poverty are disadvantaged in many ways. First, their parents or caregivers are less likely to be assertive in finding out what services are available. That means a child in poverty may miss out on specific screening for everything from vision and hearing tests to IQ tests or even tests for giftedness. Parents may not know about or understand the 1997 Individuals with Disabilities Education Act. The parents and children are far less likely to have Internet access. This means parents cannot access school-based information to help their children, and it also means parents cannot seek information for problem solving. They may not be able to access their child's homework or school announcements. In addition, poor children are more likely to have troubles in school for a variety of reasons:

- *Connection:* More affluent parents monitor their children's school progress better. In contrast, poor parents are less likely to know their child's teachers by name, less likely to know their child's best and worst subjects, and less likely to know how each child is doing in each class.[29]
- *Daily reading:* Among poor families, 36 percent of parents read to their kindergarten-age children each day, compared with 62 percent of those from upper-income families.[30]
- *Involvement:* Fewer low-income parents are involved (36 percent) at school in three or more activities on a regular basis compared with 59 percent of those above the poverty line.[31] Children from families in poverty were less likely to participate in activities than were children whose families were at or above poverty.[32]
- *Teachers:* Children in poverty are more likely to have less qualified teachers. For example, 27 percent of high school math teachers in low-income districts were math majors in college. This is 16 percentage points below the level in the middle- and upper-income school districts, where 43 percent of the math teachers have a math degree.[33]
- *Violence and anger:* Poor children are more than twice as likely to report seeing weapons at school or physical assaults.[34] Children in homes with less parental stability are more often victims of violence. Domestic violence is associated with lower IQ in young children.[35]
- *Disabilities:* Being from a low-income household is linked to a greater likelihood of poor health and development in young children, poor performance in school, and a variety of poor outcomes in adolescence.[36] The Special Education Elementary Longitudinal Study (SEELS) findings confirm the results of earlier research on students with disabilities, which found that they may be disproportionately exposed to the potentially negative effects of poverty.[37] More than one-third (36 percent) of students with disabilities lived in households with incomes of $25,000 or less, compared with 24 percent of children in the general population ($p < .001$).

Students with disabilities were significantly more likely to be living in poverty than those in the general population. Almost one in four students with disabilities (24 percent) were living in poverty in 2000, compared with 16 percent of students in the general population.[38] Almost two-thirds of students with disabilities (64 percent) in households with incomes below $25,000 were in poverty, as were almost 2 percent of students in households with incomes of $25,000 to $50,000.

- *Size of school.* The evidence is clear that between two schools providing equal services for those in poverty, the one that is smaller generally mitigates the negative effects of poverty better. The Small Schools Project (www.smallschoolsproject.org) emphasizes the value of schools with fewer than four hundred in student population, and such schools share a core set of characteristics. The case for small schools is compelling; student achievement goes up, students are recognized by their teachers, and as a result, discipline problems and dropout rates go down, while attendance goes up. Even the cost per graduate is generally lower in small schools compared with larger, more comprehensive high schools. It's likely that the increased positive social contact, more attention, and different school philosophy of smaller schools makes the differences.

In sum, we can see that a wide array of disadvantages creates a difficult web of negatives that requires tremendous personal effort to overcome. It's not that it's impossible, but you may be starting to get an idea of what low-income parents and children are up against. That leads to some very good questions.

Is There an Opportunity for Miracles?

Children of poverty often develop impoverished brains with a variety of difficulties. That's the bad news we don't really need to hear again and again. Is there hope for something good? *Yes* is the emphatic answer.

Many problems can be overcome through environmental enrichment. Though adoption studies are not something that can or should be replicated across the board, these studies tell us about why we should be hopeful.

Recent studies create a useful baseline of possibility by showing material increases in IQ for children born to low-SES parents and adopted early by middle- or upper-SES families. A positive adoptive environment for children adopted after four years of age is effective in boosting low IQs to near normal.[39] This "enrichment response" was found by starting with the files of 5,003 adopted children. Sixty-five highly deprived children, defined as abused or neglected during infancy, were selected because they met two criteria. First, they were adopted between four and six years of age, and second, they had IQs below 86 before adoption. The effects of their enhanced upbringing was dramatic. They had an average IQ gain of 13.9 points, and even higher (19.5 points) when they were adopted by high-SES families. This study was introduced not because it's a viable, inexpensive everyday option, but because of one thing. It shows that the effects of poverty can be ameliorated by an enhanced environment. In other words, the brains of kids of poverty are not lost forever.

Educational interventions can be effective in changing the IQs of children living in low-SES families. Many researchers think that the earlier the interventions the better for three reasons. First, there may be a "sensitive" time for the brain when it's more receptive to big rewiring changes. Second, we have more access and opportunity to make massive changes in the brain when the child has not yet discovered the opposite sex, freedom, autonomy, and roving peer groups. Finally, the longer the intervention the better. Here are four ways that we can significantly change lives:

- Hope
- Head Start program
- Skill-building programs
- Changing the environment

Hope

Years ago a multimillionaire in the Bronx was making a graduation speech to the sixth graders at an underperforming primary school. Inspired by the possibilities, he tore up his rah-rah speech and made a pledge that he would pay for the college education of any of the kids from that class who went on to graduate from high school (six years away). The parents and the students at this high-poverty school were shocked and struggled with the explosive meaning of that statement.

During the next few years, the teachers, the curriculum, and the policies at that school weren't any different. But you can bet the parents were different. Could you imagine the conversations happening at the dinner table that night? It's likely that many were along the lines of "You *are* going to college, and you're going to start studying right now!" The benefactor was serious, and years later, he made good on his promise. Children who never dreamed of going to college suddenly had a date with destiny. Hope is a powerful thing for both parents and kids. Years later the school had a higher graduation rate than it had ever had. This is a true story, and although a study was never published in a quality peer-reviewed journal, it suggests that hope is very, very powerful.

Some people may be tempted to pooh-pooh the value and power of hope. But surprisingly, it's science that may prove them wrong. Far from being some esoteric, wistful state, hope (and other powerful emotions such as stress) may influence gene expression.[40] How? Remember that earlier we said gene expression goes *both* ways. It emanates *from* genes to, ultimately, behaviors, but we now know it goes the other way also: behaviors trigger proteins that can influence gene expression.[41]

Our daily and hourly life experiences, thoughts, emotions, and behaviors can modulate both gene expression and neurogenesis in ways that actually can change the physical structure of the brain. In fact, "Behavioral state-related gene expression and immediate early genes are bridges between body, brain, and mind."[42] The science of hope suggests that hope, affirmations, prayer, celebration, and expressions of gratitude may do more than make you feel good; they may be changing your brain (which in turn supports different behaviors). This includes the possibility for us to make even more brain cells (neurogenesis) than normally would be predicted! When we say hope changes the brain, it's becoming backed by science more than ever before.

Head Start Program

Head Start, the main federal preschool program, provides economically deprived preschoolers with education, nutrition, health, and social services at special centers based in schools and community settings throughout the country. The program has been well researched, and even the longitudinal studies on the effectiveness of the Head Start program indicate that students who participate have higher educational outcomes and lower occurrences of criminal activity in later years.[43] Many people have been critical of the program because it has not delivered the extremes of positive outcomes that some think it should, but its impact is nonetheless encouraging.

The Head Start Bureau says that nine hundred thousand children were enrolled in Head Start programs in 2002.[44] The difficulty of trying to manage a program of that size is unfathomable. Another study followed children in the High/Scope Perry preschool study into adulthood and found there were still some positive differences.[45] The wide range of potential stumbling blocks makes it very difficult to control. The good news is that it's much better than the alternative (which right now is nothing). The fact is, early care programs do make a difference, and they are worth supporting.[46] These programs have a high likelihood of creating that "enrichment response" because they fall well in line with our primary tenet: a positive contrast from the child's prevailing environment. In addition, with plenty of positive factors in place such as social factors, positive emotions, nutrition, activity, and complexity, the chances for positive gene expression and brain changing are high.

Skill-Building Programs

To maximize achievement, skill building should continue outside of the classroom. Teachers are busy and have multiple, conflicting priorities for academic, social, and emotional skill building. Options include summer enrichment; tutoring; after-school programs; and specialized, targeted skill building during school in pullout programs.

One organization put together an enriching after-school program designed to help poor students living in public housing. The program was set up as specialized tutoring outside school, close to the kids' homes. This off-campus strategy may have worked for many reasons, but it could have been as simple as the fact that it provided transportation and met parental wishes. The follow-up data collected thirty months after starting showed the following:

- Improved reading, verbal skills, and writing skills
- Better overall school performance
- Stronger interest in class material
- Better school attendance
- Higher grades compared with a control group[47]

These data lend strong statistical support to the provision of educational enhancements in nonschool settings for at-risk youth. Summer programs are very effective, as is specialized tutoring. To find out if after-school programs really work, a meta study (combining the results of many studies) is often a way to get more reliable data. Motor activity early on helps support better cognitive activity by the start of school. Figure 5.3 shows the cascading process.

After-school, out-of-school programs have virtually no standardization, so it's difficult to compare them fairly with each other, much less against a "control" group of kids who simply play after school. Using a well-designed four-group study, a long-term program for disadvantaged youths with 599 students showed strong positive effects in both motivation and academics.[48] This matches what we've seen in other studies; that many areas of a student's life are changed, synergistically.

In Colorado, the Mid-continent Research for Education and Learning Group (McREL) looked at 371 studies of after-school programs. Only 56 of those studies met high standards for quality and rigor in how they were designed or used control and comparison groups. Overall, McREL researchers found that the student asset-building strategies had a meas-

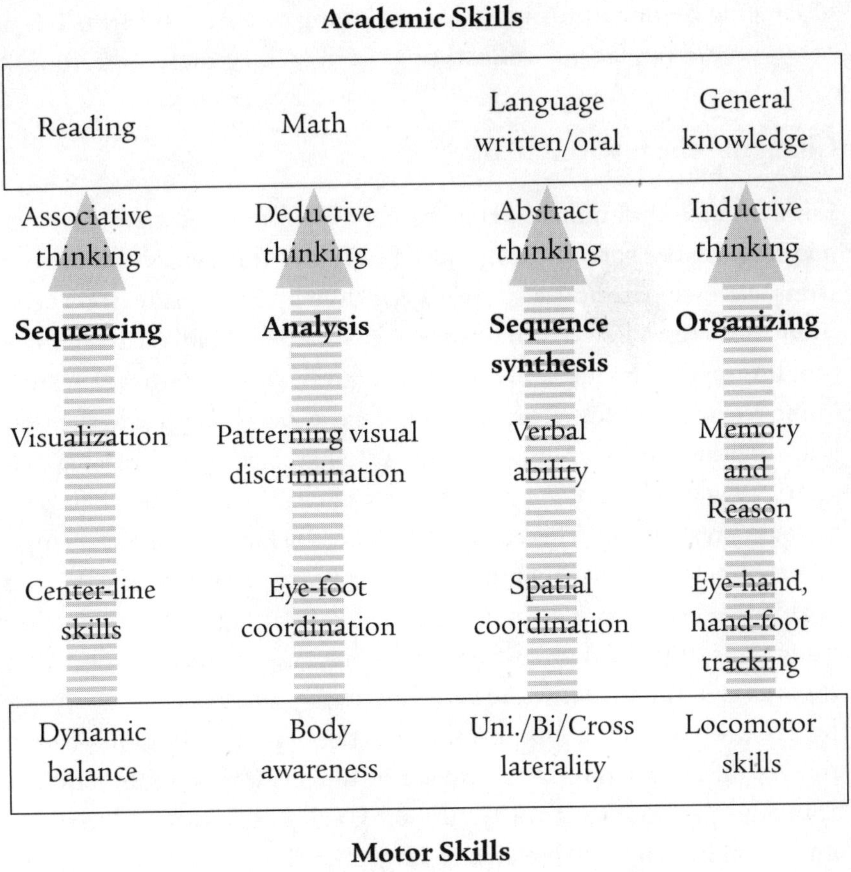

Academic Skills

Reading	Math	Language written/oral	General knowledge
Associative thinking	Deductive thinking	Abstract thinking	Inductive thinking
Sequencing	**Analysis**	**Sequence synthesis**	**Organizing**
Visualization	Patterning visual discrimination	Verbal ability	Memory and Reason
Center-line skills	Eye-foot coordination	Spatial coordination	Eye-hand, hand-foot tracking
Dynamic balance	Body awareness	Uni./Bi/Cross laterality	Locomotor skills

Motor Skills

Figure 5.3. Motor Skills Support Academic Skills.

urable, positive effect size.[49] They found the following as a useful gener-alization:

- After-school or summer programs can work, but the effects vary. Skill-building strategies have greater positive effects on the achievement of low-achieving or at-risk students in reading and mathematics, when traditional measures were used. This suggests the law of contrast once again.
- K–2 students are more likely than older students to benefit from strategies to improve reading, and middle and high school kids benefit more from math strategies.

- One-on-one tutoring for low-achieving or at-risk students has very strong positive effects on student achievement in reading.

Changing the Environment

Studies show that many of the risk factors of poverty are present at home. When the parents change just a couple of the factors—say, reduce stress, clean up the house, increase available light, or make other relatively minor and low-cost modifications—student results can change, too. Improving the home environment (contextual environment) was found to moderate the negative biological process of damage to the subjects. In other words, among students who have had bad things happen (abuse, neglect, lack of support) a positive change can alter their own biological responses.[50] This can happen with any kind of positive change. The change possibility includes creating a safe place to study, setting goals for school, working with a mentor, changing diet, and getting study skills help. It doesn't take winning the lottery; small changes that are consistent and positive are very powerful.

First, we laid out an important case: the brains of those in poverty are very different from those who are from a healthy environment. It's not about just money; poverty cuts across all of life's areas, including emotional health, social relations, linguistic abilities, financial status, medical conditions, careers, and psychological health. But the good news is this: smart, directed, and extended interventions can and do work. The brain can change, and it can be changed dramatically. Yes, you can get the "enrichment response" from brains in poverty. Now, we turn to a different type of brain; one that can exist at any income level.

Profiling Different Learners

The phrase "special needs" can apply to any students with disabilities, regardless of their income bracket and even if they're otherwise regular-education or gifted students. And, conversely, some students with disabilities also have extraordinary gifts (for example, mathematical savants). You can't have an atypical human with a typical brain; it just doesn't happen. Here's an example:

> Stacy complained that school was *boring*. Her mother applied to get her into a gifted and talented class, which would require an intelligence test, and her teacher suggested that she get another test, too. The results were a surprise; besides being highly intelligent, Stacy had a learning disability.
>
> She had sensory integration issues. Suddenly, all the pieces began to come together. Stacy had always been hypersensitive to touch, and she often went out of her way to avoid the middle of a line, preferring the front or the end. She disliked sitting in chairs at school and often slumped over, waiting for the moments when she could get up and move around. In addition, she was never affectionate with her family, preferring to be told she was loved than to receive a hug.
>
> However, she often came up with solutions that her classmates missed completely. She had most of her assignments done in half the time, and spent much of her class time talking to her classmates, who were ready enough to stop work even though they weren't finished. As a result, Stacy was not recognized either as gifted or as having a disability—but her teacher had noticed enough anomalies to suggest testing for both once the issue arose.

Surprisingly, many children are like Stacy, with strengths that mask their difficulties and difficulties that mask their strengths. The focus here is twofold. First, we'll explore the nature of the differences involved in "special needs"—whether economic in origin or inborn—then I'll present the evidence as to whether those differences are fixed or variable.

Elementary school students with disabilities are better assessed, monitored, and served than those at the secondary level, so it's possible to put together a much better database on them than on the whole preschool and K–12 population. And there are plenty of kids to look at; it turns out that one in nine of all students between the ages of six and thirteen can be regarded as having some form of disability.[51] Although the SEELS report included students with a dozen different primary disability classifications, three-fourths were classified as having either learning disabilities or speech and language impairments as their primary disabilities. Another 9 percent of students were classified with mental retardation, 6 percent with emotional disturbances, and 5 percent with other health impairments. Students in every other disability classification made up fewer than 2 percent of all students with disabilities.

About two out of every three students classified as having special needs are boys. For example, although boys constituted approximately 56 percent of students with hearing impairments, mental retardation, and visual impairments, they constituted 80 percent or more of students with emotional disturbances and autism. As a rule, African American students are slightly overrepresented and Hispanic students are slightly underrepresented among students with disabilities relative to the general population. There is a higher rate of poverty among the households of students with disabilities, relative to the general population.[52]

The special needs population includes those who are victims of neglect, trauma, learning disorders, and behavioral disorders. It includes those who suffer from fetal alcohol syndrome; developmental delays; and emotional, sexual, and physical abuse. Other sources put the total even higher; according to the U.S. Surgeon General's 1999 report on mental health, about 20 percent of school-age children have a diagnosable mental disorder.[53] About 10 percent have serious, impairing mental illnesses, such as major depression and anxiety disorders, and fewer than 20 percent of that group receive treatment. These proportions are high enough to have a serious impact on any school. Mental health has significant effects on cognitive processing. One cannot, for example, separate depression from academic issues.

What Counts as a Learning Disability?

Assessing those who may have a learning disability is not an easy task. Several hundred assessment tools are in use. No decision should be made from one tool, and other factors besides paper-and-pencil instruments should be included in the process. Schools generally use one of three primary models: test performance compared to IQ, test performance compared to grade level, or a review of the scatter-plot variations within a test score. What's important is to know the local parameters for disabilities. Using any of the following definitions, it should be apparent that a given student with a learning disability could also be considered gifted. In addition, many with serious problems might escape the definitions or may not qualify as needing special services.

IQ Cut-Off

Some schools limit the criterion solely to a discrepancy of 1 or more standard deviations (approximately 15+ points on a bell curve with 100 as the mean or 3+ points on a bell curve with 70 as the mean) between achievement scores and "intellectual potential" as measured by standardized tests.

For example, suppose you have a student with a verbal IQ of 100, who is thus considered to be of average intellectual potential. (This sets aside whatever you may think of IQ tests!) If that student is unable to earn a standard score of more than 70 on a standardized reading comprehension test or vocabulary or writing test (two standard deviations below the mean), that student is likely (it depends on the school) to be considered to have a learning disability.

Grade-Level Cut-Off

In other localities, there must be a difference of two grade levels or more between potential and actual performance—also as measured by standardized tests.

The same student with an IQ of 100 would be expected to be able to do grade-level work. If that student was instead reading, writing, spelling, or doing math at a level two years or more below grade level, the school would deduce the presence of a learning disability.

Inconsistent Performance

Still other schools recognize *intra-test scatter* as indicative of a learning disability. For example, on a standardized test of intelligence, one would expect a student with overall delayed development or mental retardation to have scores below average in all areas.

In this view, students with a learning disability may have some average scores and some below-average scores. There may be a significant discrepancy between the verbal and performance scores on an IQ test, such that the full-scale IQ is not an accurate indicator of "intellectual potential" at all. Such a student may even have a subtest score or two in the above average or superior range, some in the average range, and others below average.

Are Disabilities Increasing?

Many indicators suggest that not just the raw numbers, but the percentages of children with disabilities are increasing. The number of reported disabilities has skyrocketed. Other disorders have also gone up, such as stress disorders (depression, anxiety, trauma, and so on), autistic spectrum disorders (autism, Asperger's, and so on), and language delays.[54] This may suggest that we are getting better at identifying and reporting disabilities, or that there are simply far more of them (or quite possibly both). In 1999, students with disabilities made up 11 percent of all students between the ages of six and thirteen. There were twelve primary disability classifications, and three-fourths of the students were classified as having either learning disabilities or speech or language impairments as their primary disabilities. Another 9 percent of students were classified with mental retardation, 6 percent with emotional disturbances, and 5 percent with other health impairments.[55]

Lifestyle elements are clearly connected to many disabilities. For example, environmental toxins, head injuries, and abuse all influence learning capabilities. Many investigators believe that widespread lifestyle changes like those discussed in Chapter Four may be contributing to the increase in numbers. Potential threats to brain development surround almost every child in the modern world. It is a more toxic, more stressful, more mobile, and in many ways, more scary world than ever.

Do Atypical Brains Cause Learning Differences?

How much are brains really different in children who have lower intelligence scores from those of children with average scores? What about the brains of those with disabilities? Are they different from the brains of children with no disabilities? What kinds of differences have been found in the population that has a low IQ? Remember, you can't have functional-behavioral differences without some kind of corresponding change in the brain. As understanding of the causes of those differences improves, researchers will know better where to more effectively target treatments.

As background, it is essential to remember that there are learning differences among *all* children. Talent is the compatibility between biology and environment, and learning differences only become learning disabilities through specific environments. A given variation from the norm may be debilitating, it may be more of a nuisance and inconvenience, or it may even be an advantage.

For example, in many professions that don't require reading, dyslexia is not a disability. It makes reading very difficult, but in some cases, it can even be a gift. Being a poor reader may force one to compensate by improving other skills, but that's rare and not the real gift. Neuroscientist and child disabilities specialist Gordon Sherman believes that those with dyslexia are overrepresented in the arts, science, architecture, and entertainment. Spatial, depth, and parts-to-whole relationships seem easier to grasp for those with dyslexia.

Environmental differences are everywhere. Upbringings differ. Exposure to resources, toxins, different parenting skills, and different peers creates wide variations in brains. So we have both a genetic and an environmental influence to behaviors. These variations lead to different brains, creating different learners.

Learning, emotional, and behavioral issues are connected. Many learners who have learning disabilities get frustrated and act out when their disorders are not treated. Many who have behavioral disorders are unable to focus on the learning because of poor attention spans or inability to form positive relationships.

Brains with Special Needs

Once again, biologic differences among brains are common and significant. It isn't surprising when one child learns 20 percent faster than the next, even though the slower one has no known learning disability. But as noted, differences in connectivity, myelination, brain volume, prior knowledge, nutrition, and a host of other factors may all influence learning, and a wide variety of combinations can come together to cause difficulties in school. Three of the most common types—discussed in more detail in this section—are dyslexia, learning delays, and attention-deficit/hyperactivity disorder.

Dyslexia

Reading involves getting meaning from print. *Dyslexia* is an imprecise term used when a student has severe difficulties in reading acquisition, despite an otherwise normal intellect *and* despite access to instructional, linguistic, and environmental opportunities. The term does not encompass all reading problems, because reading disorders can also be caused by other brain dysfunctions (such as hearing problems, environmental deprivation, visual problems, educational deprivation, and disease). Dyslexia is not outgrown; it persists into adulthood, although some students compensate and become reasonably proficient readers. As of today, dyslexia is considered treatable.

The brains of those with dyslexia are different from the brains of those without dyslexia. During development, neurons in the fetus migrate from the neural tube to their eventual lobes. With dyslexia, for some reason (many believe hormones are involved) the migrating neurons go to the wrong place. This prevents the cells from being in the right place for readiness when exposed to the traditional reading process. Dyslexia is widely considered to be a brain-based, language-based disorder because there is a breakdown in how auditory language sounds (phonemes) translate into written language symbol sets that represent those sounds (graphemes). Many people with dyslexia hear the spoken word just fine and may even have superior oral vocabularies, superior storytelling abilities, and exceptionally good memories for what they hear.

SYMPTOMS.   Because there is no one standard test for dyslexia, the diagnosis is usually made by comparing reading ability with intelligence and standard reading expectations. Developmental dyslexia is frequently associated with mild visual impairments and unstable eye control. Students with dyslexia are often, but not always, poor spellers. Remember, many good readers are also average or poor spellers. One test that may be particularly useful in diagnosing dyslexia is the auditory analysis test, which asks the subjects to segment words into their underlying phonological units and then delete the specific requested phonemes from the words. If the student does poorly on this test *and* has reading difficulties, dyslexia can be suspected. Yet, even though phonological awareness is the best predictor of reading ability, lack of it is not the only indicator for dyslexia. Functional neuroimaging studies have shown a deficit in the neural mechanisms underlying phonological processing in children and adults with dyslexia. Note that the practice of using IQ tests, which require a fifteen-to-thirty-point deficit for intervention, is not sufficient because the symptoms can range from mild to severe. And those with milder symptoms need intervention, too. Remember, no one single symptom makes someone dyslexic.

TREATMENT FOR DYSLEXIA.   The appropriate intervention for dyslexia is not only hope or an enhanced environment, but more important, an overall *skill building*. Use intense phonics instruction with high-interest reading material over the long term. Students need letter knowledge, word memory, and phoneme practice. Usually training in these three work well.[56] Start early and be persistent. Many programs can work, including the Orton-Gillingham, the Lexia, or the Wilson reading programs. What is needed are two strategies: (1) remediate reading by teaching the student to read more productively and (2) accommodations that teach the student how to compensate for reading problems and keep up with the rest of the class despite reading difficulties.

In some cases, phonological processing programs and a skill-building remediation program work well in tandem. Some programs, such as Fast-Forward, focus on auditory processing and oral language training. One computer game study used children with dyslexia to increase activation in the left temporo-parietal cortex and improvement in oral-language ability. The results show that this kind of brain-based exercise can and does change the brain.[57] MRIs revealed improved function in brain regions associated with phonological processing, which had earlier shown up as disrupted. In fact, pretests showed less processing and additional compensatory activation in other brain regions.

Learning Delays

The terms *learning delay* and *delayed development* are used to describe a child's failure to make the usual developmental milestones on time. Critics call them a euphemism for mild mental retardation. However, because of the enormous plasticity of the early human brain, many children who are delayed will catch up later. Of course, many don't catch up—and although something (thinking, motor skills, emotional development) may be preserved, many other areas may end up with moderate impairment over time. There are many subtypes of learning delays, including developmental delays, mental retardation, acquired or traumatic brain injury, fetal alcohol syndrome, nonverbal learning disability, Fragile X, Williams Syndrome, and numerous others.

Countless reasons for delay may affect a child: genetic defects, poor prenatal development, abuse, brain insults, and other bad postpartum environments. Fetal alcohol syndrome, or FAS, now seems to be the number one cause of mental retardation in America. The specific links to delayed development commonly include mothers with a history of schizophrenia, poverty, cocaine abuse, paranoia, anxiety, depression, or borderline personality disorders. In addition, mothers who use tobacco, other drugs, or alcohol tend to have at-risk babies. Children receiving less stimulation, living in overcrowded homes, or facing exposure to neglect, malnutrition, or social deprivation can be delayed, and sometimes deaf children can be delayed as well. Fathers who abuse or don't support the family obviously affect children, too. Parents who interact too little with their children, have high numbers of in-poverty children, or are abusive typically raise at-risk children.

The brains of those with learning delays are different from the brains of those without learning delays. A number of brain insults could have caused the delays. The learning-delayed brain may have any combination of fewer connections, fewer neurons, too many synapses, smaller-than-typical brain structures, or even a lesion or area of neural damage. Whether such a brain can be "repaired" and by how much depends on a host of factors. They include how much skill building is done, whether there is hope, if enrichment is offered, the quality of nutrition, physical activity, and levels of stress or support. In general, the enrichment response is very appropriate for students with learning delays.

SYMPTOMS.   The most common symptoms are deficits in speech and language. These students often have difficulty understanding spoken and written language beyond the literal level, have difficulty with thinking skills such as brainstorming and problem solving, and are truly challenged by mathematical calculations. Their handwriting is laborious and may be illegible (unless overlearned), and the quality of their artwork generally is substantially less than what one would expect from typical students of their age. Other symptoms may include difficulties with tactile and visual perception, psychomotor coordination problems, tactile and visual attention deficits, and nonverbal memory lapses.

These children are often far less athletically capable than their peers; they have difficulty with motor planning and with sequencing moves in an activity, inability to coordinate bilateral movement and rapidly alternate movements, and lack of coordination. Some have persistent fine tremors, minimal precision of movement, difficulty with fine motor tasks such as buttoning clothes, tying shoelaces, using scissors, and completing paper-and-pencil tasks. While a few of these things may be symptoms of other difficulties, learning delays are suspected with most of them. These children also tend to have working memory deficits and trouble learning and applying academic skills, and to need assistance with self-care activities beyond the expected age for independence in those activities. Their social skills also tend to be delayed.

TREATMENT FOR LEARNING DELAYS.   The first step in working with a learning-delayed child is testing to rule out other possibilities. The C.O.A.C.H. Assessment ("Choosing Options and Accommodations for Children" by Michael Giangreco) is a great tool for assessing what the student doesn't know, what the student's family feels are priority skills, and how these skills can be taught in inclusive environments. The eventual plan will include a combination of accommodations by parents and teachers, specific skill building, and general enrichment. Early and continued intervention often can close the gap. The accommodations will include dozens of simple helpful strategies such as repeating directions, giving extra time, using assistive technology, giving study guides in advance and less lengthy assignments to read, using advance organizers, and the like.

The specific skill building should include functional skill instruction as part of the daily routine. This may include vocabulary, reading, life skills, and language and study skills. Many of these students will need help in basic functions such as changing money, finding resources, and communicating needs. Skills will need work three to five days a week, thirty minutes a day in elementary school, sixty minutes in middle school, and up to ninety minutes at the high school level. Anything less than intense, attention-focused, feedback-driven practice on meaningful skills and learning projects is not using the brain's capacity.

Traditionally, enrichment techniques were never offered to students with learning delays. But the research suggests that the lower the IQ and the worse the family background, the greater the value of enrichment. In this case, to create enrichment would mean improved nutrition (with supplements daily); physical activity (very important for brain function); and being in complex, meaningful, and low-stress environments, as well as increasing social support and being sure to make the learning experience a positive one. Mental retardation is not a death sentence. Many individuals who have this condition lead happy, fulfilled, and productive lives. The goal always is to enable all students to achieve the fullness of their own unique potential. This three-part program can be part of the success.

Attention Deficit/Hyperactivity Disorder

Attention deficit disorder (ADD) is the most common type of disruptive behavior disorder. It is a chronic dysregulation of the brain that presents itself as impulsivity, poor short-term memory, inability to delay gratification, and temporal processing deficits. This means that typically (but not always) people with this condition blurt out things without thinking, don't reflect on their past mistakes, forget what was just said, do poor planning or none at all, and would rather have a smaller reward now than a bigger one later. ADD with hyperactivity disorder (HD) means that the students have difficulty sitting still and would rather get up and move around or walk than sit. AD/HD is estimated to affect 4 to 6 percent (other estimates range from 2 to 15 percent) of American students. It will affect five times as many boys as girls and far more whites than African Americans, Hispanics, or Asians. Almost two million children are on AD/HD medications (3 to 5 percent) in the United States. The rate of the U.S. population aged five to eighteen years making office-based visits documenting a diagnosis of AD/HD increased from 19.4 per 1000 in 1990 to 59.0 per 1000 in 1998, a threefold increase.[58]

Although some think of it as a harmless form of impulsivity, AD/HD does have its dangers. It is often the carrier for other, more serious problems. It doesn't cause them, it simply makes it easier for them to surface. Only 3 percent of students with ADD in one study had no comorbidity (that is, no other disorder occurring at a time). In fact, 11 percent had a lifetime history of one comorbid condition (that means two in total), 12 percent had two, 18 percent had three, and 56 percent had four or more comorbidities. Males generally have higher rates of conduct disorder, antisocial disorder, stuttering, and alcohol and drug dependence than females; females generally have higher rates than males of depression, bulimia nervosa, and simple phobias. A vicious cycle often develops in which aggression and drug abuse become part of the equation. Eventually up to 65 percent of those with ADD or AD/HD will next develop oppositional-defiant disorder. Later, between 40 and 60 percent of those will be diagnosed with conduct disorders.[59]

That means that eventually between 20 percent and 30 percent of those students diagnosed with ADD or AD/HD will develop conduct disorders. In short, when attention deficit means impulsivity, and if it is not treated early, problems are going to get worse, not better. For both boys and girls, ADD is highly correlated with learning disabilities in one or more academic skill areas (for example, reading, math, or handwriting) and oppositional and sensory integration disorders. Students with ADD also tend to have a higher incidence of sleep disorders. This suggests the possibility that they'll be less efficient during the nighttime encoding of the day's learning into long-term memory.

The biological causes of AD/HD have been studied and are complex, even for a neuroscientist. Lesions in the reward (pleasure seeking) and striatal (habits) pathways are common. Typically there are dopamine (a key neurotransmitter involved in working memory and pleasure) irregularities, and EEG readings show excess theta (low brain wave arousal levels). The frontal lobes are low in amines (the "wake-up" chemicals), and typically the prefrontal cortex is unable to shut down impulsive actions. However, as the frontal lobes mature (ages twelve to twenty-five), there is better regulation of self-control and less need for specific interventions for some. Those with moderate to severe AD/HD carry it into adulthood.

SYMPTOMS OF ADD.   Children with ADD show poor application of cognitive abilities, highly variable behaviors (and performance), and poor planning. They are apt to be out of synch with others and weak at implementing strategies. These students rarely finish their work or call out answers in class; they have difficulty waiting for their turn, blurt out seemingly irrelevant comments, and are easily distracted. They show an impaired sense of time passage, wanting everything right away. They tend to have very messy desks, which seems to reflect their state of mind; inability to reflect on the past to learn from it; deficits of working memory—can't hold much at a time—and lack of hindsight and foresight; insensitivity to errors; inflexible behaviors; and weak nonverbal working memory. Such students will have trouble concentrating and sustaining an appropriate level of alertness for the task at hand, and will simply not notice details such as messy papers. They tend to refuse to re-do work, or to produce a second product that is worse than the first. They may excel in one or more areas not valued by school, but otherwise have difficulty applying themselves, and getting started on tasks. They seem to process information either superficially or too deeply, depending on level of interest and other factors.

SYMPTOMS OF AD/HD (ADD WITH HYPERACTIVITY).   With the addition of hyperactivity, children with ADD often display fidgeting and tactile manipulation, occasional antisocial behavior, and a lessened need to sleep. They are always on the go, engaging in high-speed actions instead of caution, and they characteristically prefer standing to sitting, walking to standing, and running to walking. They are restless and emotionally immature, and inclined to ignore routines and rules and to overdo simple tasks.

TREATMENT FOR AD/HD.   This is a condition that can be successfully treated. The best treatment for students with AD/HD is a combination of accommodations and skill building. The accommodations needed are often very simple:

- Supply prompts for upcoming events or changes, and memory assist devices such as organizers, day-timers, and calendars.
- Show such students how to cover up the work they have not got to yet with a piece of paper when they have a list of problems or things to read, since exposure to too many problems, too much content, or too many issues can be overwhelming. They work best one at a time.
- Provide helpful self-check criteria. Direct them to check their work before turning it in.
- Organize, establish, and use daily checklists; help students start a homework notebook, with homework assignments listed with due date and textbooks and supplies needed.
- Write out things, say them twice, and let students write out the key words in the air for better attention and recall. Learning stations can help manage info flow.

- Break up the future into small, external chunks (calendar, Post-it notes, and the like).
- Externalize time (use prompts, pointers, neighbor timekeepers). Don't surprise these children—give ample warnings.
- Help control impulse: urge students to work with a buddy to help slow down when completing answers. Provide an extra set of books to keep at home and don't let books go back and forth.

The skill-building part of the intervention may be a combination of impulse control, counting techniques, and meta skills to improve social and academic functioning. Neurofeedback can be helpful. In this case, the goal is to get the frontal lobes to manage their physiological state for alertness, instead of drifting into the spacey theta state so characteristic of students with ADD. Studies support the lasting effects.

Only certain characteristics of ADD or AD/HD warrant consideration of medication. If you have a student who is using medications, remember that AD/HD meds are amphetamines. Just because a student is on medication does not mean the condition is treated; it is being managed. No single ADD or AD/HD drug always works for every student, and doctors need parents' and teachers' input in prescribing medicine for ADD or AD/HD. Sometimes more than one drug must be tried before a student's behavior improves, and side effects always need to be evaluated. These are impulsivity, difficulty sustaining alertness and consistent mental effort, and comorbid sleep disorders. Treatment is more effective when any use of drugs is combined with behavior, environmental, and social modifications.

Can Learning Difficulties Be Repaired?

Yes, all of them can, to a degree. With any disorder or condition, there are three options: ignore (bad idea), accommodate (help the student survive), or intervene (offer either enrichment, hope, or skill-building efforts). Every single student with special needs should have an individual education plan (IEP)—and should be getting the combination of accommodation and intervention that fits the needs diagnosed and recommended in the IEP. There is *no* cookie-cutter plan that can fit every student. Your goals may be more process-oriented (How many times was a good effort made?) or more bottom-line-oriented (Reading speed goal is 90 wpm.). The three learning difficulties I touched on briefly in this chapter are only a few of the many possibilities. Each has a different biological basis, and each presents differently.

Key Questions

In general, a plan should include the type of action (accommodation, skill building, or enrichment) and answers to some of the following questions:

- Who?
  Who is on the intervention team? Who has responsibilities for what?
  Who is notified? If what happens? By what method?
  When are the meetings? Who will attend? What's the agenda?
- When?
  When does the team meet? Where? Who will lead the meeting?
  What are the necessary milestones (indicators that things are on track)?
  What are the goals? When are they expected to be reached? (Goals are end points for certain behaviors.)
  What are rewards (if any)? What are consequences?
- Where?
  Where should a particular child be seated?
  Where can the student meetings be held?
  Where can the "team" meetings be held?
  Where can the behaviors and changes be kept track of?
- What?
  What should be told to the class?
  How much are the other students involved in this?
  What rules will be overlooked, and which ones will be enforced?

What school behaviors will be enforced at home?

What activities does or doesn't this student participate in?

What are the options if this student can't be helped?

- Worst-Case Scenarios

  What should be done if this child disrupts class and annoys others incessantly?

  What about fights or major temper tantrums?

  What about profanity or threats of suicide or running away?

  What if this child taunts another who has learning delays?

- Best-Case Scenarios

  What strengths can be built on?

  What kind of skills are being built? What's the time line?

  What are the long-term prospects? What are the goals?

Prospects for Remediation

Yes, many (though not all) of the students with special needs can benefit from enrichment. Academic and social failure typically begins *before* kindergarten and becomes increasingly difficult to remediate beyond primary grades. A recent study showed that a significant percentage of student interventions were failing. Why do existing programs commonly fail to reach such a high percentage of kids (upwards of 80 percent)? Here's what the research says:

- *Bad timing:* Many interventions start too late (preschool and first grade are the best times to begin).
- *Excessive difficulty:* Some interventions are too hard for teachers in a classroom to use—to work well, many programs require intensity (thirty to ninety minutes at a time), interval training (three times or more per week), high daily feedback, motivational interest, constant monitoring, and personal relationships—these components are a lot to ask of a teacher with twenty-five kids in an inclusive classroom.
- *Narrowness:* Many interventions are not comprehensive enough to meet all the facets of the disability (social relations, family,

emotional cognition, environment, nutrition, motor skills, and the rest).

- *Oversimplification:* Many interventions lack attention to fluency development, transfer, and maintenance (the brain does not transfer most learning to other domains).
- *Lack of staying power:* Some programs are dropped too early— remember that learners need time. (Neurons must be recruited to new tasks, and they are at a premium, especially as children enter adolescence!)
- *Misguided pedagogy:* Without qualified and well-trained staff, even the best of programs may not be implemented the way their designers intended them to be and the way they were used in supportive research. Many programs have a good track record in delivering potent enrichment. Network to find the ones that could fit for the audience you work with.
- *Overprogramming:* Research suggests that it is best to allow "fragile brain" learners to *control task difficulty,* work in small interactive groups of no more than six, use directed response questioning that allows students a chance to learn while they think aloud, and always encourage!

The real message is of hope. There's been a great deal of study on the influence of hope on the human psyche and why positive beliefs are powerful.[60] We can reach more students than we have reached in the past. Schools, classrooms, and teachers create busy, complex environments that trigger complex responses. Some symptoms may occur only under specific conditions. Some conditions may require immediate medical treatment, some may require psychological or other related service, and some may require specific curricular and instructional approaches and modifications that can be done in the classroom. It is important to maintain optimism for many reasons, just one of which is that it has powerful positive effects.[61]

As with every topic, it's best to find multiple sources of quality information to ensure you are doing the right thing. Here's the most crucial information you can have: the brain can and does change every day.

Brains can become enriched, regardless of the student's IQ, brain health, income, or circumstances. Enrichment may be achieved in different ways, but the brain is designed to modify itself as a result of experiences. As long as the experiences are positive, the brain will change for the better.

Summary

Here we've explored two profiles that have a clear need for some type of enhancement. The profile of children in poverty is that of overwhelm, with an array of synergystic adverse factors. Yet as heartbreaking at it is, this is a student for whom getting the enrichment response is a perfect fit. The other profile here, that of a special needs child, commonly overlaps the one from poverty. But special needs may occur with any student, including those of middle and upper income as well as those identified as gifted. Again, we see tremendous opportunities for positive change by embracing and targeting the enrichment response.

6

Exploring Exceptional Brains

IN THE LAST CHAPTER, WE ASKED THE QUESTION, "DOES MAXIMIZING THE BRAIN make sense for children in poverty or those commonly labeled as special needs learners?" The answer is a resounding, "Yes!" The fact of the matter is, *all* brains can become enriched, some more laterally (a wider range of knowledge, skills, and values), some more vertically (greater intelligence). But why not just enrich those with special needs or in poverty? In this chapter, we'll explore those brains that are exceptional for different reasons. This chapter is about those people who display an extraordinary amount of talent. Yet are their brains really all that different from the norm? Or do they simply work their tails off and get farther based on hard work? Let's examine the evidence.

As a generalization, yes—the brains of the gifted *do* show differences from those of the general population in both structure and processes. Multiple factors have been found to cause the differences. But how much does the brain really differ in one who has higher intelligence scores? What kinds of differences have been found in the population known as gifted, talented, and just generally smart? And are these differences fixed—or can any ordinary person become more gifted?

The questions surrounding giftedness are well worth attention, especially in the educational community, even though they tend to make some people uncomfortable because of the apparent suggestion of elitism. Here you'll discover that although most education is geared for those with "typical" brains, those labeled as gifted actually have a right to get an appropriate education based on their *special needs,* too. All our children—including the gifted—have a right to an education that helps them reach their own potential.

Selecting Brains for Giftedness Services

Our discussions of appropriateness for any giftedness services depend on the question of *which individuals* to include in the "enriched group." Being gifted and talented suggests having either a high level of *g* (general intelligence, as discussed in Chapter Two) or of a domain-specific ability such as music.[1] Dr. Robert Plomin, a researcher at the Institute of Psychiatry and a decades-long advocate for the genetic basis of IQ, maintains that he has isolated the first specific gene for human intelligence.[2] However, this is preliminary and a far cry from identifying the single gene or group of genes that make people smart. Clearly some innate talents show up very early in gifted children, before any training or exposure to extraordinarily enriched environments. Similarly, the brain differences that have shown up are both early and measurable.

Still others might argue that gifted children have intense motivation, making them achieve more. But this supposition is challenged because many gifted learners are often demotivated by poor environmental support for their interests and ambition, becoming underachievers compared to their potential. Another profile of gifted children is that most of them are emotional basket cases, with social and emotional difficulties that set them apart or even make life miserable.[3] This has some truth to it; but it's true as well that students with learning disabilities also have a higher likelihood of social and emotional problems. This suggests that some of the problems may be a result of the brain differences or they may be a result of being labeled as "different." It could also be a result of the constant frustration experienced when one does not fit into the world.

Who Is Gifted and How Do We Know?

In a larger sense, all of us have gifts to offer. I truly believe that everyone on this planet has "gifts of humanity" to contribute. These gifts may be of skills, faith, knowledge, values, talents, or spirits that can and do have a significant impact on others. They are what can help make each of us special, and feel worthy, wealthy, and unique. Everyone involved in education ought to have an ongoing agenda to discover, strengthen, and nourish those gifts. To the extent that parents or educators do not attempt *educare* (the original Latin word from which we derive the word *educate*), that is, attempt "to bring forth" those gifts in each youngster in their care, the system has failed that human being. That, in fact, is what parenting and schooling ought to be all about.

Having said that, being *gifted* in the neuropsychological assessment context is different. It involves the possession of particular abilities and specific needs that must be met or problems will occur. In fact, it means that if those needs are not met, the specified population is disadvantaged. Most people involved with gifted education agree that a cut-off number is needed for labeling. Those qualifying for gifted education must meet the resulting criteria. If the criteria are watered down to include any and all students with potential talents, high motivation, special skills, and high grades, it becomes impossible to argue that the population thus defined would be disadvantaged without concentrated attention to unique needs. Let's look at the numbers.

Most of the top experts in gifted education, such as researcher Camilla Benbow, use 3 percent as a cut-off, meaning that a gifted student is "smarter" than 97 percent of the remaining students. That means, on the two standard IQ tests (Stanford-Binet or Wechsler), that although the average is 100, the gifted range would begin at 130 to 140 and higher. There's no doubt that children in either the top or the bottom 3 percent of *any* population are very different. After all, students at those levels have atypical developmental patterns and require differentiated instruction.

There may be many more gifted people than you think. One of the greatest minds of all time, John Stuart Mill, who was reading Plato with ease at age ten, supposedly had an astounding IQ of 200. Yet a consultant to parents of gifted children in the Denver area has found more than forty-two people with an IQ above 200 since 1979. Unless you believe the Denver area is attracting an extraordinary number of "off the charts" exceptionally gifted people (possible, but not likely), the numbers for Denver may be somewhat generalizable to other major U.S. cities. In other words, there may be many more exceptionally gifted in the population than have emerged in school testing. Some tests are unreliable; gifted children's IQ scores often become depressed at approximately nine years of age due to the artificial ceiling effects on the test. The ideal age for testing is between four and eight. But testing for giftedness should never be based on an IQ test alone.

One reason that IQ scores alone should not identify the gifted population is that creativity is one of the greatest gifts from higher-ability students, not computational skills, which are becoming lost in the shuffle of faster computers. In her latest book, *The Creating Brain*, neuroscientist Nancy Andreasen argues that the most creative in our society are just below the IQ designation for giftedness.[4] The highly creative people are intelligent, typically in the 120–130 IQ range, not at the 140–145 Mensa cut-off. These creative types are constantly oriented toward divergent thinking, taking a variety of nontraditional responses to a challenge. This quality does not show up on traditional IQ tests, though other instruments can measure divergent thinking.

Giftedness Identification

Despite the clarity and supposed definiteness (top 3 percent on IQ tests seems pretty straightforward), IQ tests have limitations. First, no single testing instrument is a perfect predictor of intelligence. We need to be especially careful when assessing underserved gifted students (younger children, culturally diverse students, linguistically diverse students, economically disadvantaged students, and students with other special educational needs). Minority language students, for example, may be unable to express themselves in English despite being very gifted. Therefore, today's researchers urge that great caution be exercised in using English standardized tests for the identification of linguistic and cultural minority students. The most effective and equitable means of serving gifted students is to assess them fully and individually, with a trusted testing practitioner. Be sure to select and use tests that reduce cultural and linguistic bias, and employ a mediator who is likely to ask culturally sensitive questions.

Gather data from many sources (caregivers and families, teachers, students, and others with significant knowledge of the students) in different ways (observations; performances by the student in arts, math, and the like); products (many gifted students create useful products for the marketplace during the K–12 years); portfolios; interviews; and in different contexts (in school and out-of-school settings). Other commonly used methods include self-reports, autobiographies, and case histories.

Again, no single test or instrument should be used to include a child or exclude a child from gifted education services. Interviews are often scheduled as part of the identification or selection process to determine a candidate's general fitness for a program and provide information for instructional planning. Parents can be helpful, too. They may suspect giftedness if there's a rapid progression in their child through the developmental milestones in the first three to four years. Although all these varied procedures can be time-consuming, they at least can provide a more valid basis for decision making. Early identification of advanced development is as essential as the early identification of any other exceptionality. Just as you're far likelier to optimize results if you identify an autistic spectrum disorder in a child at one year of age and begin rigorous interventions well before school begins, you can promote optimal development in a gifted child if you spot the patterns early.

One of the more practical ways to identify the gifted comes from the team of Joseph Renzulli, director of the National Research Center on the Gifted and Talented, and Sally Reis, past president of the National Association for Gifted Children and author of many books for the gifted. Their Three-Ring Conception of Giftedness suggests that it takes (1) above-average ability (no surprise), (2) creativity (novel ways of seeing things), and (3) task commitment (an essential ingredient for the real world) to express qualities of giftedness.[5] We all know of kids who seem to be very smart, but can't get off their rear ends to actually do anything. We know of those who are "calculator smart" but not creative. Renzulli's Three-Ring model suggests one must have all three elements or there will be no giftedness.

Who Is Underrepresented Among the Gifted?

The spread on IQ test results shows that many groups are underrepresented but especially those in poverty.[6] Research indicates that compared with the percentages in the population at large, the proportion of blacks, Hispanics, and American Indians identified as gifted is only half that expected.[7] Caucasians and Asians are overrepresented. The scores of Asian Americans are slightly lower than those of whites, yet their collective scores and achievement are greater than would be predicted by their IQ scores.[8] The mean intelligence test scores of Hispanics typically lie between those of blacks and whites. Native Americans test lower than their ethnic counterparts.[9]

Many of the differences in the identification of giftedness may be attributable to differences in culture. The more traditional values found in Asian culture help influence achievement and obedience to authority. In some Native American cultures, individual achievement is less valued than group decision making. In some Hispanic cultures, respect for elders is often valued more than precociousness, which can be seen as disrespectful. In some African American cultures, in-context performance is valued far more than any paper-and-pencil test. Commonly, those who are not native English speakers will underperform or be unable to express themselves in English.

Certainly all the factors involved in poverty influence the identification of giftedness. Here's an example. A group of 483 children were tracked from birth, and a complex amount of data was collected, including family structure, resources, and home environments. Then the children were assessed using the Wechsler Preschool and Primary Scale of Intelligence. Researchers compared the differences in intelligence test scores of the black and white five-year-olds. Although a one standard deviation difference appeared in the raw data, once the differences for poverty and home environment were factored out, the IQ scores were similar.[10]

There are gender differences in testing, too. On standard IQ tests, females do better on the verbal portion; males do better on the math portion. On the SAT, among high scores on the European history test, the ratio of males to females was greatest, 6:1. The next most sex-differentiating test was physics, 2.9:1, followed by elementary-level mathematics (mainly algebra and geometry), 2.5:1. Other ratios favoring males were, in 1991, chemistry (2.4:1), American history (2.1:1), biology (1.8:1), precalculus mathematics (1.6:1), Latin (1.6:1), and French (1.4:1). More females were high scorers in literature (1.26:1), and none scored better at the lopsided ratios we saw when compared with males.[11] This matches up with the work of Sally Reis, who finds that it is harder for girls to "show giftedness."[12] She asserts that it is cultural stereotyping; media-enhanced sex roles; and different, conflicting messages that contribute to the underachievement of gifted women. The more one digs, the more one finds that discovering who is and who is not gifted is not quite what the numbers seem to tell you.

But keep in mind that all these groups are underrepresented for a reason. IQ test scores are designed to be *predictors of academic performance* only. For that, they do reasonably well. The test is not biased in predicting school results. But it does suggest that if you're looking for giftedness, you might have to broaden your assessments and use other means to ensure no one is left out. To get a reliable reading on a current IQ test, WISC-III is not appropriate (low ceiling), but the Stanford-Binet 5 is suggested. Another test used for the precocious is the College Board Scholastic Aptitude Test-Mathematical (SAT-M), and the Raven's Progressive Matrices.

Who Is Not Gifted?

If you use the Renzulli Three-Ring model or even a standard IQ model of the top 3 percent of the population, it's clear that not everyone, not even the twinkle in the grandparent's eyes, is gifted and talented. Specifically, three populations are *not* gifted, though they are often given a "gifted" label:

- Savants and calculating prodigies (who do not follow up on or widen their talents)
- People with multiple talents and abilities (who do not develop an expertise of great depth)
- People who are very good at a specific task; healthy ones are considered experts in their specific domain (who fail to get beyond simply being good at something)

Savants and prodigies can do amazing calculations or perform other specialized feats, but this does not indicate giftedness as defined here. Evidence appears to support the hypothesis that savant skill is related to excessive and erroneous use of cognitive processing resources, a matter of failure in central executive control mechanisms and not of unique effectiveness. Typically these people are autistic, similar to the character played by Dustin Hoffman in the movie *Rain Man*, a role modeled after Kim Peek, an autistic with prodigious yet narrow reading and memory skills. Savants actually overuse certain brain areas because their frontal lobes don't inhibit and direct brain function as they should. And though they share two other traits with the gifted (mental focus and weaker social skills), their overall mental capacities are not in the same league when tested thoroughly.

Other people are exceptionally talented in some areas—say, playing the piano, teaching, organizing, and finances, coupled with an encyclopedic knowledge of Broadway musicals and needlepoint. That surely sounds gifted! But the capacity to have multiple talents and abilities is far from unique. It is more likely to be seen in the top 10 to 20 percent of the population at large, not the top 3 percent.

When many programs expanded by adding the phrase "and talented" after the word gifted, suddenly parents all over the country were determined to get their talented child into the program. Why? For many, it's the latest upper-middle-class ribbon of parental prestige. If their child is admitted to the school district's Gifted and Talented Education program, many parents feel proud. The gifted label is an educational status symbol for parents in certain neighborhoods. But the label makes the parents happy, not the kids. Many parents push to have kids labeled as talented who have no business in the program. One late-thirties mother of a first grader admitted in a local television interview that the gifted label is important. "To a certain degree, I feel my daughter's success as a student is a reflection on me and my parenting."

Finally, people who invest endless time in a particular skill—not dozens but thousands of hours—achieve expert status and can be wholly admirable, without being *gifted* as defined neurologically. A famous memory specialist named Rajan has learned tens of thousands of digits of the mathematical ratio known as pi (3.14159 . . .). That's part of the formula for calculating the area of a circle. He's also capable of learning lists of fifty digits with virtually perfect accuracy in about a minute of study. Nonetheless, a researcher who has studied talent, expertise, and giftedness spent much time with this amazing man, and concluded that years of practice were responsible for Rajan's abilities, not any giftedness.[13]

In the first chapter we reminded you that excellence is just as often the extensive, relentless pursuit of perfection, which often becomes obsessive. At the Music Academy of West Berlin, a wide range of practice hours per week may be the real secret to extraordinary performance. Those that became "good" students averaged about nine hours a week, but those judged as "superior" and most likely to become a concert performer averaged twenty-four hours a week of practice. It is the deliberate, intense, solitary quest to reach higher levels of skill that sets performers apart.[14]

Closer to home, many parents feel their child "has a gift" or is highly talented. But when you assess the number of hours actually spent to get good, these children compare to others of average ability in the same field.[15] What many perceive as gifted or even genius in highly successful individuals is largely the result of a hunger to be excellent at the task.[16] The hunger manifests itself as an intense focus, doggedness, relentless persistence, and sustained concentration, as well as intense curiosity in how that domain is mastered. Many successful people simply want success more and are willing to put in the hours to get there. Although there's no gifted label here that can be justified, such a motivated student will go far in almost any society!

What Makes a Brain Gifted?

As I've said, you cannot have functional or behavioral differences (such as being smarter) without some kind of corresponding difference in the brain from a more typical brain. As understanding of the causes of those differences improves, researchers will know better how to identify and develop them. On the whole, brain differences fall into four distinct categories. They are morphology, operations, real estate, and electro-chemical cellular functions, or M-O-R-E as a way to remember them easily.

- *Morphology:* Size, quantity, and shape of brain structures
- *Operations:* Neural efficiency and speed of internal connectivity in the brain
- *Real estate:* Strategic differences in which or how brain areas are used
- *Electro-chemical cellular function:* Differences in electrical and chemical activity

The difference most associated with gifted children is the effectiveness with which they learn; as a generalization, they pay closer attention, absorb information, stay focused, learn the interrelationships more quickly, and remember longer. Those are the observable consequences of the four differences I just described. The following sections describe how each of them plays out.

Morphology

The first category—brain morphology—refers to the shape, size, and boundaries of structures within the brain. Some correlations suggest that more brain volume equals more computing power.[17] Total brain volume accounts for about 16 percent of the variance in general intelligence scores. If this study was true, you'd also expect overall head size to correlate with intelligence, and it does.[18] Interestingly, students with AD/HD have both lower overall IQ scores *and* smaller brain volume, by 3 to 4 percent.[19] Data like this suggest at least some kind of a correlation between overall computing capacity and the brain's morphology. Bigger head size does increase the chances for greater IQ. This obviously does not mean that all melon-headed kids are geniuses, but the correlations are well above chance levels.

Another set of animal studies measured (postmortem) the total number of both neurons and glial cells (the highly important support tissue) in rats. In the gifted, there were far more glial cells (more than double!) as compared with the nongifted learners. But what about humans?[20] As a vivid example, when Marian Diamond studied a sample of Einstein's brain tissue in the mid-1980s, she found that his brain had more glia per neuron than did the average brain (73 percent, compared with eleven others) in one area: the left inferior parietal lobe (Figure 6.1).[21] This difference exceeded the expected ranges for both age and individual variability and may be typical for the frontal area of exceptionally gifted people—or it may have been the specific area Einstein used for complex mathematical theories.

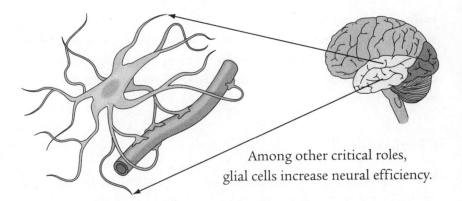

Among other critical roles, glial cells increase neural efficiency.

Figure 6.1. Einstein's Brain Had Higher Counts of Glial Cells in the Left Parietal Lobe.

As a historical note—and evidence of the difficulty many have in accepting the idea that exceptional brains can differ physically from the norm—it's interesting to observe that Diamond's paper ran into a firestorm of publicity. Her fellow scientists concocted headlines based on her findings ("Einstein's Extra Brain Cells: The Secret to His Genius!") as icebreakers in their presentations, setting crowds of skeptical researchers roaring with laughter.[22] Diamond herself never generalized her results to all geniuses, merely saying that they were potentially meaningful, and her work has since been vindicated. Today, we do know that larger numbers of glial cells are correlated with improved learning and memory.[23] In another study with highly gifted individuals, there was a significantly greater level of individual variability, especially in the right hemisphere.[24] This may reflect space, time, and sensory processing skills.

Surprisingly, gifted brains also include larger proportions of "extreme neurons"—those very small and very large neurons. These are ones that seem to either start off that way, enabling a greater number of connections, or develop in ways that may have some additional processing capacity. In another study that compared people with strongly creative, highly gifted talents to a control group of average performers, postmortem evidence revealed a much more customized and specialized brain.[25] More cortical fields were streamlined, there were greater numbers of pyramidal neuron glial cells, and there was much greater distinctiveness of how the neurons were grouped. This suggests the extensiveness to which gifted people use particular areas of the brain. All told, the giftedness may be more likely a combination of differences or a threshold that needs to be reached. There are correlations for it in a larger-than-typical brain or in those with unusual neuronal development, and it may have more glial cells than a typical brain.

Operations

When our brains do things that we ask them to (tie our shoe, turn on the lights, figure out the change from a ten-dollar bill, type a sentence in our computer, or calculate the tip in a restaurant), we call that "brain work" an operation. Some operations are merely functional (brushing our teeth or driving our car, and so on), and others are strategic (solving a problem, calculating the odds on a decision, or figuring out how to approach a problem from another's point of view). Gifted people are usually better at working memory and attention span.

Even though the functional operations seem like they are more physical, they still involve our brains. But those can be and are typically learned by people at most levels of intelligence. The more strategic operations are different. Strategic operations are done faster and more efficiently and often more creatively by those who deserve a gifted label. The mental computations are not just "fun work" for their brains; they often do them enough so that they become automatic and fast.

CONNECTIVITY.   There are between seventy-five and one hundred billion neurons in the brain and nearly a trillion glial cells. Each neuron has between several hundred and tens of thousands of synaptic connections, depending on where in the brain it is. Overall, this means the human brain has several trillion connections that enable everyday life. Neurons are linked to one another both locally and at a distance.

For comparison, think about all the technology that surrounds you right now. You needn't be deeply into the high-tech life to have a computer or two in the house, along with several phones of various types, a few TV sets (probably with DVD player and VCR), TIVO, Internet access, videogames, an iPod, and any number of other devices, from a PDA to a talking oven. Each device has different needs and varying capacity. In most homes, these separate systems don't talk to each other. Could you imagine the work in networking together all those devices in just one house, your own? This would mean a complete wireless network within your house. Let's say you did have the savvy to interface all your different types of systems into one streaming, trouble-free, seamless network. That would be tricky, but it could be done. Now add this: next you're making every bit of technology in your home talk to every bit of technology in someone's home down the street. Now add this: you're making every bit of technology in your home talk to one in three homes around the world. You've just bumped your home-networking problem into a global challenge of near-biblical proportions. If that sounds complex, that's the equivalent of what every human brain does! The gifted brain simply does it all quicker.

Does the gifted brain have a much greater number of connections as compared with a more typical brain? The answer is not known for sure, but there is speculation that the gifted brain does work faster and has up to 10 percent more connections. One wouldn't want too many connections. The human brain uses probably 30 to 40 percent of the total possible connections already.[26] But a brain with too many connections would not be any smarter. In fact, at an extreme case, a child with the Fragile X Syndrome has way too many connections and is severely mentally retarded.[27] Computer modeling simulations show that having some unused capacity in the brain is actually a smart concept. It gives a computational advantage for a brain that needs a high degree of flexibility in responses at the more global level.[28]

Therefore, it's likely that a gifted brain has the right combination of sufficient connections in the right places and high processing speed. Any brain system that has both reciprocal and sparse connections can learn faster and integrate a great deal more information than a brain that is 100 percent interconnected.

CONNECTION AND PROCESSING SPEED.   Why is speed so essential? Greater complexity creates greater possibility of confusion without another key feature: connectivity. Once all the connections are in place, the next ingredient needed to make it functional is speed.

The gifted learn things more quickly, they develop and use more connections, and they have faster connections. It's as if they are using high-speed Internet access while the rest of the population is still struggling with dial-up lines. In fact, there's a decrease in cortical usage with increasing intelligence: electrical-chemical activity from pretest to posttest correlates negatively with intelligence. This suggests that the higher the subjects' general competence, the larger the decrease in the amount of cortical activation.[29] These findings suggest intelligence-related individual differences in becoming neurally efficient. The brains of the gifted are just flat out faster at processing. That means they can move larger quantities of signals around more easily.

Other researchers have been more concerned with speed of processing. Two studies found different results. One found an inherited (genetic) correlation between intelligence and speed of information processing.[30] But in a practical manner, higher processing speed did not always mean faster decision making. Another group studied peripheral nerve conduction velocity and found no relation to IQ.[31] In fact, in a very practical study testing for memory and speed, the higher-ability participants devoted *more time* to stimulus analysis and planning than did lower-ability participants, suggesting more processing time on an activity.[32]

Generally, the gifted have the ability to acquire new and complex information more rapidly than their average-ability peers in situations involving simple acquisition. Multiple studies have shown a stronger focus ability in those with higher IQ, suggesting an ability to filter out distractions. Higher-ability people's effectiveness in controlling attention and gating sensory information seems to be a critical factor.[33] It differentiates and identifies those individuals with complex cognitive abilities.

Some correlations also show up between mental speed of processing and specific abilities. For example, musical ability, as one might guess, is correlated with higher mental speed.[34] But I would also expect competencies in martial arts, race car driving, and videogames to correlate with mental speed, too. This suggests that many people who have faster mental processing may have chosen to use the advantage in nonacademic arenas. So far, human intelligence seems much like a mental juggling act in which the smartest performers use specific brain regions to resist distraction and keep attention focused on pieces of information that *they regard* as critical, which may or may not be anything involved with their schooling.

GLOBAL CONNECTIONS.   One of the keys to understanding cognition is understanding the networking operations of the brain. For the various brain areas to be most efficient, they need rapid and thorough communications. Most research has found clear links between intelligence and brain activation patterns in the frontal lobe. These make for higher-order cognitive functions. The brain has to be able to activate, process the learning, and then wait for the next activation. Sluggish learning won't work in the gifted brain. This "transient response plasticity" occurs over a very short time scale and is typically considered to be a property of higher-order, more cognitive brain regions such as the prefrontal cortex.[35]

It's a bit like a city; the more roads, highways, and alternative routes available, the faster anyone can get to any other place. The fewer the connections, the weaker they are, the more sluggish they are, the slower the traffic. In the brain, if you want general intelligence, connecting to the right place at a high speed is a must. As an example of connectivity, consider the brain of the severely retarded savant; the savant has great connectivity in one neighborhood of the brain, but a gifted brain is far more globally connected.

In general, the brain typically called smarter or gifted has different neural wiring (Figure 6.2). One study measured interaction between the left and right hemispheres in mathematically gifted adolescents, average-ability youths, and college students. The task showed hierarchical letter pairs in three viewing conditions: (a) only to the right hemisphere—to the subject's left side, (b) only to the left hemisphere—to their right side, or (c) bilaterally—to both hemispheres at once. Participants had to make quick letter-match or no-match judgments, and some did much better than the others.[36] These data suggest to us that greater interhemispheric traffic may be a functional characteristic of the mathematically gifted brain.

Real Estate

In general, it's difficult to say that gifted people consistently use their brains differently from more typical learners. But what the research tells us is that a slew of efficiencies in the gifted brain help it use the right areas, use areas that it is very good at, and use the smallest amount of brain real estate necessary to do the task. This is important in looking at imaging studies, because the area of the brain may not light up in the same way it would for a more typical or disadvantaged learner. In fact,

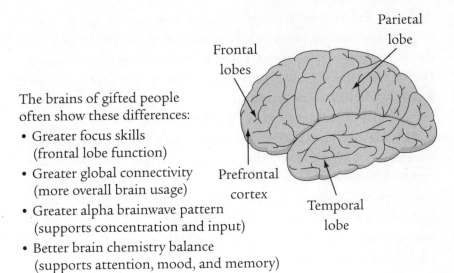

The brains of gifted people often show these differences:

- Greater focus skills (frontal lobe function)
- Greater global connectivity (more overall brain usage)
- Greater alpha brainwave pattern (supports concentration and input)
- Better brain chemistry balance (supports attention, mood, and memory)

Figure 6.2. Exceptional or "Gifted" Brains.

it may give a contradictory story that has a temporal component. Many gifted learners seem to be switching gears constantly, like an old-time car transmission, trying to get the right task into the right part of the brain. This means that the areas activated will change more dramatically during a task than would be likely among other more typical learners.

FOCUS THAT BRAIN! The amount of brain activation in each network depends on how skilled individuals are in verbal or visual learning. In other words, the more skilled we are in the strategy used, the less brain activation or effort is required to perform higher-level thinking tasks. When given a choice as to which thinking strategy to use, the brain often uses the method that requires the least effort, namely the strategy in which the individual is most efficient. This means that it takes greater skills to manage your own resources, even if it means damping down the emotions. Those who test higher are typically less influenced by affect (that is, by emotional state). Feeling ecstatic, very sad, or anxious all create competing stimuli for the brain to deal with. Problem solving and other processes require focus, and too much affect slows us down. In fact, neutral affect is associated with faster learning because the emotional processing is dampened.[37] Having some positive affect enhances thinking, but too much affect will negatively influence cognition.

Those who are gifted tend to use their frontal lobes very effectively and to manage incoming sensory information better than those who have a lower IQ (Figure 6.3). This area is used to filter the incoming data and then figure out the task, then things literally slow down. Generally, the higher the subject's overall mental ability, the more quickly the task is mastered, and the larger the decrease in the amount of cortical activation as the subject shifts gears. These findings suggest intelligence-related individual differences in becoming neurally efficient.[38]

Effectiveness in controlling attention and gating sensory information is a critical determinant of individual differences in complex cognitive abilities.[39] To be effective at a consistently high level takes the constant engagement of higher-order brain functions to sort tasks, focus, move tasks, switch brain areas used, and process tasks quickly. Generally, those with higher and more flexible, fluid intelligence keep distracting information at bay by activating regions in both the prefrontal and parietal cortexes, as well as a number of other regions. Naturally, how well subjects perform in any given situation depends on the complex interaction of many abilities, but frontal lobe execution is paramount.

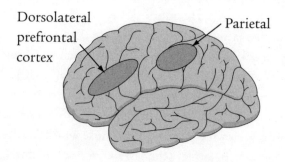

Dorsolateral prefrontal cortex

Parietal

Figure 6.3. Areas of the Brain Dedicated to Attention and Focus Skills.

To confirm this theory, we could ask if those who have difficulty with focus and impulsivity regulation (both frontal lobe functions) do worse on IQ tests; they do! Studies of students with attention deficit tell us that for overall intellectual ability (Full Scale IQ), scores were lower for those with AD/HD than for healthy participants.[40] Of course, many highly successful adults have AD/HD, but these results may tell you that they were able to compensate and beat the odds. This is just one of the many differences that crop up between paper IQ scores and real-world success.

TRY LESS, ACCOMPLISH MORE.   The relationship of the more gifted with brain usage is complex and often delicate. Gifted adolescents often have a developmentally enhanced (closer to a college age) state of brain activity.[41] This typically gives them unusually strong focus, motivation, and concentration on tasks for their age. In general, they have a greater "force of will" as characterized by greater left hemisphere alpha brainwave activity levels (8–12 Hz per second). As a generalization, those with lower IQ use certain areas more, to try harder, even though their efficiency in using that area is not strong. In one study, the higher-IQ subjects were found to be using an entirely different part of the brain to do a given task as compared with the lower-IQ subjects.[42]

Again we see the same pattern. It's not just using the frontal lobes, it's being able to use them successfully that counts. One high school boy had moderate mental retardation, with an IQ in the 70 to 80 range. But he also had exceptional calculation abilities and was referred to as a savant. When asked to perform, he actually used the frontal lobes excessively, suggesting that it was his previously diagnosed obsessive-compulsive nature combined with a probable failure in his brain's central executive functioning.[43] This shows the dual nature of skill and deficit; his sheer will (obsessive, in fact) forces his frontal lobes to work overtime at tasks. As you may have guessed, one could be both gifted and have a learning disability.

Overall, there appears to be support for the idea that gifted people have more balanced thinking ("whole brain" was the buzzword years ago). Some researchers contend that enhanced right hemisphere involvement during cognitive processing is a correlate of mathematical precocity.[44] In addition, the general pattern of activation observed tells us that those of higher ability more effectively coordinate left and right hemisphere processing. Later studies have supported this lingering notion that gifted males have a greater reliance on their right hemisphere as a physiological correlate of mathematical giftedness.[45] One older but very interesting study using EEG showed that, as compared with lower-IQ subjects, greater symmetry between hemispheres is associated with superior performance among those more gifted.[46] Again we see that those with greater intellectual prowess are literally using "more" of their brain at times, while at other times they are simply integrating its areas much better.

It is also believed that the gifted use the spatial-temporal areas of the temporal lobes to support higher-level functions. Under the supervision of physicist Gordon Shaw, a group of researchers in Irvine, California, used a very challenging videogame to understand spatial-temporal reasoning. The game is based on the mathematics of knot theory and was used for understanding DNA structure prior to this application. Some elementary and middle school students showed game mastery so quickly that researchers conjectured that the spatial temporal reasoning capacity is innate.[47] Is there a way you could test this theory? Could someone influence intelligence by changing where in the brain they are processing a task? Yes—in one experiment, researchers in Sydney, Australia, used electromagnetic pulses to suppress the left frontal temporal lobe for a task, forcing the brain to use the right side. In a statistically significant number of subjects, there was an increase in drawing skills (typically thought of as more right-brained) and even proofreading (very sequential task).[48] These studies suggest that some strengths would be available to all of us, if we could get our brains to use the right areas for the right jobs.

Electro-Chemical Cellular Function

It turns out that brains do differ right down to the electrical and chemical levels. Researchers at the University of Tennessee did an interesting experiment using cortical event-related potential (ERP). That's the one where the subject wears that fashionable little cloth polka-dot skullcap (usually with thirty-two or more electrodes connected to the scalp) to measure electrical current. Then a stimulus is presented, and the speed, amplitude, and location of the brain's response are measured. Sensory ERPs can successfully predict differences in working memory span and fluid intelligence.[49] This suggests that electrical activity is one of the indicators for efficient or effective cognitive processing.

One study used learning disabled, gifted, and typical control children of ages eight to twelve. The common "distracter" stimulus consisted of random nouns generated 80 percent of the time. The target stimulus was animal names presented the other 20 percent of the time. The research was designed to find out what differences, if any, would appear among the subject groups. There were differences, and—as you might guess—the gifted performed much better than those with learning disabilities and the typical subjects.[50] But the study differences suggested the possibility of delays or gaps in the attention and information processing for those with learning disabilities. Again, it was the speed and ability to filter out and focus that made the gifted subjects do better. The electrical-chemical capacity of their brains helped create a more efficient response.

What about hormone levels—are they correlated with intelligence? The best-researched hormones are the stress and sex hormones. It is believed that those who are more intellectually curious have a lower baseline of cortisol—that's a hormone related to stress. Higher levels of cortisol are associated with a more contracted response. When we feel too stressed, we are less likely to show exploratory, curious, novelty-seeking behaviors. Those who do show this early habit of curiosity, even as three-year-olds, turn out to be much more competent intellectually in later years.[51]

Using saliva samples, researchers measured the testosterone levels of 247 children, 100 of them gifted and the others randomly chosen. Lower salivary testosterone levels were found in intellectually gifted children of both sexes (all females have some testosterone). There was an overall negative relationship between testosterone levels and cognitive abilities in preadolescent children.[52] Greater levels of salivary testosterone are correlated with lower student achievement. This is not to say that athletes are dullards; it suggests that testosterone comes with a price. Remember that with any population sample, you'll see a bell-shaped curve. Some with higher levels of testosterone may have a dozen other, far stronger factors that support a gifted brain, including high motivation and better concentration.

And finally, certain neurotransmitter levels are associated with greater intellectual performance. Having just the right levels of dopamine is associated with better frontal lobe function. Too much dopamine (the "pleasure" or "reward" neurotransmitter) is associated with schizophrenia.[53] The brain's frontal lobes need just the right amount of dopamine to fuel working memory. Excess dopamine is counterproductive for cognitive processing.[54] However, too little is bad, too.[55] Dopamine is known as an upper for the brain; in the same way that amphetamines, cocaine, and caffeine ramp up the activity of the prefrontal cortex, dopamine does also. It just does it in a more sane way.

There's no doubt that highly intelligent, gifted thinkers display a greater degree of cognitive flexibility. Gifted thinking requires just the right amount of serotonin. That's the neurotransmitter associated with mood, memory, and attention. Those with little flexibility typically are lower in serotonin. Studies show that cognitive inflexibility is typical after prefrontal serotonin depletion.[56] Serotonin depletion can be influenced by dietary changes. Foods with a higher amount of the amino acid tryptophan (used to make serotonin in the brain) include bananas, turkey, milk, and avocados. Creative problem solving is improved when serotonin is at the middle healthy level. Together with increased dopamine release for better processing speed and attention, serotonin improves the flexibility needed for maximum cognitive achievement.

Overview of the Exceptional Brain

No one single difference makes someone gifted. In some cases, being very strong in one area allows the gifted learner to compensate for being less gifted in another. As a generalization, the gifted brain is better designed to pay attention, filter out trivial information, learn quicker, and remember longer. It is stronger in the frontal lobes, and tends to work on tasks there quickly, then farm them out to other areas. The gifted brain is more likely to use both hemispheres to solve a problem, not just one, and is more neurally efficient. It may have more connections, but not an extraordinary amount more. It is faster and more cognitively flexible. It's better regulated by hormones and the right balance of neurotransmitters. On the whole, an aggregate of factors make the gifted brain both unusually effective and unusually efficient at neural processing.

What's going on inside gifted children? No single profile can be drawn that describes all the gifted. But they do share some strong common tendencies. Conversations with teachers and parents of gifted children as well as with authors and consultants in this area revealed five personality traits or qualities that are most consistent with giftedness:

- *Perfectionism:* They want to get it right and dislike sloppy work. This also means they can be very critical of themselves.
- *Creativity:* They are constantly attracted to novel and creative ways to see, hear, and do things.
- *Sensitivity:* They can be emotionally intense and often have a greater moral, ethical, and social awareness of the world and its dangers. As an example of this awareness, gifted girls often hide their abilities and learn to blend in with other children. In elementary school they may typically focus on developing social relationships at the cost of notoriety for "smarts."
- *Intensity:* They have a dogged ability to focus relentlessly. They can be high achievers because they're willing to put in the effort. This often works against them in the social world, since there is a social likeability price to pay for isolation and focus.

Many parents and educators of gifted children note an advanced vocabulary, a tendency to ask complex questions, a preference for older companions, perceptive observations, high creativity, a strong problem-solving ability, and excellent memory. Many gifted people also display an aptitude or talent in a specific area such as mathematics, language arts, or music. We've all heard about other qualities associated with giftedness such as a natural concern with moral, ethical, and social issues. But those concerns will develop only in a supportive environment.[57]

As I've noted, those who are truly gifted are not just faster or more accurate at a task, they really do think differently. Surprisingly, most of the gifted who were high in math giftedness got no outside tutoring or training. We all know that nearly anyone can become good at mathematics. And if they're willing to put in the hours, anyone who works hard at it can become a mathematician. Now, for a moment, think of the kind of mathematical genius seen in the movie *A Beautiful Mind*, which portrayed 1994 Nobel Laureate Dr. John Nash. That kind of genius is different, and only a few are "born with the gift" and can become truly great. Here are some examples to clarify the differences:

Mathematically Gifted	*Typical Student*
Prefers elegant solutions	Takes any solution
Views world mathematically	Disconnected from world of math
Switches strategies easily	Tends toward inflexible thinking
Studies hard problems first	Jumps into hard problems quickly
Recalls problem structures	Recalls contextual details
Generalizes quickly	Slow to generalize
Long chains of reasoning	Simple reasoning
Reverses methods easily	Has trouble working backwards

Many excellent books have been written about the gifted learner. One of my favorites is Susan Winebrenner's *Teaching Gifted Kids in the Regular Classroom*.[58] In this book she notes the following characteristics:

- *Coping mechanisms.* The gifted have varied ways of coping. Gifted girls often hide their abilities and learn to blend in with other children. In elementary school they may typically focus on developing social relationships. In middle school peers value appearance and sociability more than intelligence. Gifted boys are often considered "immature" and often get held back when they don't socialize with peers with whom they have no common interests.

- *Discipline.* Many gifted students act out in class from frustration. Although they can appear to be troublemakers or unmotivated, they often feel that class time is wasted for them. You may see symptoms such as disruptiveness, restlessness, and inattentiveness, often confused with AD/HD. The gifted are more likely to challenge authority figures by questioning classroom rules that they feel are unfair.
- *Disabilities.* One-sixth of the gifted children may have some type of learning disability. Both the disability and the giftedness often go undetected because giftedness can hide disabilities and disabilities depress IQ scores. For some with disabilities, strong abstract reasoning helps children make adjustments and compensations for weaknesses, making them very much harder for others to uncover.
- *Sociability.* Gifted children are introverted at twice the rate of typical children (60 percent versus 30 percent). Of those who are highly gifted, the introvert numbers go up further, to 75 percent. Introversion correlates with introspection, reflection, the ability to inhibit aggression, deep sensitivity, moral development, high academic achievement, scholarly contributions, leadership in academic and aesthetic fields in adult life, and smoother passage through midlife; however, it is very likely to be misunderstood and "corrected" in children by well-meaning adults. Social self-concept improves when children come in contact with true peers.

Making the Case for Gifted Education

As I've said, any attempt to profile the gifted can get a bit controversial. Some people view all such discussion as a thinly veiled attempt to justify an elitist position for those who hit the genetic lottery. Nothing could be further from the truth. In total, far more gifted students come from middle- and lower-income families than from upper-income families; that's where the largest populations are! The discussion deserves to be held, the research has to be done, and policy has to be implemented that supports this population.

There are many public precedents for specific national policy changes for an underserved minority. Head Start, the 1997 IDEA (Individuals with Disabilities Education Act), and the congressionally mandated and funded Title I, Title II, and Title IX acts have all been targeted educational legislation. The question is, Why?

Most important, these acts were not implemented to level the playing field. You can't level the playing field unless you make equal the impossible: socioeconomic status, parental knowledge, love, parental education, environment, family history, safety, genes. These legislative actions are all attempts at ensuring that no one segment of the population is unfairly treated, discriminated against, or disadvantaged by educational policy.

That distinction is important. In today's schools, being gifted is commonly a disadvantage. For a child who already knows the material being presented to the class but has no choice but to sit through the lesson, the day stretches out unbearably—and no education whatsoever takes place. Quality education, after all, works by a simple principle: contrast. If there is no difference between what you already know and what is offered, there is no contrast and there is no new learning. Netscape guru Jim Clark and comedian Chris Rock were two high school dropouts who thought school made no sense for them. Jan and Bob Davidson, authors of *Genius Denied,* say that up to 20 percent of dropouts are "gifted" but quit school because they feel ignored and unchallenged, bored, and frustrated.[59] As the Davidsons point out, if you taught the alphabet every day to senior high school students, they'd not only learn nothing and be insulted, over time they would lose ground. That's what gifted students are up against.

If we take the attitude that those on the margin (or even the extremes) are to be ignored, then one could argue that we shouldn't have special needs classes, either. This is dead wrong. And although everyone is important, an argument could be made that the gifted make unique contributions to society. The numbers show that they are overrepresented in the arts, in higher education, in research, economics, science, and other highly valued fields in society. In addition, they stay married longer, pay more taxes, and use fewer social and medical services than their more typical counterparts.[60] This supports a position that says, just as others who are disadvantaged in school should be supported, so should the gifted.

The key here is that without contrast, there is no learning, no enrichment, and no point in being in school. If there's no contrast in the schooling from the home life, no enrichment can take place. The children who are truly most disadvantaged by current schooling are those in the top 3 percent of the population. If you broaden the concept of gifted to include the top 5, 10, or 15 percent, the resulting group is less different from the more typical student, so there's less reason to differentiate or provide enrichment.

In the current climate of identifying students who have special needs, it is critical that gifted populations get their share of understanding, attention, and policy support. The gifted advocates are simply asking that the same rules be applied to everybody.

Summary

Can anyone become gifted? One view holds that giftedness is all about training the brain. The thinking goes that, "If anyone provides enough resources and training, the child receiving it will be gifted." This turns out to be somewhat true, somewhat false. A strong positive environment has been shown to be able to raise a child's IQ by 10 to 20 points, but it may take months or years to do this. It's probably only likely if the child starts with an IQ in the below-average range. For the moment, there's no evidence that you can turn a moderately retarded child into a Mensa (IQ of 165+) student by enhancing his or her world (although futurist Ray Kurzweil may disagree). By the way, you still want to enhance his or her world in a dozen other ways; improvement comes in many forms and formal IQ is just one indicator. The improvement may not be in the

IQ area, but might be more lateral (social, emotional, and practical skills are powerful, too). Everyone can get the enrichment response; it just shows up in different ways.

If you combine some of the innate brain differences typical of gifted learners in a positive resource-laden environment, with good encouragement, you'll get a strong achiever. Will the child be on the dean's list, a Mensa regular, or a MacArthur Foundation "Genius Grant" winner? That's possible, but not at all guaranteed. However, you are likely to have a productive student who grows into a happy, resourceful adult: someone who is more likely to attain a higher education, be married longer, earn more money, and have greater life satisfaction than others in the class. Any fewer of the positive variables for being gifted and you'll get (maybe) less of a star—but you'll nonetheless have the satisfaction of building toward and not diminishing whatever potential was there. Remember that everyone can and should become enriched. That should be the whole point of school; to turn one into what one is capable of. There is no middle ground; you are either making headway toward an enrichment response or losing ground toward a neural wasteland.

7

Enrichment as
Educational Policy

THE ETHICAL, MORAL, AND BIOLOGICAL MANDATE FOR ALL SCHOOLS IS TO MAX-
imize human potential. We will only get this effect when we get serious
enough to create policy that works for every learner across the board.
Right now, when there is no commitment to enrichment, many schools
are shortchanging human potential. In this chapter, we take the challenge of enrichment more broadly; we can take it to the level of policymakers. That includes anyone in the position to make a decision to
either (1) create enrichment with contrast or (2) impoverish with the status quo.

In the home, the parents (or caregivers) are the policymakers. At a
school, although it seems obvious that a principal, headmaster, or vice
principal is the policymaker, there are others. Classroom teachers, support staff, counselors, school boards, school supervisors, and paraprofessionals make countless decisions that may either enhance or maintain
the status quo. It's all about contrast. This means that school time (five
solid hours) and the kids' "off time" (five hours) are both about the
same. That's approximately ten hours a day or fifty hours a week that
are "up for grabs" for many students. When those fifty hours are enhancing, the sky's the limit! Having said that, the focus of this chapter is to
pose and answer two sets of questions:

1. Why should there be a broad, across-all-levels enrichment policy at any school or district? Where is the evidence that it might work? Would it be worth doing?
2. What would that policy look like in action? Are there any existing models? What programs would be in effect?

Why Provide Enrichment for Everyone?

In the past, the standard enrichment protocol for most educators has been to offer enriching environments to the "lucky few" in a gifted program and ignore the rest. This is unscientific education policy. I have shown in earlier chapters that those in special education and those from poverty can benefit greatly from the enrichment response. I have shown that the gifted student can benefit because without enrichment, he or she *will actually go downhill.* The population that has not been addressed so far is the rest of the school; the so-called typical students.

Many critics are quick to dismiss the positive, enhancing effects of effective child care or school-based programs as merely "catch-up" programs. The old theory is that you can only increase human potential up to the statistical mean. This prevailing, old-school thinking says that when we create an "enrichment response," we are merely bringing a subpar brain up to the average, healthy standard. As their reasoning, critics cite that there are no animal studies that show you can take a genetically modified mouse (the C57 is an example; it's the "Doogie Howser" or artificially smart breed) and get an enrichment response to make it any smarter. They cite human studies that show you can't take a gifted child and make him or her any smarter either. But that argument is faulty, and here's why.

• In rodent studies, typically two behavioral measures were being used; a standard radial arm maze or the Morris water maze. These present far too narrow a range of possibilities for change. What we don't know is, What skills or knowledge would be behaviorally relevant to a mouse other than spatial navigation or memory tasks? In this case, the conclusions from the animal studies are missing the wider human expressions of competency. It is worthwhile noting, as mentioned earlier, that there are a slew of biological changes that did occur as a result of the enrichment response. If you measure only two tasks for rodent intelligence, that's all that could ever possibly show up.

• In human studies, the only measures used to support the position of "No improvement to healthy, typical brains is possible" are test scores (state, national, or even IQ tests). Yet in the early part of this book, I've already dismissed IQ when it's used as either a *solitary* or a fixed measure of intelligence. It's only one of many potential measures. In fact, in the large scheme of things, it's a very narrow measure as an indication of human potential. We can go broader or deeper. What if you opened up the measurements to a much broader set of indicators? As an example, we might agree that one's life be enhanced if he or she

1. Had a more optimistic attitude and enjoyed life more
2. Got sick less often, and for a shorter time
3. Enjoyed consistently better-quality relationships
4. Had a strong love of learning
5. Had a stronger, more resilient response to distress
6. Was better able to self-regulate mood without drugs or alcohol
7. Participated more in life
8. Ate well enough to slow the aging process
9. Had extraordinary persistence and determination
10. Was able to adapt well to changes in housing, school, and relationships

You might say, "Well, sure, those are nice indicators, but that's not enrichment!" Now you understand the catch-22. If we define enrichment response narrowly enough, we can ensure that very few deserve it, qualify for it, or get it. What I'm arguing for is to drop the notion that many humans cannot be biologically enriched; they can. Why do I say this? Humans change as a result of experience. Contrasting positive experience promotes positive change in humans. The enrichment response occurs in the brains of those in contrasting coherent environments.

What Is a Schoolwide Enrichment Policy?

A typical curriculum at school leaves many students bored. But if kids are bored, how does that prepare them for the future? In fact, what if being bored was bad for the brain? Neuroanatomist Marian Diamond has shown that rats will actually have brain cells in the cerebral cortex thinned by the experience of boredom.[1] If children are stressed, upset, or learn to dislike learning or school, how does that prepare them for the future? That's exactly what happens at schools that ignore their real mandate. If we're sold on the idea that enrichment is either simply smart education or at least worth a try, how do we go about making it happen?

The first thing to understand about policy is that someone has to implement it. Implementation won't happen unless everybody else is on board and sold on the idea. Plus, if others don't understand the policy, it won't happen—teachers are very pragmatic, and policies have to be straightforward, make sense, be relatively easy to implement, and show results quickly. The first thing that should happen is to allow plenty of time for the priming effect (just light introductions, no mandates). Allow staff time for questions, discussion, and brainstorming. What is it that would actually be discussed? Here are some questions to ask staff members:

1. Do they believe the human brain is malleable and can change continuously?
2. Do they buy into the premise that all kids (special ed, poor, gifted, and so on) can improve?
3. Do they understand and believe that a more contrasting curriculum for all kids will result in less boredom, more challenge, and fewer discipline problems?
4. Do they buy into the possibility that kids who are in an integrated, contrasting, enhanced environment will produce better test scores, although not immediately?
5. What new learning, curriculum changes, or scheduling options are they willing to make? How open is each staff member to co-creating a model school for kids?

These questions are absolutely essential for discussion before any plans or models are introduced or, heaven forbid, forced upon any educator.

What Does Enrichment Mean?

Few schools and teachers understand enrichment and brain plasticity and use the knowledge properly. Most people, inside or outside the educational community, are at best barely beginning to understand the new science of the brain. New research is coming out daily that redefines what the human brain is and what it can do. Brain function benefits most if the enrichment programs provide a clear improvement over a baseline, prevailing environment in ways related to the measured outcomes. As an example, if a child comes from severe poverty, attending a Montessori preschool can and has worked wonders, all the way through middle school.[2] Remember our definition:

> **Enrichment is a positive biological response to a contrasting environment, in which measurable, synergistic, and global changes have occurred within the brain.**

As educational policy, enrichment means more than a commitment by policymakers and educators to create a specific climate at school. Enrichment means that curriculum, assessment, environment, and instruction all will have to be revisited. Any program will have to meet the criteria of enhancing that we introduced earlier to get the "enrichment response." Exhibit 7.1 puts the seven "golden maximizer" factors into a school context.

The Seven Golden Maximizers

Before the maximizers are detailed, let's make sure we're on solid ground in our research. With the recent emphasis on "scientific teaching" is there a solid basis for each of these factors? The answer is "Yes," and the

Exhibit 7.1. Seven Factors or "Maximizers" for Contrasting Environments.

1. Physical Activity (voluntary gross motor)
2. Novel, Challenging, and Meaningful learning
3. Coherent Complexity (not chaotic)
4. Managed Stress Levels (not boring or distressful)
5. Social Support (at home, school, and community)
6. Good Nutrition (balanced and healthy with supplements)
7. Sufficient Time (not rushed, plenty of sleep)

evidence is broad-based. Here are each of the factors and a quick review of the powerful science behind them.

Physical Activity

Exercise helps increase the release of brain-derived neurotrophic factor (BDNF), which supports learning and memory function and the repair and maintenance of neural circuits. Fernando Gomez-Pinilla and his team at UCLA found that voluntary exercise increased levels of BDNF in the hippocampus, a brain area involved with learning and memory.[3] Some studies have found strong evidence that in mammals exercise increases the production of new brain cells, and they become functional.[4] In addition, exercise leads to increased calcium levels in the blood. That calcium is transported to the brain, where it enhances dopamine synthesis, making the brain sharper for both cognitive problem solving and working memory.[5] For example, one study found that joggers consistently performed better than nonjoggers on learning and memory tests that required the use of the prefrontal cortex.[6]

Now all this brain stuff may sound good, but does this evidence translate to the real world? What happens to student achievement when schools engage kids in quality physical education? First, it improves self-concept and reduces stress and aggression.[7] Second, it improves academic performance.[8] Various states have mandated physical activity and spoken out in favor of it. And finally, it regulates mood. Some evidence suggests that it may be a protective factor against depression, which is becoming increasingly prevalent at the secondary school level.[9]

A preliminary analysis conducted by the California Department of Education shows a significant relationship between academic achievement and the physical fitness of public school students.[10] In the study, reading and mathematics scores were matched with fitness scores of 353,000 fifth graders, 322,000 seventh graders, and 279,000 ninth graders. Higher achievement was associated with higher levels of fitness at each of the three grade levels measured. Exercise is consistently a part of any successful enrichment program.

Recommendation: A solid body of research suggests that at the K–5 level, twenty to thirty minutes of recess (or its equivalent) should be mandatory daily. Any district that mandates this must then *create a climate that encourages and supports it.* In California, one hundred minutes a week of physical activity is the law at the K–5 level. But it does not happen in many classes. Teachers, who don't know the research, are tempted to cut out the recess. Mixed messages and testing pressures mean that many teachers skip recess out of fear of lowered test scores. In the United States, more than two out of three secondary students (68 percent) do not participate in a daily physical education program.[11] At the 6–12 level, the research supports a daily choice of voluntary gross motor activities including power walking, swimming, jogging, team sports, cycling, treadmill, or similar choices. But again, this rarely happens. If the physical education program seems "broken," then fix it; do not throw it out.

But what about students who don't want to do exercise or physical activity? Find something they do like. It is *that* fundamental to the brain. The goal is to get students to participate in daily gross motor physical activity *voluntarily.* So offer a range of choices: team sports such as soccer, treadmill, stair climber, bicycling, power walks, jogging, swimming, cycling, or dance or ballet. More options increase the likelihood that something will be attractive to each student. The key is that *they choose* to do it.

When done well, athletic programs have coaches that instill self-discipline, high personal standards, positive attitudes, and a quest for excellence. The students learn to improve reaction times, cardiovascular capacity, muscle strength, body coordination, speed, and stress responses. Most interestingly, good athletic programs, even daily recess, can improve cognition and academic outcomes.[12] This is relevant because it verifies that enrichment responses create a global, not a specific effect.

Novel, Challenging, and Meaningful Learning

The human brain is designed by nature to survive. Learning is the only way to do that, since we live in a world far more complex than one of simple stimulus-response. It seems that physical activity may enhance the *production* of new cells, but it is the novel learning that appears to *increase brain cell survival* and *functionality*.[13] Novel, meaningful learning is key, and quality schooling changes our brains.[14] Relevance is critical because meaningless tasks provide no enrichment. Just basic stimulation alone does not drive an enriching change in the brain; it has to be behaviorally relevant.

This creates the essential "cortical imprinting" needed to release the acetylcholine necessary to form the memory to "save" the new learning.[15] We need a meaningful context for an activity to get purposeful changes in the brain, and studies show that more relevant, meaningful learning is better.[16] All of these factors, like novel, relevant learning, allow us to make better-quality predictions. In fact, the primary strategy for school-age survival is to predict likely outcomes and respond appropriately.

Recommendation: The most critical ingredient is contrast, so the curriculum and instruction must feature contrasting choices for students. This is a key factor for keeping kids in school. The five dominant strategies used by schools to match up learners and instruction have been

- Choice by students of what and how to learn
- The use of differentiation
- The use of pullout programs
- The use of acceleration
- Using prescreening testing to match students with curriculum

Let's walk through these suggestions that may enhance the enrichment response.

Choice. The first option is to allow students to pick their own learning, challenges, and grade requirements. I would argue against students at any grade having a *total choice* over their curriculum. School-age kids do not have mature frontal lobes, and their ability to make decisions with long-term consequences in mind is a bit suspect. Some moderate choices are acceptable.

Differentiation. The second option is differentiation; here teachers use instructional strategies to modify and adapt the curriculum for various ability levels within a given classroom.[17] The concept can work for certain talented teachers with student populations having more narrow ranges of ability, in smaller size classrooms. This is one of the more widely accepted educational theories in the past ten years.

Pullout programs. In the third option, students are pulled out of their regular classes for special tutoring. It's primarily for those needing improvements in skill levels (reading, writing, math, and other basics).

Acceleration. Acceleration allows students to move quickly past units of content if they are able to pass the exam. Students might spend half the time on the same content as other students if they are ready to move on.

Prescreening. The last option allows schools to mix and match students at the right school based on the student's abilities and the level that the school offers. Any of these five could work, but the last one is the most ideal because of its reliability.

Coherent Complexity

Complexity is a big part of what challenges the brain. It requires shifting from one cognitive factor to another, allocating resources such as working memory and stress management. The stress issue is huge because if the complexity crosses the line into chaos, the potentially good learning event becomes stressful. Neurons under distress become conservatory and won't grow or communicate properly with other cells under distress. Their dendrites, the branch-like extensions from neurons mentioned earlier, were reduced by 18 to 32 percent in one animal study that exposed them to stressors.[18] The opposite condition, boredom, can also create a retracted or withered dendrite, from underuse.

This factor is a bit tricky, because it always rides the edge between boredom and distress. Complexity is a school experience in which students see school as a busy (but not chaotic), interesting (but not threatening), and challenging (but not overwhelming) experience. Two strategies are suggested to make complexity saner. First, allow a graduated level of complexity that builds over time as the human brain develops the capacity to handle multiple levels of curriculum, social structures, and the necessary emotional responses. The second strategy is the building of student assets. This includes emotional intelligence, resiliency against stress, study skills, and time management.

Recommendation: This factor means that students need to have the kinds of options that they perceive as "juicy" and "cool" subjects. That includes the arts (theater, photography, dance, music, and so on), sciences and problem-solving (talent fairs, special projects, Odyssey of the Mind, math league, debates, and so on), and exploration (field trips, internships, mentoring, community service, and so on). Without these types of options, not only can students lose interest in school, but you'll never find out what they're good at doing.

In theater, drama, dance, and other performance arts, subjects improve emotional intelligence, timing, reflection, respect for diversity, and even SAT scores.[19] In fact, compared with those taking no arts courses, those taking theater and drama scored thirty-five points higher on the math part of the widely used college entrance test and sixty-six points higher on the verbal portion. In case you're thinking that sharper students simply self-select into arts (a possibility), that too has been debunked.

Showing that it's the time spent in the arts that matters, the more years one is in the arts, the greater the difference on the SAT. This suggests that it's *the work in the discipline,* not the selection process, that contributes to the SAT difference. The first year, there's an average differential of ten points between the mean scores of non-arts students and a first-year student in drama. But by the fourth year of arts participation, the difference is close to forty points.[20] This is a clear example of the enrichment response. Students start out above the average (ten points) and yet, still gain an additional thirty points on the SAT over time.

Managed Stress Levels

Many students experience daily stress that is over and above the healthy limits. It comes from bullying, rude teachers, overdemanding parents, and life's events. When there are unpredictable stressors, the brain's capacity to learn and remember is severely impaired.[21] Animal studies show that behavior stress modifies and impairs a key learning structure called the hippocampus and reduces learning capacity. In fact, the actual brain cells in the prefrontal cortex become disfigured with chronic stress.[22] In general, students learn best in a classroom climate of moderate stress (I prefer the expression, "healthy concern"). But that's just a generalization; there are plenty of exceptions. For example, many students with disabilities need lower stress or their learning shuts down. Examples include those with autistic spectrum disorders, reactive attachment disorders, attention deficit, oppositional disorder, dyslexia, stress disorders, or learning delays. So for a portion of the students, low stress *does work* better. Healthier students can thrive under much more demanding conditions. Figure 7.1 shows how stress affects various parts of the body.

Recommendations: Schools should adopt a three-part strategy. First, all staff should be taught and should participate in stress reduction strategies to help better manage responses to adverse events. This may include skill building, reframing, treadmill, or power-walking activities. Second, students should be taught life skills, which include time management, study skills, and emotional intelligence. They need to be taught about how their body experiences stressors and what to do about them.

Establish an environment that would typically inspire and challenge the learner. Make it less chaotic, uncomfortable, or overwhelming, and more predictable. Ensure that the physical environment has the best possible acoustics and lighting. Offer the possibility of movement, rich wall decorations, choice, open windows (if appropriate), and going outside. Give students the life skills to deal with stressors. Teach self-regulation strategies such as meditation, exercise, yoga, better nutrition, and reframing outcomes more positively. Students need the skills and mind-set to believe they can influence their environment.

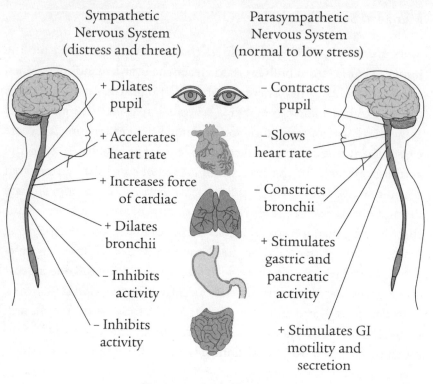

Figure 7.1. Stress Responses.

Social Support

Student brains never mature in a vacuum. They become human-friendly in the context of a social environment. School stress that is associated with bullying and violence hurts achievement. The stress also impairs test scores and attention span and increases absenteeism and tardiness.[23] Community violence exposure—an unsafe home neighborhood or a dangerous path to school—also contributes to lower academic performance.[24] It is discouraging, but many high school students either stay home or skip classes due to fear of violence. Students who have to worry too much, especially over safety concerns, will underperform academically.[25] And plenty of recent evidence shows that stereotype threat reduces working memory capacity in students.[26]

Recommendation: Schools that provide enhancement use the following: mentorships, peer counseling programs, cooperative learning, clubs, and team sports. They use whole-school assemblies and class meeting models, and ensure that every single student in the school is assigned an adult or older student as support.

The key is a sense of belonging, invitation, and connectedness. School leaders and staff that make schools a place for a positive social climate do things differently. They typically make sure the staff is prosocial and respects relationships. They use daily rituals and traditions, they hold assemblies and community functions on a schedule. They respect diversity and openly discuss diversity issues. They'll have morning homeroom meetings with familiar agendas. Students have room for expression in voice, art, and sports. The schools embrace the culture of the students with familiar themes that students, staff, and community can align with.

People also need social connectedness—the store of social capital that gives them access to a network of caring human services. Connectedness is an important enrichment factor because it can regulate stress levels up or down. If our relationships are positive, they tend to have buffering effects against stress. If they are negative, it increases our stress response.

Schools ought to foster positive social connectedness for many reasons. But the main reason is that it may keep students in school. Of those in school, it increases their likelihood of having better friends, fewer illnesses, less absenteeism, and a more positive attitude. For many kids, the main reason they're in school is because it's the law and their friends are there. Social contact can influence gene expression; improve student health; and reduce discipline, bullying, and violence. How many more reasons do school policymakers need to mandate positive social structures?

Good Nutrition

Why support this factor? The more we know about the value of both basic and enhanced nutritional support, the more important nutrition becomes for enrichment. Multiple studies show that good nutrition improves mood and behavior.[27] One public school in Arizona ran a randomized, double-blind, placebo-controlled trial, giving supplements to half the children and placebos (pills with no nutritional value) to the other half. Pre- and post-testing showed a statistically significant increase in nonverbal intelligence, with some increased as much as 10 to 15 IQ points.[28]

The average student, from kindergarten through high school, will have the opportunity for 2,340 lunches, which, at five hundred calories each, would contain over *one million* calories. Those meals will either support or hinder student cognition and behavior. Since positive nutrition is also a factor for enrichment, schools have to take the big step and make food healthier. In the initial animal studies in the 1960s, food was considered an automated, fixed element, and researchers simply ignored it in the studies.

Recommendation: Positive student nutrition needs a three-part approach. First, educate parents about the true cognitive and behavioral impact of nutrition. Give parents low-cost options and be specific. Second, educate students about how their brain works and how nutrition influences it. Teach them which foods have the effects of uppers and which foods can induce calm. Teach them about vital cognition-boosting nutrients, too. Third and finally, be sure to implement the modifications in the school food services. Empty calories and fatty, saturated foods do no good for the growing brain. Exhibit 7.2 shows some nutritional suggestions.

Sufficient Time

With the exceptions of trauma and surgery, significant changes almost never happen in the brain in an instant or even overnight. Why? Most change is the result of large-scale aggregates made up of millions of molecules and cells responding to environmental input. Both behaviors and learning create changes in the brain. To make the changes happen, we use up resources, including glucose, which needs to be replenished. Brains also need time to recycle proteins, which are used to create new

Exhibit 7.2. Suggestions for Healthy Nutrition.

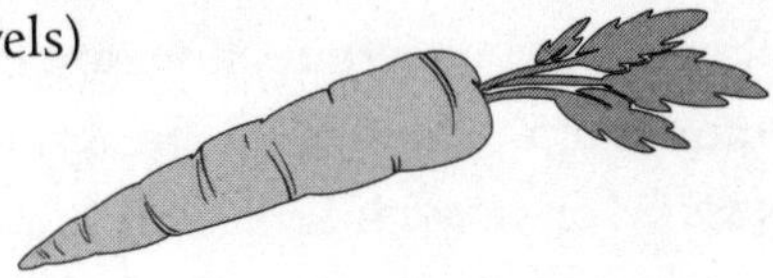

- Nibbling diets (manage glucose levels)
- Available water
- Healthy snacks
- Five essential brain nutrients:
  - (1) Protein (early in the day is best)
  - (2) Minerals (c-m-s-z)
  - (3) Complex carbohydrates
  - (4) Vitamins (B, E, C, A)
  - (5) Essential fatty acids

connections between brain cells. All of the learning processes require resources, and that takes time. New connections are being formed within fifteen minutes of new learning, but it takes from one to six hours to solidify the new learning. Smart policymakers give students enough time for transition between classes and enough time for lunch. Many teachers complain of overwhelming numbers of school announcements that eat into instructional time. That's why we must consolidate them, keep them restricted to the minimum, and give enough time for teachers to do what they do best—ignite learning!

Recommendation: Students need time to develop their interests, talents, skills, and passions. They need a daily schedule with time to reflect, socialize, and review. They need homework that asks them to solidify already learned material, not figure out new concepts. Finally, they need some options in the speed at which they proceed through school. Most important, policymakers have to make the commitment to long-term change. This is no quick fix for a few weeks to get test scores up. It's a commitment to optimize human potential throughout the schooling process, from day one to graduation.

Establishing an Enrichment Program

Providing the seven maximizing factors can make any school a fabulous enrichment experience. Perhaps that's what your school already does. If so, you or your children are at a terrific school! But most schools have strengths and weaknesses in different areas. The perfect school experience is one that keeps students loving to learn, hungry to learn, and getting just enough mental nourishment that instead of becoming satisfied, they simply develop a bigger appetite. When parents don't feel that their schools are providing this experience, many seek alternatives.

Examples of alternative options include those designated as charter, private but noncharter, online, and home schooling. Collectively, these four alternatives combine for over six million U.S. students.[29] This number should send chills down the spines of traditional public school policymakers. The watchword in twenty-first-century education seems to be "choices." In some cases, parents get the new mix just right for their child; in other cases, they do not. Yet it should be clear how badly parents (and kids) want just the right educational experience. They'll risk a completely new model of education to get it. What policymakers do at their school influences parent and student decisions about themselves and their future. Enrichment is one of the strongest selling tools a school can have! The rest of this chapter is directed to policymakers and describes how they can design and implement enrichment programs.

How would an enriched school work? Can anyone include all of the enrichment factors across the board in a single school or even a school district? It's not easy unless we remember what makes enrichment work: contrast. What's needed is to employ for all kids the mentality that's now used for students who are identified with learning disabilities.

Instead of just throwing random programs out and hoping for a match, an IEP (individual education plan) can be created by a team that knows the child best. With a team usually composed of at least one parent or guardian, a school counselor, special education teacher, and the teacher most involved, IEPs make sense. The huge challenge of enrichment brings us to the core concept of IEPs for every student.

Changing the Paradigm

The most effective way to provide enrichment to every student at a school is already in front of us. All children, in all schools, should have an IEP. Grade levels in classes should be eliminated. High-stakes testing should be dropped. Lockstep schooling should be eliminated. There should no longer be "third grade" or "tenth grade." All students should work toward mastery learning. When they have mastered a skill or a subject, they move on to the next one. When they finish the required and elective curriculum, they graduate. Slower learners are never "held back." There is no "back" to be held to. There is no grade to be in. Gifted kids are no longer in pullout programs or accelerated learning programs. They work at their own pace, moving through the learning at the pace at which they can show they have mastered the curriculum. For everyone at the school, the learning is enhanced and the likely result is enrichment for all.

Old Paradigm	New Paradigm
One size fits all	Customized IEPs for all
At grade level for one year	Students move at own pace
Graduate after sixteen years	Graduate when curriculum is done
Pullout programs	Always in pullout enriched class
Grade promotion	Content-mastery promotion
Stressful grading	Mastery-level achievement

At the heart of the enriched school is the IEP. Only the IEP can ensure that each student is constantly in an enriched environment. An academic, social, and extracurricular path is chosen, and meetings every two weeks with peer counselors and monthly with teachers help guide and manage the process. Students will still have a host of subjects that are mandated by the state. But there will always be two other things as part of the IEP. First, students should have some electives to help develop talents and abilities. Second, they will have skill-building sessions in small breakout rooms to work on specific skills. A surprising number of students need help in reading, note-taking, writing, summarizing, test-taking, and time management. Effective assessments will tell the IEP team what the strengths and weaknesses are in each student. Because all learning now becomes customized, every student has the possibility for enrichment.

The IEP specifies the opportunities and concerns, plus it sets the short-term and long-term goals for each child. The IEP becomes a template, a blueprint with milestones for measuring student progress. Students are not compared to all other students—that's absurd. They are compared only to their own past achievements. Many private schools are already using IEPs for all their students. If more schools wanted to reap the benefits of enrichment, they would adopt an individual education plan approach. Once the logistics are worked out, it becomes no harder to manage than any other system. If you think it would be too tedious, or time-consuming, you haven't added up all the hours educators currently spend on the standards-based system and high-stakes testing. Now that's a pretty big vacuum of time.

Using Better Assessments to Identify Studies

Instead of investing time on trying to beat the system with high-stakes testing, a better option would be to design a school from the start to customize its education for all students. Nearly every school district uses some form of standardized achievement or intelligence test in the identification and screening process for programs and services. Tests are also valuable for assessing students' needs and for designing programs and services based on these needs. But testing instruments alone are not infallible predictors of intelligence, achievement, or ability, and they should be used carefully. Although critically important in all assessment, this precaution must be given even greater consideration when underserved gifted students (very young children, culturally diverse students, linguistically diverse students, economically disadvantaged students, and students with other special educational needs) are being assessed.

Because the IEP is so important, no single measure should be used to make identification and placement decisions. That is, no single test or instrument should be used to include a child or exclude a child from any level of services. Testing situations should be culturally sensitive, help students feel comfortable and relaxed, and meet any special needs of the student. Naturally, multiple measures and valid indicators from multiple sources should be used to assess and serve all students. As I recommended earlier, when students are being assessed for giftedness, information should be gathered from all the key sources, in a variety of ways and in different contexts. The school personnel who administer, use, or advise others in the use of standardized tests must be trained and qualified to do so. Once the tests are completed, they can form a key part of the basis for the IEP.

Gather Your Data

The very first step is knowing who's in your school. That may not be a welcome suggestion; many proponents of data-driven instruction will swear that teachers are historically "data phobic." If you think data are a bit too quantitative for your qualitative classroom experiences, remember that understanding in detail where each of your student's strengths, interests, and areas of weakness will support the matching up of the student and the curriculum so that it finally fits like a glove is essential to designing an enrichment program. There is no enrichment without contrast. Only by knowing the existing condition can you propose an enriched one.

It can be challenging to gather sufficient data. You need a wide range of data to meet the issue at hand. Data tell you whether students are doing well or need extra help. But data are not always prescriptive; they do not always tell you what to do next. That information may need to be pieced together. You'll develop hypotheses about what's going on and what to do next based on the data clues. They may need different data if they're trying to reach a specific population. Any specific test is typically valuable only for a specific purpose, so data should be used carefully and thoughtfully.

Ideally, all educators would be given the time to learn, to think about data and how to use the tools well. Teachers ideally should be able to walk through each of the necessary steps involving inquiry, data acquisition, management, analysis, application, and evaluation of data. They can request permission to get training in those skills if they don't have them yet.

For enrichment efforts to succeed by contrast, every student needs an IEP (individual education plan) created by a team made up of the people who know the child best. This team should include at least one parent or guardian, a school counselor, a special education teacher, and the teacher most involved.

The IEP outlines student strengths and weaknesses, and sets a plan in motion. In it, the IEP team will want to set up clear, measurable goals. These may be set for weekly, monthly, and annual checkpoints. To match student progress with these goals, you'll need a wide variety of data to establish benchmarks. Besides standardized testing, sources for benchmarks may include

- Attitudinal pre- and postsurveys
- Portfolio progress
- Interviews with the students
- Weekly reports from peer groups, teams, cooperative learning
- Grade-level content exams
- Journals, reflection activities
- Interviews with the school team working with the student
- Parent surveys, phone contact, or e-mail
- Weekly quizzes, autopsies of the quizzes
- Observation in class from teachers

These are formidable masses of data. But many teachers already keep this much on students. Those that do not do so now can build up to it over time. After a year, the portfolio goes with the student so the next teacher does not need to re-create everything from scratch. Thus the first year will be the most challenging in data gathering, decision making, and follow-up. Until you or your whole school gets used to it, data gathering will seem like a lot of work. But it pays off big time. Everything you can learn about your students is helpful.

Matching Students with Instructional Needs

Enrichment requires matching the right students with instruction targeted for specific needs. Before you think in terms of what to do, let's start with *who* is in your class. We have introduced the concept of IEPs (individual education plans) for all students. Knowing your students by way of an IEP is critical, but if your school does not use the process, you'll need to do some homework for yourself. Create a simple questionnaire (informal works best) that you administer over time. Each time you give it, you'll ask slightly different questions. Each time, you'll learn more and more about your own students. Exhibit 7.3 offers ten sample questions that would help you discover where your opportunities are for contrast.

As you might guess, those students that answer more of the questions with "a" or "b" answers will need a different type of contrast than those who answer with more of the "c", "d," or "e" answers. All your students deserve contrast, but once you start understanding who they are, you've got a better shot at creating contrast. You'll hear this concept over and over. It's not *what you do* that creates the "enrichment response." It's the *positive contrast*. And you can't create contrast unless you know about your students.

Problems Created, Problems Solved

The whole notion of a customized education for every single student may well seem crazy. But we already do it for many special needs students—and what I'm arguing is that *all* students have special needs. Talk to parents, and they'll tell you how special *their* child is. Some gifted children benefit more from association with peers; some need skill building in social skills. Approximately one-sixth of the gifted children also have some type of learning disability—often undetected before the assessment—such as central auditory processing disorder, difficulties with visual processing, sensory integration dysfunction, spatial disorientation, dyslexia, and attention deficits. That should tell you how important an IEP is; without it much gets missed. Exhibit 7.4 shows how a customized approach might fit into the school schedule.

Exhibit 7.3. Sample Questionnaire (modify for your age group).

1. How much do you like the following?
   Time to get up, move around, and do things
      (a) a little (b) some (c) a lot
   Plenty of one-on-one time with the teacher
      (a) a little (b) some (c) a lot
   Time to talk to other students
      (a) a little (b) some (c) a lot
   Extensive use of audiovisual equipment or computers
      (a) a little (b) some (c) a lot
   Time to work by myself on things
      (a) a little (b) some (c) a lot

2. In class, most of the time:
      (a) Class is too fast, it's really hard to keep up.
      (b) Class is a little fast, but it's OK.
      (c) I am keeping up just fine, but bored with the content.
      (d) I like the speed of class and what I learn just fine.
      (e) Class goes way too slow for me.

3. At home, what do you like using the most?
   Television
      (a) a little (b) some (c) a lot
   Movies, games, DVDs
      (a) a little (b) some (c) a lot
   Videogames
      (a) a little (b) some (c) a lot
   Phone
      (a) a little (b) some (c) a lot
   Computer
      (a) a little (b) some (c) a lot

4. At home, whom do you learn from the most?
      (a) mom or dad
      (b) another relative
      (c) a brother or sister
      (d) best friend or cousin
      (e) no one else, mostly books or the Internet

5. How often do you eat any of these:
   chicken, yogurt, eggs, meats, soy, cheese, or fish?
   (a) not very often
   (b) a couple times a week
   (c) I have one of those almost every day
   How often do you eat any of these:
   potatoes, pasta, breads, rice, or noodles?
   (a) not very often
   (b) a couple times a week
   (c) I have one of those almost every day

6. How much do you like to read at home?
   (a) not much
   (b) some magazines or comics
   (c) a lot—I read a book and several magazines a week

7. How much homework do you do at home each night?
   (a) I have the time, but I can't concentrate.
   (b) I would, but have no time to do it.
   (c) I try to do up to an hour.
   (d) I usually do way over an hour.

8. Tell me about your friends.
   (a) I don't have as many as I would like.
   (b) I have a couple of friends.
   (c) I spend over an hour a day with my best friend.

9. Where have been your favorite places to visit?
   (a) I don't go outside that much
   (b) neighborhood, malls, movies
   (c) other cities, states, parks

10. What are your favorite things to learn about?
    (a) anything
    (b) friends, other people
    (c) stuff on TV, the Internet
    (d) school
    (e) my own hobbies

Exhibit 7.4. Sample School Schedules.

Elementary School (schedule is 8 A.M.–2 P.M.)

Opening (30 minutes): All students at all levels begin their day in a mixed-ability homeroom (community is created, lessons are reviewed, goals are set, IEPs are kept up, announcements are made, student sharing occurs, peer counselors are used).

A.M. *content:* School curriculum, differentiated instruction including the use of acceleration and compacting

Physical education (30 minutes): Required

Lunch (30 minutes): Required

P.M. *Skill building* (IEP mandate): emotional intelligence, arts, learn-to-learn skills, reading skills, other specialized programs

Closing (30 minutes): All students end their day in the same mixed homeroom (community is re-created, goals are checked on, partners help with review, relationships are strengthened).

Secondary Schools (schedule is 9 A.M.–3 P.M.)

Homeroom (30 minutes): All students at all levels begin their day in a mixed-ability homeroom (community is created, lessons are reviewed, goals are set, IEPs are kept up, announcements are made, student sharing occurs, peer counselors are used).

Content: (rotate two to three times per week with another content block) IEP is designated: could be accelerated or review class

Physical education (30–40 minutes): Required

Lunch (30 minutes): Required

Skill building (IEP designated) or Elective class fifty-minute session (every day)

Homeroom ending (30 minutes): All students end their day in the same mixed homeroom (community is re-created, goals are checked on, partners help with review, relationships are strengthened).

While this looks like "nothing new," it's actually all customized. Kids take content that fits for them, they take physical education that they have selected, and they get skill building only in areas in which they are deficient. After-school activities may be appropriate for some students.

What Would Change

What we are proposing is a commitment to make schools customized for every student. As soon as you think it's too tough to do, take a few minutes and think about all the things you should not have to be doing right now:

- Comparing students with each other
- Teaching to the test
- Worrying about where your school ranks
- Trying to meet the needs of all students through simple instructional changes such as differentiation
- Coping with parents who want their child's needs met
- Pacifying school boards who want higher test scores

The whole notion of "no child left behind" only makes sense in a school that can respond to the needs of all students. Think about the steps needed to create a customized school. Is it feasible? Can it be done? My guess is that for every problem you face, another one would be eliminated. Consider your options and I think you'll vote for an enriched school.

How all the variables play out in your school may be a delicate financial, political, and philosophical issue. You'll want to ensure that everyone is on the same page when it comes to enrichment. At a staff meeting, a qualified representative from the gifted community should help profile the gifted, and equally qualified representatives from other underrepresented populations need to speak to your staff. Someone should address language-minority students, those with disabilities, and those representing culturally and ethnically diverse populations, too. The point is, you want your staff to understand that every child is unique. No one-size-fits-all teaching approach can work. Once the staff sees and hears from multiple advocates, they'll be more ready to make a plan and jump on board.

Implementing the Enrichment Policy

When it comes to implementing the "enrichment response" programs, there are three ways it can happen. They are top down, bottom up, or a combination of both. The top-down approach means that the program is supported or mandated by policymakers, administrators, and executives in the positions that direct implementation of policy. The bottom-up implementation means that the real doers (teachers, child-care providers, and parents) begin taking actions unilaterally, regardless of the "official" policy. The combination approach means that while immediate actions are taken to begin maximizing brain possibilities, there are additional efforts in process simultaneously, to affect public policy. As a rule, the most effective way to make change happen is the combination approach.

First, Three Myths to Explore

There are three major myths that typically hold back this process. Many in the education community share these ideas, and that makes it very difficult to move ahead. One belief is the idea that most policymakers *already* understand enrichment, both what it is and how to create it, and are offering it right now (especially to the gifted students for whom it is supposedly best suited). Others believe schools are utterly powerless to do anything but drill and kill to get higher scores on standardized tests. The third is that it's all too much work, time, or money to make it happen. I'll label those three beliefs as follows.

THE MYTH OF DELUSION.   "We already do it." How can a school "do it" if you don't even know what "it" is? The false belief is that many *already understand* what enrichment is. It's such a new topic, for which there's so much "ripped from the headlines" in the past few years, that it's unlikely many key decision makers understand it. As an example, most still use phrases such as, "we have enrichment classes" or "we have an enrichment school" when, as described earlier, you don't *do* enrichment. You need to *find the contrast* in student's lives and make an orchestrated *and committed effort to sustain those differences* with as many of the seven factors for contrast as possible. At some point, you *will* get the enrichment response in students, but you can't just snap your fingers; humans are much more complex than that.

Yes, enrichment is already happening at a small number of savvy schools and for a minority of fortunate students. But it's not universal and it should be. Elaine Yagiela is the executive director at New Morning School, a pre-K–8 school in Brighton, Michigan. She uses IEPs for every student. They use small-group instruction, but blocks of the day are used for students pursuing their individualized academic plan. No school's perfect, but her staff seem to love their job, rave about how excited the kids are at school, and point out that they're doing well on the tests. Her school is one of many that already use IEPs for all. We know some schools *do* get the enrichment response, as a school, but most do not. By the way if you *really* already are enhancing with maximum contrast, your test scores, attendance, personal growth, and satisfied parent numbers are "off the charts!"

THE MYTH OF REDUCTION.   "Less is more. If we narrow our focus to test scores, we'll meet our mandate to educate children and prepare them for tomorrow." If you think narrowing the focus of learning will broaden the child's life, you're mistaken; the research does not support this premise. This belief says that policymakers and practitioners are trapped like agonizing, prehistoric creatures in a subsuming tar pit of overwhelming regulatory and scholastic pressure.

The truth is, the enrichment response is so powerful that any and all expectations of an "improved" or "enhanced" student are probably *too low* unless you're doing a scientifically based contrast-driven enrichment program. In fact, much of the current body of knowledge of enrichment is both new and unexpected; enrichment is synergistic—it can only be created, but not offered. And the beauty of it is that every child on campus can benefit from it, though in different ways. Without enrichment, school is in fact for many a neural wasteland. Kids who get bored, frustrated, and drop out, do so for a reason. The outside world is offering a much more compelling scenario than the daily life at school. It's time to face the music and it's playing our song: "Enrich or waste away; there is no middle ground!"

THE MYTH OF POWERLESSNESS.   "We can't do it. There's not enough time, money, or expertise." The fact is, there are schools that create enrichment pretty well already. It is not free to change; it does cost time and money. But the return on investment is astronomical. First of all, the enrichment response in the brain does not necessarily come from a more expensive curriculum, nor does it mean more of it. It means different and better; and that takes vision, will, and time.

This lie may be the deadliest of all. It strikes to the core of our hopes, dreams, fears, and institutions. It maintains that schools are mammoth institutions that change about as often as desert rock formations. Many people actually foster this belief because it means schools need not be particularly responsive to their constituents. Many new teachers in schools of education believe that they have to accept the education they are getting. New teachers should be asking how the brains of their students could change for the better. Teachers should be asking about neuroplasticity and altered gene expression. Parents often don't have time to solicit changes in their school to help their own children because they're so busy themselves, but there are things they can do.

The beautiful thing is that many successful schools have already followed the template or plan that confirms what enrichment looks like and feels like in the real world. Many school leaders have read the research, done the trial-and-error, or simply followed the lead of other successful schools. The good news about educators and parents is that there are already many success stories and models that work. We don't have to invent the wheel when it comes to smarter schools. We only have to take the core principles and connect them to the schools that have shown how it works. The research is solid. The only issue is, "Are there any schools actually doing this stuff anywhere?" The answer is a resounding, "Yes!" Schools now have multiple enrichment options; thousands of schools do a fabulous job in offering smarter choices for students.

Existing Program Models

For those skeptical of the possibilities of across-the-board enrichment responses, here are two examples (one public, one private) of successful programs that have changed human potential not just for those in poverty or with special needs, but for the average or even the above-average student.

One of the best-designed and most researched public programs is the School Enrichment Model developed by Drs. Joseph Renzulli and Sally Reis at the University of Connecticut (access this model at: www.sp.uconn.edu/~nrcgt/sem/semexec.html). Over time, this research-based model has been shown to promote both challenging and enjoyable high-end learning across a varied range of school types, academic levels, and demographic diversity. Renzulli and Reis have used well-tested curriculum strategies to help those labeled as high ability achieve up to their capacity.[30]

Renzulli and Reis have codeveloped this model with a beautifully detailed blueprint for schoolwide improvement. They endorse using well-designed ability grouping strategies, which show strong results.[31] Yet Renzulli suggests we still have much more we can learn from and research among all populations, especially those identified as gifted.[32] In this format, teachers need to have clarity, certainty, and confidence in any plan that is offered. Renzulli's plan is smart because it is based on the critical ingredient, contrast. Remember, we will only get the enrichment response when we create contrast for every learner, and he understands that.

In efforts to either be politically correct or save money, many schools put wide varieties of mixed abilities in a single classroom. This is called differentiation, and it could work (1) with highly talented teachers, (2) with lowered expectations of getting the enrichment response, (3) in smaller classes, and (4) without today's climate of testing pressures. Differentiated instruction in an inclusionary classroom is much better than no options at all. But the real enhancement comes from an integrated continuum of service delivery components that allows students to move, on their own accord, through the network. Renzulli's School Enrichment Model has an elaborate matrix that ensures that students can move up at their own ability levels, not when the teacher discovers they're ready. There must be options for rapid or superior learners as well as wide-ranging learning tasks that are meaningful to the students, making all curriculum available at every variety of levels.

There are many private "enrichment for all" models already developed; one is SuperCamp®. I cofounded it in 1981 with two partners after seeing the transformative possibilities. SuperCamp is a ten-day residential academic enrichment program for students ages eight to twenty-two that typically incorporates nearly all of the "golden maximizers" for a consistent enrichment response. Although some students arrive at the program with a history of chronic demotivation, many are average and some are already highly successful students. Yet after attending for just ten days, students often graduate as insatiable learners who go on to improve their grades, their school participation, SAT scores, confidence, relationships, and self-esteem. Years of follow-up have shown that the benefits of this program lasted long after the ten-day program itself.[33] Today, two generations later, this program boasts over forty-five thousand graduates from around the world. Although I have since sold my half of the business, it continues to be guided by the philosophy of "enrichment for all" by its two caring partners, Bobbi DePorter and Joe Chapon. Students at this academic program (www.supercamp.com) have a nearly universal positive experience. In addition, students' grades and school participation went up, and the students reported greater self-confidence. The teaching methods used have been evaluated and shown to be highly effective by an independent firm.[34]

What You Can Do

Individuals within the educational community—a term that must include concerned parents as well as educators at all levels—do have the power to influence local schools, staff developers, school boards, and universities. There are already many existing partnerships between parent groups and schools. One of the many sites you might visit is www.projectappleseed.org. This site can provide you with ideas, project examples, strategies, and tools to make your school improvement project successful. In addition:

- The Internet can allow you to reach and mobilize hundreds or thousands of like-minded supporters, and find vast amounts of useful information.
- The Freedom of Information Act can allow you to get quality information to help build your case.
- Although schools, school boards, district administrators, and politicians do not listen to isolated voices, they do listen to dozens, hundreds, and even thousands of focused, mobilized citizens with a clear, specific agenda for change. They can't afford not to listen. It is not easy, but change does get done by those who are relentless in their pursuit of change. Your path is simple:

Why: Develop a big "why" reason and passion for pursuing change. The process will take time. Your why is all about maximizing the brains of *all* children.

Who: Find out who are the decision makers and get contact information. Introduce yourself and let them know about your passion and your agenda.

What: Do your homework and know the facts, the issues, the law, the unions, the constraints, and the budgets. Know your facts and know the facts for others' points of view, too. Decide what is a first small, reasonable step in the right direction.

Where: Be flexible and meet with decision makers wherever they are, whenever they can, and begin a dialogue.

When: Set up a time line for small, measurable steps. Use your parent support and stick to it!

Every individual's role is to nudge schools where and when it's appropriate. Running a school is a tough job, and changing its operations is never easy. You must have a real, not imagined reason for change. You'll need to get many others on board, so it must be an issue that cuts across many demographics. Once you've got the ball rolling, let school officials know that you're not their enemy. Even though you may become a thorn in the side, it doesn't mean you're against them. You are simply the impetus for a change that might have happened . . . someday. To you, the time is now!

Summary

Enrichment is the whole reason for school. Enrichment is about making daily improvements; it's about growing all of us into better human beings. You can't do that by producing someone who will only pass a single instrument each year in school. We are missing out on the entire range of human possibilities. The IEP-for-every-student concept will customize school and allow students to become the best they can be.

But it is not just a neurobiological question as to whether those programs can help when done well. UCSD developmental neuroscientist Terry Jernigan says, "We have to look at the cost-benefit ratio. In cases where there may be substantial upside gain with little downside, we should try out those ideas in school."[35]

Having said all this, if your only goal is raising the traditional IQ, I must acknowledge that efforts to create enrichment have significant limitations in school applications. I'm hoping that you're interested in far more than whether the IQ is raised or not. I'm hoping you're interested in a host of improved outcomes including happier students, better health, higher graduation rates, higher acceptance rates for four-year colleges, less likelihood of mental or psychosocial dysfunction, and enhanced reading and language skills.

If you're interested in all of those outcomes, enrichment efforts are still the way to go. We don't yet have any evidence that they can enhance intelligence dramatically in those who are not disadvantaged in some way, but we do have evidence that many other good things will happen. And they will certainly reduce any risk of cognitive backsliding among students who have made a strong start toward healthy and productive lives.

School must be all about hope, backed up by the practical skills, relationships, and knowledge to support it. Getting the enrichment response provides the best hope possible. The research is clear; we can and must enrich the students we work with. We must enrich all of them, too. This chapter has shown what the enrichment research means in terms of policy changes—and made some suggestions as to *how* exactly a school could implement the changes. In our next chapter, we'll start naming some specifics in even greater detail.

8

School and Classroom Solutions

ONE OF OUR FIRST PRINCIPLES IS THAT THE BRAIN IS NOT STATIC; IT'S ALWAYS IN A state of flux. Many educational authors have argued that teachers have an inherently brain-changing job.[1] For example, Zull argues persuasively that because learning is a biological change and good teaching begets learning, teachers are, in fact, "brain changers." I hope that by this stage you've seen that the enrichment response is both desired and possible for every single student in school. Could all students become enriched, every single day? It's possible! If that goal sounds a bit ambitious, keep in mind that many schools already do this. They are set up for generating enrichment, and that's all they focus on.

Remember, no enrichment means there's not much of a point to school since there is nothing offered of contrast to the student. Think less in terms of what *one thing you can do* and start thinking in terms of *creating conditions for contrast.* Enrichment is what happens in the brain of someone who enters an environment substantially richer than his or her baseline or accustomed one. It happens in an environment with opportunities to explore and grow, but one sufficiently secure and supportive to make the experience welcome rather than impossibly stressful. You can't "enrich" anyone on cue—you can only be purposeful in setting up conditions of contrast, and then allow the magic to happen. Remember, enrichment is *an effect* and not a cause. Putting up pretty posters and mobiles, or playing music are all good, but actually may not be very enriching to some kids who are already working on an upcoming school musical. Remember, it is not *what* you do, it is the *conditions for positive contrast* that you create. This chapter will deepen your understanding of those conditions and offer examples of how others have done it.

This chapter, directed at policymakers and educators, is focused on making every single classroom into one that fosters the good in students. Whether your entire school, district, or state embraces the enrichment response (or not), you can do things smarter. It should be clear that no given situation will be equally enriching for every student—but equally clear that it is worthwhile to try to make every situation as rich as feasible. Enrichment, after all, requires the provision of stimuli that are over, above, and beyond what would be typical and characteristic for each individual child. A key tenet of a schoolwide or classroom enrichment commitment is realizing that human potential can be maximized deeper (higher academic scores) or wider (stronger life skills). This is critical because there's good evidence that those with better life skills do better academically. If you only push, push, and push academically, you'll not only rob students of their real human potential but still get worse test scores!

Part-time enriching conditions, just a few hours a week of contrast, is better than nothing. There are a total of ten hours each school day (five in school and five outside of school) that are up for enrichment "grabs," or fifty hours a week. If school lasts for forty weeks, that's over two thousand hours of enriching contrast per year. That's more than enough for miracles! But you won't get the perceptible intelligence jumps of enrichment unless you can make a clear improvement in conditions. A full-time enrichment program is most likely to get the best results for students.[2] The question is, "How can you make contrast the norm?" There are many ways to do that; let's jump right in and get some answers.

A careful reading of the responsibilities and roles tells you that enrichment takes a good deal of work to envision, implement, support, and manage. One of the lessons here is that although it's easy to say,

"Oh, our school does enrichment," chances are that no one would argue with the criteria or even question your intent. But if you really do want the enrichment response at your school, it takes a fair bit of sustained, purposeful study and work to make it happen.

The Enrichment-Driven Classroom

This section discusses ways to make contrast the norm in your school.

Know Your Students (and Student Self-Knowledge)

Data gathering on your students, including creating IEPs, is absolutely essential. Understanding your students allows you to make the decisions that create the contrast needed for the enrichment response. Having said that, it's not enough. You can't (and don't want to) do this alone. You'll want, to the degree possible, your students to know themselves well, too. When students know themselves, they can be allies in the enrichment pursuit instead of passive players on the academic chessboard.

Many students struggle through school, never finding out what their learning styles are, their passions, their strongest talents, or their preferred modes of communication. This puts them at a tremendous disadvantage because it is their strengths that will help them cope and even thrive in this world. When students know their own strengths, it does more than build their self-concept and self-esteem. It allows them to see themselves in the bigger picture of school and at home. It lets them see how to succeed in life by asking for help without judging themselves as stupid.

In the previous chapter, we included a sample survey that can help determine how to best create contrast needed for the enrichment response. Elementary students can discover their strengths simply by selecting from a variety of offered activities at specially designed learning centers. Teachers can set up a row of tables, each with a different type of option. Tables might have a computer, selected books, science props, a musical instrument on one, and theater costumes on another.

Students in secondary school might Google the words "student inventory, learning styles" and discover many free surveys on the path of self-discovery. Remember that self-knowledge may reveal many areas of weakness. This is important to you because nonacademic weaknesses are just as essential to remediate as are the more academic ones.

Passion

Passion in teaching is core to the enrichment possibilities. You can have all the knowledge and strategy in the world, but without the passion, you'll get few student "takers." Passion is the electricity, the energy, and driving fire behind learning new things. It makes you smile, become animated, and be excited over the smallest detail. Passion sells your students on the "why" of school. Passion means you'll be

Varying your facial expressions
Nearly exploding with interest and curiosity
Constantly using voice inflection, volume changes, and range
Always selling students on the content and themselves
Using student interests to make a point
Evangelizing your topic to others
Bringing in new things from home all the time

The "why" of school is not just to graduate kids who can get a job. The real "why" is the process of bringing out a passion for living, a joy for learning, and a desire to have an active role in society as a contributor. It's passion that makes life vibrant and exciting. You may have students who have never, ever, seen the passion from the joy of discovery or the thrill of insight. Role model this experience for them or they'll never know it exists. Learning can be exciting, so get passionate about it.

Passion is important because it sells students on themselves, on the subject, and on learning. It usually takes a conscious effort to encourage students to take part in enrichment activities—and not just a few well-directed words, either, but many smart policy decisions and actions. Surprisingly, not all students will gravitate to or find the enrichment options in your school. Even when you offer fabulous, contrasting conditions, not every kid will be excited. Here is a range of strategies that have been used to encourage students to take part in enrichment activities:

1. Talk about the brain and enrichment! Make clear to students the benefits of participation by sharing the science behind enrichment.
2. Boost the expectation that students will participate. You expect everyone to become excited about the joy, thrill, and passion of discovery!
3. Hold private positive talks with individuals to introduce them to activities that interest them and are relevant to their future plans. You can bring up former students' statements about the value of the contrasting, enrichment experience.

Classroom Instruction

Classroom instruction for learning enhancement is both the easiest and the hardest of the options mentioned here. It's easy because you can be right there, directly managing the instruction. It's easy because in some cases, you can allow student choice to be the source of contrast, since few students will choose content or skills they already know. But it's also the hardest because in order to use instructional strategies that create contrast, you'll constantly be making adjustments for contrast. It's also hard because you don't *teach* that differently, you *plan and orchestrate* differently.

When you see the suggestions that follow, instead of looking for novel ideas, look for *how well these are seamlessly integrated* in your classroom. It's not *the number* of new ideas you learn that counts; it's the *quality and execution* of the ideas that counts. Let's start with your primary process for contrast in the classroom. The core instructional strategies are variety and choice. There are endless ways to carry these two out. In fact, some of these many teachers already use:

Variety of inquiry

Tiered activities

Interest centers

Independent study centers

Multiple texts and supplementary materials

Computer programs

Earlier, differentiation was suggested as a strategy but only under certain conditions. Results may suffer if class sizes are big, the teacher is less experienced, or the student population has extreme academic and behavioral "outliers." But it can be done. On the surface, differentiation seems to be simply the adjustment of the instructional strategies according to the student's learning needs. But there's far more; the more effective you get at differentiating the instruction, the deeper, more complex the process becomes. Savvy teachers typically use widely varied forms of differentiating in their instruction. The core and characteristic principle is this: When you do differentiation successfully, teachers are *not* traditional dispensers of knowledge but *organizers of learning opportunities.* Dr. Joseph Renzulli suggests using a model of five dimensions of differentiation:[3]

Renzulli Five Dimensions of Differentiation Model

- *Content.* Put more depth into the curriculum through organizing the curriculum concepts and structure of knowledge. Use graphics, mind maps, and flow charts—visual hierarchies of both structure and content to allow students to enter at one spot and move along as their competencies increase. Use these graphics to show students where they fit into the big picture. Everything from world history to higher mathematics can be mapped out from simple to complex.
- *Teacher.* Use passion and personality to share personal knowledge of curriculum topics through personal interests, collections, hobbies, and enthusiasm about issues surrounding the content area.
- *Classroom.* Influence the physical structure through the use of partitions, novel social groupings, and alternative learning spaces. We will explore more of this later in the chapter.

- *Process.* Use many instructional techniques and materials to enhance and motivate learning styles of students. This means debating, game shows, academic competition, or outside projects.
- *Product.* Enhance cognitive development and foster students' ability to express themselves. This requires options for student multimedia presentations, the building of physical models, music instruments, or other practical hands-on products.

When teaching for the enrichment response, teachers should not make assumptions that all students need a given task or segment of study. Instead they'll continuously assess student readiness and interest. In this way, the enrichment comes from the constant adjustments of contrast. The students use their self-knowledge of strengths and weaknesses and the power of choice and the teacher provides support when students need it. He or she gives guidance and new pathways when students are ready to move ahead. This constant, ongoing assessment of student readiness and growth has to be built into the daily classes.

The lack of differentiation has been a significant issue facing schools, frustrating both higher- and lower-end students. Carol Ann Tomlinson and others have advocated differentiating instruction as a process for *all* students, *all the time.*[4] In differentiated classes, teachers use variety, variety, and more variety. They use different strategies to explore curriculum content, different meaning-making activities to better understand the ideas, and different ways for students to show what they know. And it makes good sense. Realistically, differentiation takes an experienced or confident teacher to make it work, with plenty of willingness to learn, adjust, and adapt to the feedback. The ideal is a partnership with the students who have good self-knowledge, are reflective, and can make many choices for themselves. There is no perfect cookie cutter for all education. Following are examples of some of the instructional strategies listed earlier.

DIFFERENTIATED INQUIRY.   This is the process of customizing the way that students tackle the learning. I am a big believer in asking students to generate questions about the content they are learning. It's not just a good learning experience for them, it helps them understand and prepare for the assessment part of the process, too. First, put students in cooperative groups or in their usual work teams. On Friday, ask students to prepare a list of ten questions based on what was learned over the previous week. The questions can be done individually and then combined, or they may be formulated as a group activity. Once their lists are complete, ask them to add two variations to each of the ten questions; one harder question and one easier one. You can collect these, and, for your Monday review session, you can differentiate by asking different sets of questions of certain students, depending on their understanding level.

TIERED ACTIVITIES.   As an example of differentiation, you might use tiered objectives and tiered activities to give students a set of "cognitive stairs" to climb. Students see what they have to learn and focus on the level they're challenged by. This lets teachers ensure that students work at appropriate levels of challenge while studying the same overall skills and concepts. Sometimes this tiered concept is formalized in a posted visual aid for all students to see and be challenged by.

This strategy, combined with ability group learning, can allow every student to be in a class that feels (and is) personally customized. Tomlinson also adds that teachers typically will need training in other ways to meet the needs of their students from the special needs population (who may also be gifted) to the gifted (who may also have special needs).[5] For example, gifted students may need different reading assignments (not more!) to challenge them, different study questions, and different goals for paper projects.

INTEREST CENTERS.   Traditionally, interest or learning centers have been set up based either on different subjects or, more recently, on various ways to approach the same subject. Some use multiple-intelligences approaches, but with differentiation, there's anther way to approach it. Set up three levels of your centers based on degree of difficulty. Encourage students to select something that's slightly above their skill and knowledge level. This will help create the climate you want of contrast and give students a more viable choice in finding the contrast they need.

INDEPENDENT STUDY CENTERS.   Some students have a strong passion for learning, but struggle with the formal concept of school. Let them learn! The student creates goals, time lines, and accountability levels, and checks in often. You'll be surprised at the quality work you might get. At the most challenging level a student might "compare and contrast relevant differences and similarities between the Egyptians of 2000 B.C. and Greece of 2000 A.D." Let them figure out in what ways Sir Isaac Newton is still exerting an influence on the science of today. Allow students to study what conditions need to be present for agencies or countries to adopt a proenvironmental, "green" approach to global warming issues. That would be a challenge!

MULTIPLE TEXTS AND SUPPLEMENTARY MATERIALS.   With the availability of the Internet, it's tempting to dismiss the wider use of texts. But often, texts can go much deeper into a subject and allow students to dwell on it longer. Additional texts may be found in classrooms of higher grade levels, at home, in local libraries, or at nearby universities.

COMPUTER PROGRAMS.   Many teachers find computer programs helpful for two reasons. First, students can get error correction while using them, and second, most strong programs allow students to continually move upward into areas of increasing challenge. A good example of a national program that has been successful in accelerating the thinking development of disadvantaged students after the third grade is the Higher Order Thinking Skills (HOTS) program (www.hots.org). Dr. Stanley Pogrow's software program uses the principles of challenge and "controlled frustration" to encourage students to move up the ladder of cognitive activity. With all the emphasis on reading and math in today's schools, you'd think we'd have a nation of high performers. That's not happening for a number of reasons.

One of them is that progress in school requires a greater ability to deal with deeper, more complex ideas in more sophisticated and integrative thought processes. Disadvantaged students do have the intellectual ability to engage in such forms of thinking at high levels, but often don't get the experiences they need in learning, building, and interacting with academic problem solving. This has to happen with adults using complex, school-related content. Good software programs can help build these skills and customize the process. Computer programs that fail to challenge students are electronic baby-sitters that waste student's brains.

Classroom Assessment

To constantly be getting the enrichment response, you'll want to constantly gather data on student progress. That can come from a variety of forms, many of which the student can supply for you. Students can track their effort (time spent on certain tasks, choices of resources, socializing, and so on), and they can track results (how many ideas, pages, chapters, Websites, articles, and so on were consulted). This information can be posted on the wall or e-mailed weekly to ensure a contrast happening constantly. Remember, if you know where they're at, you can create situations and environments of contrast. The importance of assessment is that it gives you the data you need to make the decisions that will ensure that enrichment has a good shot. There are countless forms of assessment, and we'll touch on just a few of them.

STUDENT CONTENT JOURNALS.   These are journals that students know are going to be shared with the teacher. Commonly, the teacher only reads them and does *not* make return comments. Exceptions for this rule are when there are formal assignments such as "Tell me what you learned, how you learned it, and how you feel about learning it." "Tell me how your team interacted and what suggestions you have." "Tell me what you got most interested in and why."

GRADUATED TASK AND PRODUCT RUBRICS.   These are originally codesigned by students and either their mentor or the teacher. A rubric is basically a grid-shaped scoring tool that organizes the criteria for success in a product or process. For example, a rubric for an essay might include clarity, purpose, organization, factual details, voice, and passion.

LEARNING CONTRACTS.   These are typically proposed by the student while fitting within a set of guidelines the teacher creates for content, product, or process mastery. The student's proposal becomes a contract when the teacher approves it. It may include benchmarks that can be checked at quarter-by-quarter progress stages. Contracts may be renegotiated, but typically at a cost (sometimes more work, more difficult work, and so on) to the person asking for the changes.

ON-DEMAND MAPPING.   Graphic organizers in the form of colorful maps can be used for assessment. These are creative patterns of connected ideas, similar to a sentence diagram, a road map, or a blueprint. They use color and illustrations, and are organized from the center (main topic) outward (details on outer branches). Teachers can ask students to map out the previous day's learning or a week's learning and turn these in as a form of ongoing assessment.

PERFORMANCE-BASED PORTFOLIOS.   Many teachers are using portfolios, which are a purposeful collection of student work. Ideally, a portfolio broadly demonstrates the student's efforts, progress, and achievements in student participation in selecting contents, the criteria for selection, the criteria for judging merit, and evidence of student self-reflection.

During the past generation, the most-used format for portfolios was paper-based, usually assembled in manila folders, three-ring notebooks, or larger containers. But recently more video or audio evidence of student work is being stored digitally. The value of these is that they offer a wider, deeper picture of student efforts and usually a much more accurate one, too.

ONLINE ASSESSMENT.   This emerging tool is another way to assess learner progress toward subject objectives. The beauty of it is the
wide variety of forms such assessment can take, including

Electronic submission of written assignments (papers, projects,
   essays)
Publication of documents on the Web itself
Manipulation of online graphs and labeling of online diagrams
Completion of brief online quizzes (short-answer and multiple-
   choice questions)
Online exams with monitored and controlled start and stop times

Not all forms of assessment are done well. As an example, racial and
cultural biases can and do affect the outcome. We know that the knowledge that the person doing the assessment is racially biased against you
can change your test results, even if you know the material just as well
as the next person.[6] Fortunately, holding classroom discussion about
cultural and racial topics can reduce feelings of discomfort and improve
test performance.[7] The main point here is that simply throwing out a
variety of assessments will not guarantee that you gather accurate data.
It's the whole social, cultural, and academic picture we have to consider.

Classroom Social Grouping

Social dynamics change the entire process of learning. Socialization
alters our levels of stress, our confidence, and even our content knowledge. Make it a habit to constantly seek appropriate levels for your students. This would include, but not be limited to

- Reciprocal teaching
- Flexible grouping; pairs, groups, triads, and so on
- Group investigations and cluster groupings (at one grade level,
   the top five to eight meet with an adviser or resource teacher)

RECIPROCAL TEACHING.   Reciprocal teaching is a structured,
specialized form of peer teaching. It can be used for second-language

learning, when half the students are speaking (and learning) one language and their paired partners are speaking (and learning) the other language. The essential principle of reciprocal language teaching is quite simple: invite the learner of a foreign language to also be the teacher of his or her own language. There is strong evidence to support reciprocal teaching as an effective instructional technique for many types of learning, both second language and reading.

Reciprocal teaching can increase the kind of reading comprehension that is necessary for improved test scores.[8] Palincsar and Brown found that when reciprocal teaching was used with groups of students for just a month, their reading scores on a standardized assessment of reading comprehension increased by 50 percent.[9] Palincsar and Klenk found that students not only improved comprehension skills almost immediately using the reciprocal teaching method, they also maintained the gains a year later.[10]

FLEXIBLE GROUPING; PAIRS, GROUPS, TRIADS, AND SO ON. This type of social structure is highly dynamic and flexible. I typically use two to four variations of structures per day. Many times a student will do well in a group of four (less focused attention on him or her), but not in a pairing, where there's a bit more pressure to know it all. Some students don't have the focus skills in a group of three, four, or five, but they can pay attention better with just one partner. I find that you'll get more out of the processes if you constantly change the numbers in the grouping while paying attention to students who have either struggled in the past or been ahead and bored. Learn who does well with what and you'll be able to reach more students, more often.

GROUP INVESTIGATIONS AND CLUSTER GROUPINGS. These are groupings with a content purpose. For example, at one grade level, the five to eight volunteers might meet with an adviser or resource teacher on a weekly basis as part of a semester-long project. The students may be investigating a school-based problem (such as racism, recycling, or bullying), and their goal is to produce a presentation to the whole student body in April with key recommendations and an action plan.

This section has highlighted just some of the opportunities that come from a wider variety of social groupings. This is an important concept because the human brain is organized around being responsive to the surrounding environment. A huge part of the environment is the social conditions, because most of us want to be liked, to be respected, or to be appreciated. How others behave influences our stress levels and, of course, academic and behavioral outcomes. To a degree, we adjust our behaviors based on what others do. If the social groupings you are using are not producing miraculous results, simply keep changing them until you get what you want.

Schoolwide Solutions

Schoolwide solutions include the use of multigrade mentoring programs, school projects in the community, and school-culture-building activities such as dances and assemblies.

Matching Students to Curriculum

Here the focus is a balance among the following variables: state or local mandates, student choice, available resources, and assessment-driven curriculum instead of the reverse. The curriculum is a key element of achieving an enrichment response. It absolutely must be a match for student ability and interests, and yet still meet the standards. There are various ways to achieve this match, including student choice, curriculum compacting, ability grouping, and pullout programs for skill building or accelerated content learning.

STUDENT CHOICE.   Many school reformists have long advocated student choice.[11] With it comes responsibility and the necessity to pair up the choices offered with the maturity level of the student. Just as it's a good idea to give a two-year-old free choice (but only among several preselected options) of nourishing things to eat, it is also a good idea to give students a choice (among preselected options) that can meet their basic educational needs. The regular-ed students, special needs populations, and gifted students will all appreciate choice. Choice supports student buy-in, builds decision making, and encourages personal responsibility. It is up to you, however, to ensure that the menu that each is choosing from is one that you approve of and that fits with the mandates from the student's IEP. Students need graduated responsibility, not unlimited free options.

Here are some examples of how the choice process works. You see on Terry's IEP that he is strong in science and math but needs more help in reading. His reading skills are not terrible, but slightly below average. First, you'd ensure the student gets proper assessment to discover what the reading issues are (central auditory processing disorder, learning delays, dyslexia, tracking, and so on). After the diagnosis, a qualified reading professional may be able to suggest to the student a choice of three different types of reading instruction improvement: a computer-based program, a self-study program with worksheets and guidebook, or a tutor.

The student may pick *the type* of skill-building activity that fits his learning style, but there's no choice as to whether he will get help in the skill itself. Maybe another area on the IEP mentions Terry's strong interest in sports; in that case, any or all of the reading efforts could involve sports-related text as an option. There are countless kids who stayed in school because of this simple process: (1) find the areas of needed contrast, (2) match them up with a strength, and (3) monitor and give feedback. Kids know they're not good at everything; they want to know they can feel good about some of their strengths.

CURRICULUM COMPACTING.   Sometimes it seems as if schools are dedicated to having students all "serve their time." Initial resistance to compacting from more traditional educators was strong, but it's starting to melt away. Compacting allows students to "compress" their learning into a much shorter period of time, based on their ability to pass competency tests. This process is also known as telescoping. It is actually a very simple and effective way to meet the needs of diverse students. The three-part process goes like this:

1. Define clear outcomes (standards) for content or skill areas.
2. Carefully assess students to find out who can already meet those outcomes.
3. For those who can meet the outcomes before the traditional instruction would begin, modify or eliminate that work. Help them set suitably challenging alternative goals, materials, and procedures to follow.

Compacting is common sense because it is the same process that any teacher would use to individualize instruction for each student. That's the power and beauty of an IEP and compacting. When using compacting, teachers typically report that in reading, mathematical concepts and computation, spelling, and social studies, no significant differences separate all treatment groups and the control group in pre- or postachievement. In other words, kids who are taught less because they already know the material turn out just fine.

In some cases, qualifying students skip from 40 to 50 percent of the traditional curriculum. Yet in some areas, such as science and math concepts, the group getting the compacting did better than the ones getting regular instruction.[12] Compacting is a no-nonsense approach to both science and mathematics differentiation because of the nature of the content and skills in the curriculum. Reassuringly, it has produced documented achievement gains for students at the secondary level.[13]

ABILITY GROUPING.   Schools already use ability grouping with certain populations that have special needs. The research on ability grouping is strong; when students are with those of the same or slightly higher ability, they do better. When they are grouped with those of lesser ability, they bog down and become demotivated. Putting students in small work groups, enabling students with advanced abilities or lagging performance to be grouped in same-achieving groups, makes good sense. For gifted students, homogeneous grouping has a positive effect on academic achievement.[14] This allows them each to get appropriately challenging instruction. Just as special needs students might be ability grouped, so would gifted. The beauty of IEPs for all students is that you might have a grouping with a mixture of students who have a wide range of abilities in other areas while sharing the same level in the grouped area.

Within any classroom, a teacher can create an enrichment cluster. In this cluster, a team leader meets privately with the teacher before or after a class to set goals and manage milestones. The cluster may work as a whole unit or individually. When each student has an IEP (as I have recommended), they will know what areas to work on. The enrichment cluster may also work on a group project. Renzulli has excellent resources on how to form and manage these groups.[15]

For example, students with limited English proficiencies may be in a class with gifted students who have excellent language skills. But they both might be taking and excelling in the class in visual arts. This can increase school camaraderie and reduce the labeling of students. Grouping allows for more appropriate instruction for all learners. It will better match the needs and rapidly developing skills and capabilities of both gifted and regular-ed students. Ability grouping can be perfect for enrichment, especially when enrichment is part of an in-class ability-grouping practice. Research suggests that substantial academic gains can be made in general achievement, critical thinking, and creativity for the gifted and talented learner.[16] The National Association for Gifted Children does not endorse any type of a tracking system that sorts students and keeps them in a fixed position in the school system. They do endorse temporary grouping strategies to meet specific needs for specific learners with common abilities and goals.

PULLOUT AND ACCELERATION PROGRAMS.   Pullout programs allow for isolated small-group instruction in skills or content that are not available in a mainstream or inclusion classroom. Acceleration ensures contrast. It is designed to match general ability or specific talents with more challenging optimal learning opportunities, and it works well.[17] To do that, it continually adjusts the pace of student instruction to ensure a sound work ethic, maximizes the level of challenge, and reduces the time that most students need to complete traditional schooling.

Educational acceleration is an application of a best practices research for gifted education. It has a formidable research base, with more research supporting this intervention than any other in the literature on gifted individuals.[18] In mathematics in particular, research shows positive effects of accelerated or advanced curricula for high-ability learners.[19] A larger meta-analysis found that acceleration (when used with ability grouping) has stronger effects on student learning than just enrichment done by itself.[20]

There are many forms of acceleration. It could be as simple as a group of high school students who meet with a professor from a local university for an advanced mathematics class twice a week. These are the factors that make it work:

- Everyone on board: enthusiastic teachers
- Clear time lines and milestones
- Parental support
- Management of the process with systematic monitoring of each step of implementation

Students, gifted or not, should have the opportunity to move forward at their own pace. An example might be a streaming acceleration process in which children who are very strong in one subject area (most commonly math, science, or English) can sit in on classes at a higher grade level. While they take advanced courses with older students in just that one subject, they would still remain in their own grade for other subjects. Other specific strategies might include

- Grade skipping
- Early entrance into kindergarten
- After-school programs
- Early entrance into college
- Early honors class entrance
- Gaining secondary school or college credits by examination
- Opportunities to take and accelerate through advanced placement and international baccalaureate programs at the high school level

With grade skipping, for example, a child who has completed the third grade may be double promoted to the fifth, omitting fourth grade entirely. With careful monitoring and the use of IEPs, this student may be much happier and more likely to be productive. Some students lose motivation and act out in class when it does not fit their needs. Many people are concerned that these kids will be overwhelmed if they accelerate. But the majority of studies have shown that they do well academically.

Typically their results compare favorably with those of older students in their classes, and they commonly report heightened interest in and enthusiasm for school. If the children are well-adjusted and socially at ease before accelerating, they'll be just fine. Many report having two groups of friends, the older students and those the same age. If a given child is not socially ready, however, it's good to explore other options. Many researchers have amassed a large amount of data that support the effectiveness of acceleration. To delve into this strategy, I recommend Camila Benbow's book *Intellectual Talent*.[21]

Expanding the Curriculum

The wider curriculum path is essential for establishing both novelty and complexity as a constant. Although some may argue for a deeper curriculum, it makes sense to have more relevant, contrasting choices before you dig deeper. Many have argued that to support all the learners in the school, plenty more curricular options will be needed.[22] In an enrichment-driven school, classes are more likely to be offered not by grade level but by *type* and *degree of difficulty*. The curriculum has to offer *both* content and skill-based learning. Many students can use study skills, social skills, life skills, or improved reading skills. Those needs would only show up after full assessments, and the corresponding IEPs would help them get the services they need. Students with disabilities would continue to get the services they need. They would have the added advantage of being able to move more quickly as they master subskills, and they would lose the stigma of being learning disabled.

The good news is that both schools and communities often have those options or, working together, can create them. Here are some examples of the scope of potential options for the entire range of students, from special education, to typical (but frustrated or bored), and to gifted:

Early childhood programs
Arts education
Complex learning projects
Career-based high school options
Online coursework
Advanced electives
Honors programs
Tapping the university level
Community-based learning
After-school options

The items on this list are all familiar. But strangely, in a climate currently obsessed with higher test scores on a single instrument (statewide high-stakes testing), many of those programs are being phased out. That's a long step away from an enlightened enrichment policy. Remember, the enrichment response can be either deep (stronger intelligence building) *or* wide (emotional, social, cultural, or other life skills).

EARLY CHILDHOOD PROGRAMS.   It's worth mentioning that the curriculum begins early, even if it's just developing the basic scaffolding for the human brain through emotional attunement or motor skills. Steps on maximizing the brain for early learners will be addressed in the next chapter.

ARTS EDUCATION.   Attention to the arts may be essential for enrichment, especially when you consider what the arts can offer: novel, challenging learning that's usually coherent and relevant. Arts can be done at a *very* high level, including graphic arts that produce curriculum, industrial arts to remodel community homes much like "extreme makeover" reality shows, and visual and musical arts produced for the community to raise money.

Unfortunately, many shortsighted policymakers are eliminating arts programs to reach an elusive target of higher test scores. That's a mistake. Thousands of schools around the country are extremely arts-centered—and they're succeeding.[23] Typically, arts-centered schools have fewer dropouts, higher attendance, better team players, an increased love of learning, greater student dignity, and enhanced creativity, and they produce citizens better prepared for the workplace of tomorrow and with greater cultural awareness as a bonus.[24] In the past ten years, discoveries from brain research confirm the plasticity and enrichment that comes from music, dance, and visual arts. There are sufficient data to support the fundamental value of arts on equal standing with every other so-called academic discipline, including science, languages, and math. Arts can no longer be called a cultural add-on. One success story follows.

In the northeast, Boston Arts Academy serves four hundred students in grades nine through twelve. With a talented group of students who come from fifteen different neighborhoods in Boston, the community diversity is reflected in the school: 47 percent are African American, 30 percent Caucasian, 18 percent Latino, and 2 percent Asian American. One of the most enriching things about this school is contrast. Students study things they might not ordinarily be able to focus on, since it is so arts-centered.

Arts Academy science teacher Sung-Joon Pai says, "I see my students' commitment to learning every day—I know they want to be in my classroom. They enjoy studying science, because of the way we, the teachers, connect it to the arts. Today, one of my students, an actor, responded to my explanation of the scientific method with a quotation from Shakespeare—it is amazing to see students making connections, feeling that excitement."[25]

Students specialize in one of five arts subject areas: visual arts, theater, dance, instrumental music, or vocal music. Each student spends at least twelve hours a week in arts class, often staying after school or coming in on Saturdays to rehearse for a performance. Students' schedules also incorporate a full college preparatory course load, including humanities, mathematics, science, and a foreign language. Throughout the curriculum, a special emphasis is placed on developing writing skills. In their senior year, students embark on a unique capstone experience: writing a grant proposal to fund an independent community outreach arts project, giving something back for the extraordinary educational opportunities they enjoy at Boston Arts Academy.

COMPLEX LEARNING PROJECTS.   These may be year-long efforts that engage whole teams, specialized groups, or classes to accomplish a common goal. While these can happen at any public or private school, I'll share one example, from Minuteman High School in Foxboro, Massachusetts (www.minuteman.org). Former superintendent Dr. Ron Fitzgerald successfully directed the visionary development of his school over two decades. The success of the high school shows what happens when students get involved, hands on, with a curriculum that is relevant, global, and well-presented.

As one of many examples of what kind of good can be done, one major project involved 120 students from various departments. The students designed and built an entire house. From preliminary planning through actual construction and landscaping, the students participated at every step (under the supervision of onsite professionals). These kinds of projects are done annually at this school, showing why it ranks among the best in its field. Give credit to the staff, students, and visionary leadership. There's no doubt that, compared with what those students would have gotten in a more traditional school, their curriculum is vastly more likely to lead to enrichment.

CAREER-BASED HIGH SCHOOL OPTIONS.   Many think career and technical education is the "dummy" track for those who are not going to college. But the reality is very different. The high school students who combine work experiences from the community, apprenticeships, or service work with their education are likely to *attain higher GPAs* in their freshman year of college than those with no career experiences in high school. The National Assessment of Vocational Education (NAVE) report authors are highly encouraging of the career and technical education (CTE) track process.[26] They also agree that schools must do a better job of helping students take a specific identified track. They must emphasize either the immediate goal of education or workforce development. The enriching strategy of secondary vocational education itself is not likely to be widely effective for improving academic achievement or college attendance without significant other modifications to policy, curriculum, and teacher training. Fortunately, countless schools already do a fabulous job with CTE tracks.

Earlier, we introduced you to Minuteman High; another interesting example is David Douglas High School in southeast Portland, Oregon. It has 2,600 students, and of them, 49 percent are in poverty, 34 percent are minority, and 27 percent ESL, yet 84 percent go on to higher education. The school creates a learning plan for every eighth grader, beginning with graduation and working backward. Upper-class school leaders help the younger students make the transition through the process by mentoring and getting them a more appropriate and often specialized curriculum. Every student would be required to pass core academic coursework and state assessments, as well as amassing work samples of sufficient quality to earn a Certificate of Initial Mastery (CIM). Typically students finish this work by the end of tenth grade, and then pursue one of six broad career pathways leading to a Certificate of Advanced Mastery (CAM) during the last two high school years.

This curriculum is not less, but *more* demanding. Its students do even more coursework than you'd find in other schools. Students must pass all courses with a grade of "C" or above before they may tackle the Certificate of Advanced Mastery. David Douglas administrators call this intensive, project-based phase of their education Project STARS—Students Taking Authentic Routes to Success. They use seven broad career areas:

- Industrial and engineering systems
- Social and human services
- Natural resources
- Business and management
- Arts and communications

- Health sciences
- Hospitality, tourism, and recreation

The support as well as the curriculum is complex, meaningful, and challenging. This strategy supports the whole enrichment concept partly because it evokes massive buy-in to succeeding in school. Overall, what is this school's secret? Mentoring that works, plus more meaningful curriculum.

In 1997, A. J. Moore Academy (AJMA) was founded as a magnet high school of six hundred students in Waco, Texas. Located in a highly diverse community of more than one hundred thousand residents, AJMA has become a model for the state. It was the first high school in the district to receive the state's highest rating of "exemplary," meaning that at least 90 percent of students had to pass each of the three areas of reading, math, and writing on the Texas Assessment of Knowledge & Skills (TAKS). The percentage of all AJMA students passing all three tests was 91 percent. The students are enrolled in three clusters: business, engineering, and information technology. How did this school do it?

Many enhancing strategies were implemented, but two stand out. One was to begin with realistic career options (meaningful learning). Students in area middle schools are counseled about careers in the three clusters and then given the opportunity to enroll in the AJMA prior to entering the ninth grade. There's a dinner for parents and students before entering ninth grade, and every attempt is made to get the students into a strong social bonding support group. This innovative school includes local businesspeople and has even parents talking about innovation and school mission.

In the United Kingdom, Blackburn College includes a range of "curriculum enhancements" for its first-year advanced-level students. Focusing on employment, this school is one of many that gives students real-world experiences for particular careers. There are currently seven enrichment areas: preteaching, premedical, pre- (uniformed) services, pre-media, prelegal, outdoor pursuits, and recreational studies. Over 50 percent of the three hundred first-year advanced-level students opt for one of the enrichment tracks. There are two groups for preteaching and one group for each of the other enhancement areas. Students get up to three-and-a-half hours in the option block, and they are not restricted to taking particular subjects or combinations of subjects. They must keep continuity and work within the block they have chosen to end up with a credential in that focus.

Sacramento, California's capital city, solved attendance, motivation, and contrast problems when it opted to reorganize the school system around a school-to-career theme. Now, all twelve thousand high school students in the district get career education in micro "career academies." These programs are within the existing schools, and students study specific subject areas as a context for their studies. The program would last all four years of their high school career. Since this program has begun, attendance, motivation, and graduation rates are all up.

Many students will find challenge and meaning if they can apply what they know immediately in a workplace. A business or academic internship allows them to see what they know and don't know. Many times these programs lead to the desire on the student's part for more learning just to keep up. Some of the manufacturing businesses need qualified job applicants so badly they'll train them in a study-to-work program. Do some homework in your area. I talked with the owner of a tool and die manufacturer who was having trouble filling jobs at forty to sixty thousand dollars a year because he said kids today didn't want to go into what they perceived was a "dead industry."

ONLINE COURSEWORK.   Some teachers have found that students learn better when given the online option. At the lower primary school levels, I oppose this idea. Online work has too many negative issues involving safety, lack of social contact, and age-related security, and few young students are sufficiently mature to profit by the experience. However, if it is part of (not all of) the educational experience for secondary students, taking a class online makes good sense. On the Internet there are countless levels of curriculum that can be used for a gifted pullout or acceleration program. Several teachers who have used this strategy successfully show that when planned well it can work wonders.[27] One of the nice things about online learning is the capacity to use interdisciplinary curriculum. The Web is so interconnected, children can have the opportunity to explore wide as well as deep. Good resources include http://eduscapes.com/activate and www.edutopia.org.

Here is a sampling of the types of online projects students can do:

- Design and develop teacher Web pages
- Extend the learning of any required curriculum
- Make a scrapbook for the class itself during the school year
- Find booklets for online reading
- Teach computer literacy or Web strategies
- Use desktop publishing to produce student or school guides
- Cooperate with local weather forecasters for a school station
- Become a class researcher for other students' projects
- Create virtual travel guides and present them
- Teach other students—research, prep, and present new info

The more that students work with the medium, the more they'll boggle your mind. They have the open-mind attitude, but they're one or two generations younger. Today's secondary students are tech savvy and ready to explore; don't hold them back.

ADVANCED ELECTIVES.   Many schools limit access to electives by grade level. Effective enrichment policy often involves no more than asking the students to fill out a simple form stating why they want to attend a given class, how they think they're qualified, and what they're willing to put into it.

HONORS PROGRAMS.   Another form of higher learning opportunities is the school honors program. Such programs are a tried and true approach, but entrance to them must be made far more accessible, and for a wider variety of achievements. Special programs can include your highest-achieving students and faculty members who love to work with them. High-level discussion and standards in the stratosphere will challenge these hungry students.

TAPPING THE UNIVERSITY LEVEL.   Surprisingly many students at high school may qualify for high-level courses at a university, or private or community college seminar classes. Create relationships with local colleges that will allow students to take classes outside the school premises. Some classes may be through the extension programs and others may be part of the summer session, when requirements are more flexible.

In Randolph County, Indiana, schools are using curriculum developed by the Purdue University Cooperative Extension Service. This curriculum may or may not meet the criteria of enrichment based on whether the students are experiencing a strong contrast from their prevailing environment, the social environment, nutrition, physical activity, and other factors. But the actual curriculum has some very positive qualities. The premise is science and math learning that is challenging, novel, and problem-based, in a complex environment. Teachers get the curriculum that allows students to discover how their world works in a real hands-on way.

COMMUNITY-BASED LEARNING.   In the Austin community on Chicago's West Side, an after-school enrichment program was created in partnership with the Rock of our Salvation Church. The Circle-Rock Preparatory School is an inner-city neighborhood school and provides much-needed enrichment programs to over one hundred children, grades K–8. This campus gives kids a safe and educational place to go after school where there's no baby-sitting; it's an enrichment program that extends the church's ministry by teaching a holistic curriculum with subjects that the regular school day misses. Using a curriculum called Kid Trek, the enrichment program teaches children through all five senses. This school's curriculum includes

- An accelerated reader program (computer based) to build reading skills and reading comprehension
- Computer lab instruction (all computers are Internet-connected with appropriate content filters and firewall protection)

- A middle school mentoring program
- Regular art instruction
- Participation and interaction with scientists
- Roundtable times when social and behavioral issues are addressed
- Use of the PASS Program (Providing Assistance for School Success) to assist students with social and emotional needs that interfere with their learning
- ICPS (I Can Problem Solve)—a research-based, social competency curriculum that helps students resolve inner and interpersonal conflicts

An important concept about what this school does is complexity of coherent, meaningful options. There is no one program that equals enrichment. But the aggregate of all the programs constitutes a highly enriching climate, packed with learning, nutrition, social support, and low stress. As important as all those are, they're not the only enrichment ingredients. Possibly the biggest of all with this school is contrast from the prevailing environment. The greater the contrast from the student's life and the enrichment program, the greater the good that can be done.

Another excellent alternative program is the 4-H Clubs. These are a century-old institution that started as a way to train and support youth in agricultural communities. In 1914, O. H. Benson came up with the 4-H formula: an attitude of roll up your sleeves, put your head, heart, hands, and health into something 100 percent, and you'll get results. Since then, 4-H has grown to flourish even in major cities. There's now a 4-H School Enrichment Program (SEP) in many public schools. Dr. Ed Maxa, department extension leader and associate professor of 4-H and youth development in the College of Agriculture and Life Sciences in North Carolina, claims that teachers see huge improvements when this program has been instituted. The 4-H SEP works by having university specialists in topic areas develop curricula specifically for use in schools and in keeping with the standard course of study for each grade level. In this program, they work with grades two through seven, as specified by the state Department of Public Instruction. Teachers receive training from their county agents or other 4-H staff and then deliver the program to their students. Enrichment policy can be that easy.

The teachers who have incorporated it into their science curriculum will tell you that the SEP delivers. In fact, Dr. Maxa says that, originally, 47 percent of the teachers saw academic increases after their science experiences. Four years after implementing the 4-H program, the academic improvement numbers shot up to 84.5 percent. Homework completion went up 31 percent, he says, and homework quality went up 28 percent. And reports of science grades improving after the school enrichment experience increased from 54 percent in 1998 to 93 percent after four years. "I'd have to say school enrichment does have an impact," says Maxa. "And it's why we want to help other folks develop—or deliver what they have already developed—through this mode." For more on this, see www.cals.ncsu.edu/agcomm/magazine/fall03/4h.htm.

AFTER-SCHOOL OPTIONS.   Make access to clubs, service groups, and partnerships easier. Create a list of all offerings, then make sure to explain *what* the group does, *who* the faculty adviser is, and some cool examples of the things the group has done in past years. Students may have no idea what a "key club" does, and as a result, they might never apply. In fact, some of the most valuable programs go unfilled because kids don't understand them or don't think they're "cool" enough to bother joining. After-school extracurricular activities can be very good, when done well.

Work with local clubs (Boys, Girls, and so on). When I was a kid, the local Boys Club was my salvation. It provided a safe haven, social contact, and options for sports, intellect, and socialization. I can still visualize the library, the gym, and the games rooms today. Find a way to interface with these valuable outlets for kids.

While some students like to relax, the hungry-to-learn or disadvantaged students will take advantage of summer classes for extended coursework. These have a good track record when students are matched well with the curriculum and teachers. In some cases, the skill-building means survival for the upcoming school year.

Assessment and Accountability

While all of us believe in having accountability in schools, the argument is over which types of accountability. The more standardized the testing, the higher the stakes, the more likely you'll see a narrowed down, "drill and kill" approach. This is the opposite of the enrichment process. Students' lives are not enriched by the stress and focus of high-stakes testing. It will take new varieties of assessment to help us get there.

Assessment pioneers Grant Wiggins and Rick Stiggins are both vehement about *how* assessment is done as much as *which way* we assess.[28] First, we must ensure technical quality through reliability, validity, and fairness of classroom assessments. Students' capabilities are expressed from an aggregate of home, school, and classroom factors. For example, sometimes a novel grouping decision (cooperative group, team, project grouping, and so on) can influence academic performance by 20 percent or more. Naturally, students will all need both access to matched curriculum and the specific opportunities to get the necessary learning skills before being expected to perform at their highest level. Assessment is a critical piece of the enrichment process, since it not only provides feedback to the learner and teacher on progress, but also allows teachers to assess and manage the contrast for maximizing potential.

Social Support

Social support is critical for creating the enrichment response. Social support provides widespread encouragement, stress reduction, feedback, and a sense of community that enables learning.

SOCIAL SUCCESS OR ACADEMIC SUCCESS?   Let's say that your pretesting reveals that social skills are weak for many in your class. When students have better social skills, there are fewer classroom discipline problems and more effective instruction is likely. That means that although you may be tempted to ignore social skills, don't. There are many positive examples of prosocial programs. Social Skills Universe (SSU) is a program developed by the Houston Achievement Place. Established in 1974 by a Texas citizen group, it's a nonprofit, tax-exempt social service agency that offers hands-on learning and science-based teaching to introduce and reinforce social skills development. SSU, like many other excellent programs, deals with the reality that "getting along with others" is vital for school and life success, and the sooner we learn these skills, the better.

TUTORING AND MENTORING.   Cross-age tutoring has endless possibilities. In this sort of program, a tenth grader may tutor an eighth grader. The teaching role typically requires knowing the subject in a different, more thorough and versatile way. It requires people skills and leadership, and can be a worthwhile growth experience for the tutor while providing a much-needed role model for the younger student.

Many schools link up students with a mentor, especially at the most vulnerable years. At David Douglas High School in Portland, Oregon, upper-class students, key faculty, and counselors provide strong mentoring for the incoming ninth graders. They support them, integrate them into the culture, show them the ropes, and practically ensure that they'll succeed. Why is this so important in the context of enrichment? Think of the big picture. In addition to the other qualities, enrichment requires meaningful new learning (which a mentor can help frame and make more meaningful). Student mentorships can also work with university professors or local leaders. Many leaders actively seek out students for mentoring. To facilitate this, your role is to help make the links, set goals, and manage the process. Enrichment requires coherent complexity (mentors can help create coherence and keep the stress down) as well as social support.

Increasing Schoolwide Participation

Make your schoolwide programs attractive:

1. Start the enhancement program and maintain it with a high profile throughout the academic year.
2. Get students involved in planning the program. Get feedback from students on the activities—and adapt the program as a result.

3. Provide both formal and informal guidance on how to choose appropriate amounts and types of enhancement for individuals.
4. Do a brain "fair" with mini activities for an induction program.
5. Create an attractive brochure of enhancement activities and share it with parents, paraprofessionals, community donors, and staff.

Then, keep them in the program:

1. Have an assembly or in-class acknowledgment as a quarterly schoolwide function and issue certificates recognizing student participation.
2. Get funding for specific subject areas with the stipulation that teachers build enrichment thinking into their courses.
3. Build key skills through enrichment activities or programs.
4. Include work shadowing or work experience in the enrichment program.
5. Keep track of student participation and produce records of participation that are used for references and college applications.
6. Early on, focus on participation, not on always getting 100 percent. Continually share positive expectations, but do not expect perfection. The evidence is very compelling that expectancy shapes our experiences.[29] We want others to know we expect good things and they should expect good things from themselves.
7. Always build on strengths. All children at school have flaws and make mistakes. But those imperfections are not what will sustain them into a productive, adult life. It's up to you to acknowledge mistakes, help the child see what went wrong, support him or her in learning how to change, then move on. Support through encouragement and showing them a better way. A great book called *Stand Up for Your Gifted Child* is chock full of reminders about what builds and shapes intelligence and maturity.[30]

An Enrichment Specialist

Schools or districts that are serious about enrichment might want to include a position for an enrichment specialist. You may want to tap into the experience of school- or district-level enrichment specialists. In a larger setting, such as a district of five to five hundred schools, it's absolutely essential to have support for enrichment at the broadest level. This means you'll have someone who can help in gathering information, finding funding, sharing information, coaching, and supporting programs. This person can inform parents, work with teachers, and develop appropriate curriculum. Typically, the enrichment specialist assists the building principal and the building enrichment team in the development, coordination, and implementation of the enrichment plan. For example, in the Webster Central School District of nine thousand students, just eight miles outside Rochester, New York, the enrichment specialist works to ensure quality learning for all students. Exhibit 8.1 shows what the job description looks like for that position.

Summary

It's clear that no one is powerless in supporting the enrichment of all learners. You can make a difference even if your whole school is not on board, though having administrative backing is, of course, the ideal. Many teachers have told me they are concerned about the high-stakes testing and they don't want to change anything they're doing in their classroom too drastically. I understand that. Yet another way to think of this is to say to yourself, "If I'm not providing contrast, my students aren't getting enriched." Or, stated in the positive, "If I want my student learning to last, it's up to me to do the contrast." I know that's a bit silly, but it helps me remember it, too.

Enrichment is the lifeblood of every student; they all crave novel, meaningful, challenging learning whether they realize it or not. It's up to us to either provide that or settle for the consequences. I hope the examples in this chapter have continued to deepen your understanding of

Exhibit 8.1. Sample Enrichment Specialist's Job Description.

Description: The Enrichment Specialist is a full-time position in each elementary and middle school building. The Enrichment Specialist, in accordance with the Schoolwide Enrichment Plan, adds expertise and coaching to the faculty, assisting the school to meet the stated goals to differentiate curriculum, instruction, and/or assessments to meet student needs; to deepen thinking processes about curriculum; and to offer and/or facilitate the offering of interest-based activities.

Accountability: The Enrichment Specialist in each of the elementary and middle school buildings is directly accountable to the building principal.

Specific Roles: Educational Program

Coplans lessons and units incorporating specific differentiation strategies and complex reasoning skills with teachers in order to meet the needs of learners.

Coteaches differentiated lessons and units modeling best practices with individual teachers within the classroom setting.

Provides teachers with resources that will support the curricular areas and the complex reasoning processes to promote differentiated educational experiences.

---

what enrichment is and is not. It's the aggregate of many key factors, and more of them *are* better.

Many teachers like to share their "enriched classroom" with others. They proudly show off all the music, the affirmations, mobiles, posters, colors, and pictures on the walls as symbols of enrichment. It would sure be simple if having music, posters, and mobiles were all it took to create an enrichment environment. We now know better.

Does this mean that you should encourage bare-walled classrooms? Absolutely not! Although busy, decorative classrooms probably have debatable enrichment value, they do serve other very valuable purposes.

Specific Roles: Educational Program *(continued)*

Assists the principal in integrating the Schoolwide Enrichment Model within the overall school program.

Remains current in educational research through professional literature and workshops. Disseminates pertinent information to faculty.

Assists in the collection of student data for instructional planning as needed to provide for students' individual needs.

Provides ongoing staff development on current educational issues. Helps teachers integrate NYS Curricula with best practices.

Attends scheduled enrichment specialists' meetings, working cooperatively with other enrichment specialists to share ideas.

Conducts site-based needs assessment to help in developing a Schoolwide Enrichment Plan. Evaluates the effectiveness of the Schoolwide Enrichment Plan with the help of the building principal and the Schoolwide Enrichment Team.

Maintains parent communication related to the Schoolwide Enrichment Model.

Accepts other responsibilities related to the Schoolwide Enrichment Model depending on the needs of their particular building.

They can be a source of inspiration, affirmation, and content. They can help learners feel safe and comfortable, and even help them keep up with the learning. In fact, a rich classroom environment full of posters, mobiles, maps, pictures, and graphic organizers will be taken in and absorbed *at some level* by most students as they appreciate the complexity and messages that include "Your teacher cares." But you've seen that enrichment itself involves much more than a pretty classroom.

Creating enrichment responses requires a classroom or a school that provides a consistently high percentage of the list of contrast factors for enrichment over time. More factors, over a longer period of time, for more of the waking hours of the day, are better. That takes a great deal of intent and purpose on the part of any institution. But for those that make the commitment, the rewards are great.

Some policymakers believe that higher standards for math and reading test scores will ensure that all learners do better in school. That may or may not be true. But there is no evidence that higher standards actually produce better human beings—unless accompanied by better-quality teaching, more targeted resources, greater opportunities for underserved populations, stronger role models, high expectations, and a dozen other key variables.

However, there is good evidence, as we've seen in this book, that the enrichment response is good across the board, in all areas of a student's life. Good enrichment policies can be so successful that they become an attraction or selling point for an institution. There's no doubt about it; getting the enrichment response is one of the smartest things any educator can do at his or her school. Anything less, in fact, fails to maximize the students' brains and risks fostering the neural wasteland so common among today's youth.

9

Early Childhood Enrichment

ALTHOUGH THIS CHAPTER PRIMARILY SPEAKS TO PARENTS, PRESCHOOL TEACHERS, and other early childhood caregivers, all educators should know what contributes to an early enriched brain. It's becoming increasingly clear to neuroscientists that the first five years matter a good deal over the long haul.[1] Having said that, one thing is clear: aside from exposure to trauma, no one, single thing really matters. Avoid paranoia or obsession over childrearing. It's the aggregate of life experiences that will matter most over the first five years.[2]

Depending on when a child enters the educational process, three to five years of brain development have already taken place. It is therefore a good idea for teachers to be aware of what might have, or could and should have been happening with the children in their care and what might have gone wrong for them. While much has been written about this time period and what parents or child-care providers should do, here we'll explore strategies most likely to induce an enrichment effect in preschool-age children. Later in the chapter we'll look at effective early childhood programs.

What's the range of potential outcomes? How much do genes matter and how much does environment matter? In other words, how much can we actually change or maximize a growing child's brain? The scientific answer is that both genetics and environment are so intertwined that genes influence environmental responses and environmental responses influence our gene expression. In short, never give up and always assume that the human brain can make some kind of positive change. It may be big or small, but the fact is, the human brain is designed as an adaptive, self-organizing, highly malleable structure.

Drawing on what we've learned earlier about the brain's malleability in the first five years, we will now focus on the seven enrichment factors.

The Seven Golden Maximizers

Let's begin with our original premise of the book: all enrichment effects start with a baseline from which we can create environmental contrast. But remember, the baseline is not always obvious. The consideration of an "ultimate enrichment response" is laughable if the brain's own minimum baselines are not being met. While it's true that there are many ranges of criteria for optimal childrearing, nonetheless baselines do exist. I'm convinced many people think they're living an enriched life, when they've got a long way to go to maximize their potential. This is especially obvious in cases of extreme danger, trauma, or high-risk poverty. Here again are the seven positive factors, the ones we learned in Chapters Three and Seven, that are the contrasting factors most likely to maximize the enrichment response.

- Physical activity
- Novel, challenging, and meaningful learning
- Coherent complexity
- Managed stress levels
- Social support
- Good nutrition
- Sufficient time

A child will not be raised poorly if parents and teachers ignore some or even all of these principles for a day or make occasional mistakes. No one expects constant perfection, but young children do need constant help, and it's useful to keep these principles in mind. Every caregiver in a child's life should do as much as possible, within reason. While the human brain is highly malleable, getting a child off to a good start makes the long haul much, much easier.[3] Early child development pioneers and national experts Craig and Sharon Ramey urge us to shift the conversation away from the question of "if" early childhood programs can make a difference with high-risk children to "how" we can best design curricula, implement the ideal age of onset, and discover the best intensity and duration for treatment. In short, they say the science has already proven that early childhood programs can work. Now we turn our attention to the mechanics of how to do them efficiently and effectively.

Physical Activity

There's nothing like it on earth. The first time a baby sees you blow bubbles, open a box of goodies, or peel a banana. Or the first time an infant sets foot in snow, a warm pool, or a big pile of soft leaves. As a parent or caregiver, you'll want to promote the magic that happens when a child discovers a new aspect of the world for the first time. You'll want to be there to help your child smell a rose, squeeze a piece of fruit, or get tickled with a feather. This is the world in which the brain's senses are stimulated and the visual and auditory responses are of surprise and delight. The developing brain needs active exploration to learn the new world of senses and to connect it to its own world. That's what creates expectancy and coherence. This key principle is to foster safe and active exploration of the natural world. Notice that I did not say exploration of battery-operated toys, television, or the DVD player. The real, physical world of natural sensory stimulation is where the child's brain needs to interact.

Curiosity is a good thing for children. To prevent it from being stifled, make your house safe to explore and set up opportunities for it. For example, children will explore all day at a local park if given the freedom. How valuable is this to your child? Research found that children who are curious and seek out new adventures and experiences at age three have substantially higher IQs by the time they are preteens.[4] This exploring is essential; it encodes the love of learning, a natural curiosity, and zest of the process of discovery more than any other activity.

The most adventurous of the three-year-olds in a study of 1,795 children scored twelve points higher on total IQ when they were tested years later. They also had far better academic and reading ability by age eleven than their less exploratory and less curious peers. UCLA researcher Adrian Raine used recordings of children in informal learning situations as they explored their environment, engaged socially with other children, and verbally interacted with adults. Exploration and physical activity developed the brain better than being sedentary. Possibly further follow-up (high school or college age) would confirm the long-term results. So allow your child to explore! Instead of a diet of television, videogames, and DVDs, provide your children with plenty of free, creative exploratory playtime.

Today's infants are often baby-sat by flat-screen television shows, with little emotional or physical contact. In addition, they are strapped into car seats for hundreds of precious motor-development hours. In 1960, in more than half of all families, the mother was the child-care provider. The average two-year-old spent, from birth, an estimated 180 hours in a car. Is today's world better or worse? From 1983 through 1995, young children went from 2.65 trips a day to 4.80 trips a day.[5] Traffic has increased in most areas and now, after the first twenty-four months, today's infant has spent an estimated 350 hours in a car seat! That's almost double the amount of time.[6]

Back in 1960, hours spent in a car meant time to sleep, play games, and physically interact with other passengers. Today's car seats reduce interaction capacity. Although car seats are vital for infant safety, few parents would ever think to compensate for the confined, strapped-in hours with extra sensory activities later on. Watching a DVD in a mini-van is not enriching the brain. In other words, consider that car time is deprivation time for the developing brain. There's nothing a child would like better after getting out of the car than to go play with friends.

An active life during the first two years promotes development of the vestibular system. That's the mechanism in the inner ear responsible for balance, among other things—which needs to be activated early and often to "acclimate and set" itself in the developing brain. Great activities for it include tumbling, spinning, merry-go-rounds, slides, teeter-totter, jungle gym, and childhood games. Many scientists link the lack of vestibular stimulation to dozens of learning problems, including with reading, writing, and math. Are today's children getting enough sensory stimulation? Not usually, says Lyelle Palmer, professor of special education at Winona State University in Minnesota. His innovative pre-K and K–2 program (SMART START) stimulates children's sensory systems to develop higher levels of academic success. For over twenty years, he has shown that early motor stimulation leads to better attention, listening skills, reading scores, and writing skills.[7] How do you create the enrichment response in the developing brain? Active, guided, safe exploration and movement are the answer.

Children will want to explore anything and everything they possibly can. They'll want to pick it up, smell it, shake it, and throw it. With this "take no prisoners" attitude, a child's home will be under siege. To be an enriching environment, it must be open for exploration, so parents need to make adjustments. Attempting to use discipline to discourage a child from getting into cabinets, trashcans, refrigerators, and medicine cabinets or jewelry boxes leads to a discouraging and maddening day-long series of no, no, and more no! It's much smarter to let children simply explore as they will—but make sure anything they can reach (which is pretty much everything, once they're mobile enough to stand on chairs) has been childproofed for safety. This sounds a little extreme, but it takes only once accident and you'll be sorry for life. One of many Websites for resources can be found at www.safensound kids.com.

Strategy for Enrichment Response: An impoverished condition would be very limited and confined spaces for a child, with minimal movement opportunities. The enhanced conditions would be plenty of safe, active exploration. Ensure that the child has got plenty of novelty, engaging all the senses, and that you respond with appropriate (even a bit exaggerated) emotional expression. Plan a field trip to your own backyard. You don't need theme parks to build brains. You can get fabulous stimulation when you share the amazing miracles of blades of grass, ants, and other bugs building homes. Also use parks and playrooms, with supervision of course. Keep it safe, but encourage the exploration.

Novel, Challenging, and Meaningful Learning

The funny thing is, you almost can't stop children from birth to five from learning. Their brains are designed to learn and do learn countless things. In the context of our first few years of life, there are two specialized types of learning that we'll focus on. The first is the learning of appropriate emotional responses. That process is known as attunement. The brain is born with the capacity to express six, or maybe eight wired-in emotions. They include joy, fear, surprise, disgust, anger, and sadness.[8] But we have to learn hundreds of socially appropriate, environmentally learned responses such as gratitude, worry, appreciation, anticipation, suspicion, flirting, and others. Attunement helps children activate emotional states appropriately and in context. The second type of learning is the more formalized types of cognitive learning that parents and caregivers frequently provide for youngsters through the use of toys and games. This learning helps us understand cause and effect, addition, the alphabet, and countless other early chunks in life.

ATTUNEMENT.   The word *attunement* means becoming "in tune" with another, that is, establishing an emotional and physical reciprocity between two or more persons. The child smiles and you smile back—that's attunement. For the child, your response launches a synchronous dance between the visual, auditory, and tactile systems and the developing emotional centers in the brain. Early healthy emotional attachment—especially during the first twenty-four months—helps develop the social and emotional skills fundamental for life.[9] This is when the primary caregiver illustrates the proper and critical emotional responses, and the child learns how to express emotions in a social world (see Figure 9.1). Although all humans are born with the capacity to express basic emotions such as surprise, anger, and sadness, we are not born with the hundreds of more sophisticated emotional responses that make up our culture; they have to be learned in context, over and over. There is accumulating research that suggests that children with delayed cognitive development are not getting the *frequency of exposure* they need from adult-child transactional experiences.[10]

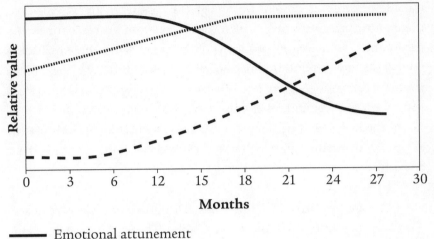

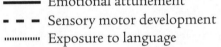

— Emotional attunement
- - - Sensory motor development
.... Exposure to language

Figure 9.1. Development Calendar.

Picture a scene like the following—one that happens countless times in the life of a child who is receiving reasonably constant care. Adult and infant play with a small toy until the infant tires of the game and slams the toy down or throws it at the adult. The attuned adult resists the temptation to teach a lesson in respect by barking "No!" or smacking the child. All that lesson really teaches is that anger and violence are the appropriate response to frustration. Instead, the adult should show a very sad face and slump over, even backing a bit away from the child. In this ten-second interaction, the infant learns that throwing toys at some-one else is a costly behavior. The adult withdraws, depriving the infant of valued attention. Plus the child learns what the human face looks like when sad. That's the way children learn appropriate emotional responses. In less than a minute the infant's brain is busy storing another new understanding of what it is like to be a social, caring human being.

There's an entire spectrum of how much attunement occurs in any adult-infant relationship. It's not an either-or situation. At the low end it could be impoverishment from neglect or abuse. In an extreme case, there's no attunement, only neglect. Below a certain level of attunement, the infant brain develops problems in the right hemisphere including poor connectivity, poor myelination, and a lack of pruning. These mean the brain does not get "wired up" emotionally the right way. Such a child will have low affect and other emotional problems later in life.[11]

At the higher end, attunement can be very enriching. Here are some examples of attunement behaviors that very young children find rewarding:

- *Emotive responses:* The infant has just figured out how to put several pegs into their appropriate holes. The mom's face lights up with a smile and says, "Good job!"
- *Face mimicking:* Smiles given, smiles returned; tongue out by baby, tongue out by mother; and similar mirroring responses.
- *Reciprocal hand games:* Peek-a-boo, patty-cake, toy telephone interaction, finger play, counting games.
- *Actions mimicked:* Hide-and-seek with a blanket; stacking cups; then follow and repeat, how to put on socks, shirts, and shoes; classics such as "This little piggy goes to market."

How does a child know what emotional state is appropriate in a given situation? He or she learns only by seeing adults role model such responses. The brain has to learn how to express emotions. This early time is not to be tampered with, and this principle is not optional. Even when children have quality relationships with nurturing adults as adolescents, those whose early years—ages one to five—had nonexistent or poor attachment experiences will find that their relationships suffer.[12] If children don't get the early exposure to proper emotional development, can they learn it later? This issue is well researched, and the answer is ambiguous, but leans toward *no*.[13] Why the ambiguity?

Although some suggest that the brain could be rewired emotionally later on, the amount of resources it takes increases and access to the child's life diminishes with every passing year. It's far easier to develop emotional skills with a two-year-old than with a teenager. Parents must

take the time to develop emotional give-and-take if they want an emotionally and socially healthy child.[14] The attunement process works best
during the first two years, because connections unused at that time are
very likely to be lost. Correct timing of all developmental processes is
essential for healthy, normal functioning in humans. Parental warmth
combined with stimulating activities help promote positive adjustment
in children, even those exposed to poverty.[15]

Some years ago, the phrase "quality time" became quite popular in
the press and especially among parent advocate groups, but it turns out
that there is absolutely *no substitute for the quantity of quality time*. The
lower end of the baseline here is that parents or loving caregivers should
have sufficient positive contact with growing children for some but not
necessarily all of the first five years. But that's far from the upper end.
It is this quantity that builds not only the emotional systems needed for
life but other basics such as the skill of paying attention.

The act of learning to pay attention is critical and highly relevant
for all humans growing up in a demanding, complex world. Why? When
we pay attention to one thing, we suppress the neurons that would ordinarily be active in distracting us to other, irrelevant stimuli.[16] Basically,
attention serves to bias the brain toward an object of intention. This
activity starts as a simple state—paying attention. But over time, it can
become a recurring property of the brain in which neurons are quick to
coalesce again and again. The more often we are in this state, the easier
and more self-reinforcing it becomes. This state is important for another
reason; mindful attention strengthens the forces of neural plasticity, one
of our brains' change mechanisms. Although the frontal lobes are immature at this early age, the skills of attention begin here.

LEARNING WITH TOYS AND GAMES.   The games and toy manu-
facturers would have you believe that children under age five should be
getting on board the electronic bandwagon or they'll fall behind early.
Nothing could be further from the truth. Kids will get more such exposure in their lifetimes than you and I ever dreamed of. If a toy needs batteries, children under age five don't need it. Will a battery-operated toy
for young children do harm? No, it won't. But a steady diet of electronic

games and computer-like products is the wrong way to feed the developing brain. No child can be raised by a TV set, videogame, DVD, or even the best-quality computer game. For a good treatise on this subject read Jane Healy's *Failure to Connect*.[17]

Videos and DVDs that are made for babies, no matter how cute, funny, coherent, and well meaning, are baby-sitters, not an enrichment program. Don't fall for the hype that says that such and such DVDs are critical for developing early learning in your kids. Ask questions such as, "Where is the supporting research using large-scale, randomized trials?" Remember, the enrichment response is all about contrast. If your only choices are (1) forcing a child to watch cartoons in a closet or (2) watching DVD cartoons in the living room contrasting with friends, well, I guess DVDs win by a nose. But neither choice is an enrichment program.

Be smart about exploration; if you can offer active exploration, interaction with other children, well-designed toys, books, or even just a big empty box, cartoons lose by a landslide. Do not use electronic media on children under five as a way for them to grow their brains; it's not going to happen. At best, you might get a child that enjoys a show for a short time. At worst, his or her receptive brain is downloading sugary cereals, terrible social skills, and violence from cartoons. A young child's brain is vulnerable, and it's absorbing its environment every conscious minute of every single day, seven days a week. Your child needs

Things that he or she can do, not watching the toy do it

Things he or she can make sounds for, not listening to premade sounds

Things he or she can customize and modify, not just hold

Parts to assemble, pull apart, and assemble again, not ones that break

The ideal games are ones that look simple (but are in fact, complex) to a child, with many colors and big pieces or parts to it. They should engage a child immediately, not by barking out irrelevant sounds or lights, but by begging the child to try it out, explore it, test it, and modify it. Children who learn to build, arrange, create, and repair their own toys develop a sense of competency that will never, ever come with punching buttons with sound effects on a dumbed-down laptop. Here's an interesting concept: the bigger the toy that kids get for Christmas or their birthday, the more they like the plain brown box it came in. A big box (with imagination) can be a fire station, space ship, queen's palace, or haunted house. Now that's a real builder of the brain!

Strategy for Enrichment Response: For enrichment, a child needs a parent or caregiver who is at home all day through the age of two and who purposefully uses a variety of quality attunement activities every single day. The ideal is an environment with interesting, colorful toys that invite the child to figure out things, not ones that require batteries, and then the child must push, listen, and play.

Coherent Complexity

From ages two to four, important cognitive functions include learning letter sounds, learning the alphabet, and getting exposed to more vocabulary. Reading is not a "natural" human ability. That's why introducing reading to young children is smart. It was invented only six thousand years ago, roughly only 240 generations from today. This is way too short a length of time for us to have developed any inherited central nervous system structures specifically for the purpose of reading. That means read with passion, reread the same books often, and make books available in the house.

If you've ever visited another country or simply listened to another person speak a language that you do not know, it's easy to feel outmatched. When you don't know the language, you're seriously "out of the loop." New languages when you have no background with them are tough. But for kids, it's even tougher. The difficulty of learning a new language is the greatest complexity that most children face. Even if some parts of a child's life may be suboptimal, that doesn't make them complex. In a child's life, the most complex part of his or her environment is language. Between birth and six months and again between six months and twenty-four months children cross several thresholds in language learning. The development of language is primarily stimulated by these activities:

- *Listening to millions of words.* The more words a young child hears, the better. The highly fluctuating tonality of "parentese" (the "goochy-goochy-goo" burble that people find themselves using without thinking about it, sometimes to their embarrassment) is actually helpful from birth to twelve months. This is the time to speak clearly, enthusiastically, making eye contact with the child. Hearing people speak normally—in "grown up" talk—is beneficial for infants at any time after six to twelve months.

- *Listening to whole sentences.* The children who had the most impoverished vocabularies and who were least likely to read were those whose parents shouted out commands, directives, and complaints. Children who hear phrases all day such as "Stop it! Now sit down," or "Shut up!" will have weaker vocabulary development than those whose parents take time to talk with them. Slow down, de-stress, remember that your child is downloading the world you create, and be as kind as you can. Ask questions, and speak slowly and respectfully.

- *Seeing words as well as hearing them.* Point out letters. Point out words when you read aloud. Point out signs on streets. In short, make the world of letters, sounds, and words very real in an everyday context. Use fingers to show letters. Sign language is often valuable for infants to learn before they have a spoken vocabulary. It can reduce their stress of being unable to communicate.

- *Speaking.* The more the better. Encourage a child to talk through things. Ask simple questions such as where, when, how, why, and who. Most important, read interesting books to your child, and talk about them.

- *Making specific identifications.* It's not enough to say to your child, "This is a hat. See this . . . this is a hat." Make distinctions so your child knows what is similar and what is different. Instead say, "This is a hat right here. And here, we have a scarf." Hold them up and point them out, "This is a scarf, not a hat. Now, here's a hat. See both of them? The hat is black and the scarf is red. Point to the red scarf."

From birth to age five, the children starting school with the weakest vocabulary had parents who spoke, on average, about one thousand words per day. Over five years, it adds up to nearly two million words, which sounds like a lot! But contrast that with those who began school with an excellent vocabulary. They had parents who spoke an average of two to five thousand words a day. In five years, that's several million more words! This gives you an idea of how much language children have to hear to be ready for school. More speaking—more quality speaking—to children is better for educational outcomes.[18]

The key to developing a child's language assets seems to be interaction, with animation, using gradually more complex vocabulary, very often.[19] In addition, speaking with loving actions seems to help even more than just talking! In one simple but elegant study, infants who received attention that was specifically prompted by their vocalization used more syllables and faster consonant-vowel transitions.[20] The study shows the value not just of talking but of listening responsively and touching gently to acknowledge the sounds.

In another study, it turned out that parents who knew more and cared more ended up with children with the best vocabularies.[21] It is not always the smartest, but those who cared the most, who loved and acted on that love every day.

Strategy for Enrichment Response: When you're with very young children, talk as often as possible (see Figure 9.2). Speak clearly and often. Use full and complete sentences. Ask questions and wait patiently for answers. Avoid "barking" out one- or two-word commands. Talk through every task you can. Talk through getting dressed, using the toilet, and changing diapers. Talk through exploring objects and playing games. One of the easiest ways to ensure that a child gets a daily dose of vocabulary is by reading aloud. Read aloud every day for at least ten to

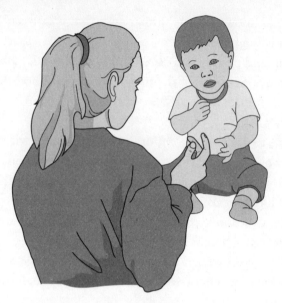

More conversational language, more coherent
speaking, more interactive language, and
less choppy, one-way, disciplinarian talk is
better for the developing brain.

Figure 9.2. Lavish the Language!

fifteen minutes. Talk with enthusiasm and remember that when it
comes to exposure of vocabulary, there are no studies that show one can
do too much. You can play the "I Spy" game. "I spy a . . . dog!" "I spy a .
. . tree." Or, "I spy a . . . shoe!" It's great for kids to learn new words while
being engaged with some suspense.

Managed Stress Levels

This contrasting enrichment factor reminds us that body and brain
respond negatively to distress. Because stress is a biological response that
results from the perception of lack of control, children are highly vulnerable to stress. They simply can't manage the variables as their brain
soaks up the world. They don't have the capacity to reframe life, debrief

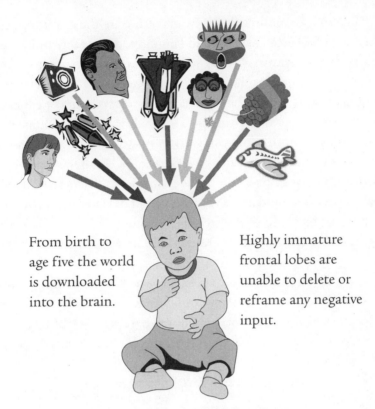

From birth to age five the world is downloaded into the brain.

Highly immature frontal lobes are unable to delete or reframe any negative input.

Figure 9.3. Mediate Cultural Download.

it, and redirect attention very well. During the first five years, the human brain is especially adept at—and therefore vulnerable to—a process called "downloading the culture." This is an amazing human phenomenon that allows youngsters to get "up to speed" in their new world.

The way it happens is so efficient, it's uncanny. Although the frontal lobes are immature, the brain is highly receptive. It is at this point that the world becomes one gigantic lollipop for downloading (see Figure 9.3). As noted earlier, the very young brain is bursting with new, receptive neurons and spending most of its waking hours in the theta state, a level of activity ideal for soaking up—and not evaluating—information about the world. As an idea of how fast the brain develops, some believe it's creating new neurons at the rate of over a quarter of a million per minute in the embryo, and it's still fast after birth!

The single worst downloads from culture are those of trauma associated with violence, distress, bad language, disrespect, and poor role models. The American Academy of Pediatrics urges parents to avoid any and all television for children under two years old. They also say that children over two should be limited to one to two hours of educational onscreen media per day. Other professionals suggest avoiding any television exposure until age five or six. Parents who want to enrich should create an electronic-media-free environment in children's lives, with the exception perhaps of certain kinds of music, as discussed further on. Ideally, parents should avoid using any kind of electronic baby-sitter.

But in what kind of electronic environment do today's kids live? Read these numbers from the Kaiser Foundation Report carefully:[22]

- Nearly all children (99 percent) live in a home with a TV set.
- Half (50 percent) of American homes have *three or more* TVs.
- One-third (36 percent) of children have a TV in the bedroom.
- Nearly three out of four (73 percent) homes have a computer at home.
- Almost half (49 percent) have a videogame player.

Children in heavy-TV households are less likely to read every day (59 percent versus 68 percent), and when they do read or are read to, it is for a shorter amount of time than for children in light or no-TV households. In fact, these children are less likely to be able to read at all.[23] The evidence is clear: more television means less reading.

Exposure to television is dangerous in itself because of the kind of passive, no-feedback absorption it involves. The more time a child spends watching TV, even if it's positive, constructive television, the less time that child spends interacting with the world. And the content that fills most of the airwaves—full of violence and the sort of vocabulary no child needs—takes an actively negative toll on children.[24] Overall, the levels of violence in primetime programming have averaged about five acts per hour—while children's Saturday morning programs have averaged about twenty to twenty-five violent acts per hour.[25]

Children learn what it means to be human by what they see around them. The evidence is overwhelming: the correlations between a tendency to act with violence and TV watching are stronger than they are for the risks of secondhand smoke or environmental lead exposure. This is long past the point of idle speculation; evidence from the studies is very strong, and it clearly shows that preferentially viewing violent television is related to aggressive attitudes, values, and behaviors.[26]

One simple thing parents can do to raise a sane child is to reduce exposure to violent visual images. The child's brain simply does not know how to filter them out. Early television exposure (ages zero to five) is associated with attention problems at age seven.[27] There is also compelling evidence that violent videogames are linked with aggressiveness in children.[28] Remember, the young brain is downloading all the violence and accepting it as "just a way of life." All of these are a result of distress. Exposure to early violence does not toughen a child up. Emotional resilience is partly heritable, but for the most part, it's what parents do early on that matters. Expose children to predictable, moderate levels of stress and that can help support the development of resiliency.

One way to soothe or regulate the early brain may be to play music to it; especially organized, soothing music. Many believe that listening to music over an extended period of time is linked to cortical reorganization similar to an enrichment response. Wisconsin psychologist and researcher Francis Rauscher found that rats bathed in music for thirty days outperformed those with no music exposure.[29] The "music enriched" rats made fewer errors and completed tasks quicker than those in a standard "no music" condition. In human studies, a daily dose of music of an hour a day seemed to enhance preschoolers' brains over time.[30] There was more integration and connectivity as shown by EEG activity.

Strategy for Enrichment Response: Mediate as many stressors for your children as you can. Remember that they cannot cope well with distress. Come as close to zero for electronic entertainment in the first five years as you can. Too much of an unmanaged electronic download is terrible for a growing brain. It's not only stressful, but a huge wasted opportunity for alternatives that could do more benefit. Instead find other children for your child to play with and make your house childproof so the kids can play with less supervision. Include social time with friends, more hands-on games, or an adult reading to the child.

Social Support

Much of the studies on enrichment suggests that a positive social environment can do wonders to enhance health and social outcomes. One of the roles that positive social contact serves is to be a go-between. Other people can buffer negative experiences and amplify positive experiences. Usually one or more of the older group serves as a mediator. A mediator is a go-between, one who serves to translate, influence, and ensure the success of a relationship.

Children need mediators—people who will mentor, encourage, rehearse, guide, limit, and celebrate the experience of life, helping them perceive and understand how people and things work. This is one of the hardest but most important principles for enriching the brain. The first five years are a time when the child has little ability to regulate his or her own brain. Life happens to them. What children need, especially from ages two until five, is a guide, mentor, and guardian to help them navigate their way through life. This is particularly challenging for today's working parents, but it is essential for enrichment.

Mediation influences the kinds of experience (and subsequent brain connections) that a child has. The development of the brain relies not so much on having enough synapses as on having the right ones for the right jobs. Most of today's researchers support a connectionist viewpoint about brain development. This model suggests that input to the brain is what alters the "weighting" at the synapses (between the neurons). The altered weights bias and then help form new, complex neural networks based on life experiences. The unused synapses disappear and the new ones get stronger through usage. If the experiences are negative, the brain is getting the opposite of enrichment—it's being impoverished. And while you cannot and do not want to prevent every single negative experience (people do learn from mistakes and errors), you want to prevent trauma and abusive experiences.

Protect your child from bullying, harassment, teasing, or physical punishment. Children this age cannot understand others' intentions, and they certainly don't know how to understand the history behind another's misdeeds. Infants especially do not need to be punished. You may say, "No," and walk away, but they don't need violence. When your child makes a mistake, keep remembering his or her age. Children's brains are not mature, and there's no way on earth that they'll understand etiquette, manners, safety, or cause and effect for social conduct or just plain mischief. Children are not resilient; they are highly vulnerable to stress, trauma, abuse, and distress. The research suggests that early adverse experience contributes to the pathophysiology of depression, more so with girls than boys.[31] Boys are more susceptible to violence. This implies either strong genetic factors or that there is a sensitive period for learning to inhibit physical aggression, generally between birth and four years of age. Many believe that there is increased vulnerability during this time.

Mediation is also especially valuable when it comes to reading. Households that value literacy and push the children to read will have kids that excel in this area. Children who listen to their mothers read them stories tend to experience greater gains in comprehension and vocabulary when their mothers interject the reading with explanations, inferences, and analogies of how the story applies to the real world.[32] Also, intervention that is print-focused rather than picture-focused works best in enhancing such reading skills as print recognition, alphabet knowledge, and word recognition.[33] You can make the difference if you set aside the time every day.

Finally, children are learning countless things every day. Earlier we talked about the constant downloading of the environment. Children download the stress, the vocabulary, and the emotions. Children are also downloading images, phrases, and actions. They are downloading how you treat them, how you treat others, and how you respond to stress. Children are downloading the love you show them, the way you treat other children, and the way you treat your spouse.

Now we get to the core: children are learning how to be parents based on how you are parenting them. Every action you take, every word you speak, and every discipline you carry out is a template. Your child is learning how to be fair or to cheat, how to be loving or mean, and how to be forgiving or vengeful. Your child is learning whether to be impulsive or patient, reassuring or stressful, hug-giving or standoffish. Think about the qualities you'd like your son or daughter to have and ask yourself if that's how you are acting. You are arranging the future at this age; your children are getting an imprint or download that tells them how to behave when they are your age. In one sense, you are not bringing up children; you are teaching your child parenting skills. It's a bit scary, isn't it?

Amplify the positives through celebrations. Celebration is key, not just to children, but also to those who live and work with them. When your child finishes a task, celebrate with a smile, clapping, and whoops of joy. Celebrate not just for the first word, or the first step, but for every little thing. Your child needs to know what you find important. But you, too, need to stop and smell the roses. Your child is making a break-through! You and your child did it! Make a point for a mini-celebration when your child

Completes a simple task
Mimics your smile, movement, or laugh
Stands up, walks, or holds an object carefully
Completes a request
Tries out a new food
Finds a toy or puts toys away
And performs countless other simple tasks

The celebration becomes an encouraging milestone. The child learns what you value and to anticipate what will be celebrated in the future—and the joy of learning itself. But what about you? You get to see the forest through the trees. You get to stop, pause, and smell the roses. You get to freeze time and say, "Progress is happening, goodness is here, we are getting there." It's an acknowledgment of your parenting as well as a celebration for the child. Remember to celebrate even the little things, and remember that it's just as important for you to celebrate as it is for others.

Strategy for Enrichment Response: Mediate the world for your child by making it safe, more interactive, and filled with laughter. Be the parent that you'd want your child to grow up to be someday. Every day, practice being loving, encouraging, accepting, and patient. Celebrate the simple milestones. With children under five, there are often new milestones reached every week.

Good Nutrition

This factor continues to linger as a potential brain maximizer. Why? Most parents believe that they already provide sufficient nutrients for their young children, but the data show otherwise. Many ignore nutrition, thinking that getting the government's minimum daily requirements is all that's needed. Growing children need much more. This is a huge opportunity for maximizing the health and growth in any child.

Many children under five years old often drink soft drinks (a no-no), eat deep-fried foods (a no-no), and get more refined carbohydrates than fruits, protein, or vegetables (that's a no-no, too). Among infants aged twenty-four months or less, 11 percent (one in nine) have French fries daily, and 24 percent (almost one in four) have hot dogs daily.[34] French fries and hot dogs are a carnival experience, not nutritious food for the delicate growing brain. Hypoglycemia has a profoundly negative effect on the hippocampus, which, you will recall, is the small crescent structure in our temporal lobes that organizes and codes explicit memory. Instead of a diet of sugar, children need nutrition-rich complex carbohydrates. Those are the unprocessed foods that take longer to break down and digest, but offer far more nutrition. They include potatoes, brown rice, pasta, yams, and eggplant.

The human brain is particularly susceptible to the effects of poor nutrition during the early years of development, and most home and preschool diets are either average or impoverished.[35] Young brains need many nutrients for learning. Here are some suggestions:

- No soft drinks should be allowed until age five; even then, make them an occasional treat (children don't need the sugar or the habit).
- Potato chips, donuts, Pop-Tarts®, and cookies are neither staples nor a balanced meal.

- Whole fruits—bananas, sliced apples, grapes, and watermelon—should be a steady part of the diet.
- Water is the best liquid; otherwise use real (not artificial) fruit drinks. (Artificial drinks have too much high fructose corn syrup, which has been linked to diabetes.)
- Avoid foods with MSG (monosodium glutamate). Studies link MSG not only with obesity and greater appetite but also with cellular breakdown. In fact, MSG is used to create obesity in lab rats. MSG is in thousands of products that are refined, processed, and enhanced for flavor. It goes by other names such as hydrolyzed vegetable protein. We are facing an obesity epidemic and this is one additive that should be avoided. Stick with fresh foods whenever possible.[36]
- Commercial hot dogs, hamburgers, and pizza are *not* staples; make fast food an exception offered no more than once a week. If you buy frozen pizzas, add fresh ingredients to make them healthier (spinach, broccoli, or bell peppers). Again, keep an eye out for MSG in foods.
- Stick with whole foods—real foods—and reduce the ready-made ones.
- Give choices—but make them minor, insignificant choices. The adult should be the real guardian of the child's nutrition, offering only positive choices.

Nutritional supplements given to children up to seven years of age have a significant impact. Pollitt and his colleagues found that greater nutrition, especially protein, was more important than socioeconomic status in measuring performance. In groups receiving a high-protein supplement, there were no significant differences in performance between subjects in the lowest and highest SES categories. Conversely, performance in placebo groups was highest among those with the highest SES and lowest among those with the lowest SES.[37]

The first thing to do is to ensure that a child is getting sufficient and balanced proteins. Next ensure there are sufficient micronutrients;

they've been exceptionally well studied. They are iodine, iron, zinc, and vitamin B-12. A summary of optimal nutrition suggests the following:

- Begin with mother's milk. As long as the mother gets good nutrition, it's the best source of early food.
- Sufficient protein is absolutely essential; offer eggs, lean meats, and yogurt. Review guidelines for the amount of protein the child should be eating per day and stick to it. Too much protein is just as bad as too little.
- Minerals and trace elements are essential, including iron, zinc, iodine, and selenium.
- Vitamins A, B, C, D, and E are essential.
- EFAs (essential fatty acids), especially Omega 3 (flaxseed oil), are beneficial.

Strategy for Enrichment Response: Include a wide range of foods for your child. Sneak some supplements or extra nutrients into the meals. Make fruit smoothies with flaxseed oil in them. Proteins and fruits are needed as well as the more complex carbohydrates (pasta, real potatoes, and brown rice) as soon as the child's digestive system is ready.

Sufficient Time

Most parents have a tendency to want to keep their children busy, and for good reason. At least they know where each child is and what's happening. But it is possible to keep a child too busy. Children need time to go at their own pace, taking pauses or breaks and doing nothing at times. As long as the area is safe, it's perfectly acceptable for your child to be doing absolutely nothing for as much as an hour a day of waking time. Why? Read what a leading expert, Peter Huttenlocher, a professor of pediatrics and neurology at the University of Chicago, says: "The brain of the young child may need some 'time out' to consolidate the information. Reservation of cortical space for the processing *of later acquired skills* may also impart a functional advantage. . . . A proper balance of early exposure to an academic enrichment environment and *time off* [italics added] may be important for optimal cortical development."[38]

Huttenlocher has made detailed studies of brain development that are classics in modern neuroscience. As much as anyone in the world he understands the complex process of a growing brain, and he maintains that it may be costly to try to cram too much too fast into a young brain. Enrich, and then allow for settling time. If the brain gets too many learning experiences too early, it may use areas that would have been better reserved for later development. The world is full of "late bloomers"— people who were average or below average early in school or even by graduation, then became substantial contributors later in life. To cite the most vivid example, Einstein was an average student up through middle school. He did not get life crammed into his daily routines and was unable to make it into the equivalent of the advanced placement classes in his high school. In fact, he struggled with basic math problems. No early blooming here; Einstein's first job was as a patent office clerk.

The "more, faster, earlier" movement has taken hold with many parents around the world. The kinds of things some are doing for their preschool kids may surprise you. Davis, the daughter of a Minnesota couple, is three years old. She's already been introduced to three languages and can speak fifteen to twenty words in both Spanish and Cantonese. Her parents have provided music lessons twice a week as part of an aggressive home schooling program. They make hundreds of oversized flashcards that introduce vocabulary words such as *hat, socks, car, Italy, computer,* and *Thailand.* In addition, there are math cards, too. Davis gets exposed to math statements such as 15 > 12 and 75 < 84. She sings the alphabet and dozens of other songs, too. Then it's time for twenty somersaults before the session ends. Her parents are working with her every single day on an aggressive regimen to build her brain. This is at an age when most children barely know how to count to ten. Is this a good idea?

There is absolutely no harm done to the brain with all these cognitive and physical activities. Some learning is clearly going on. Other things concern child development experts. Do the kids still love to learn? (This is critical.) How much free exploratory play are the kids getting?

(They need time off each day.) How is the parent-child relationship? If it is good, and the parents do these activities with love and sensitivity, again, no harm is done. Some neuroscientists think such activities are a big waste of time, however. For example, David Elkind, a professor of child studies at Tufts University, worries that children will get "burned out" on learning and lose interest in it.

The studies on this are unclear. Many of these "better baby" graduates do better the first year or two in school. But others not in the super-enriched program catch up quickly.[39] This raises other questions: Is there any possibility that other opportunities are being lost? Are other kids better at things not measured? What would happen if the better-baby brigade were tested ten years later? Maybe it's not how much you offer children, it's whether what you offer is appropriate for that child, during that week or month. One of the lessons here is that enrichment is not about cramming in as much as possible per minute of life. It's the whole package. It means avoiding harm, keeping stress down, giving some free quiet time daily, and managing the download so it comes in amounts the child can use constructively.

Strategy for Enrichment Response: Avoid cramming high-speed activities into every waking hour of your child's day. It's acceptable to let children simply sit, rest, observe, explore, and take naps. Find a balance between guided activity and quiet time. Remember to allow for simple relaxation or passive observation. Even more than adults, children need a chance to consolidate their gains and find uses for them that are personally rewarding.

What Effective Early Childhood Programs Do

If this enrichment response is the real deal, there should be evidence for it; and there is strong evidence. The place to do the best studies is in early childhood, because many kids who are starting first grade are not ready for school.[40] Although the more obvious complaint might be that kids are cognitively behind, the fact is, many are behind socially and emotionally. That's why the seven enrichment response factors discussed in this chapter are wide in their reach—they're not all academic. The first thing to understand about effective programs is that it's not easy. Just following the seven factors seems simple, but executing them is not a piece of cake. One reason is that for any early childhood program to be effective, it must either keep up with the anticipated or typical developmental trajectory of healthy kids or make up for lost ground if the kids have been exposed to adverse circumstances.

If genuine catch-up is needed, the program must produce results that exceed the normative rate so that the kids catch up. It can be scary; the shorter your time in any child-care service, the more crisp, powerful, and effective the intervention must be. There are many good resources that describe the brain's progress during the developing years. For the first eighteen months, I recommend *Right from Birth*.[41] For a book covering childhood up through adolescence, read *Your Child's Growing Mind*.[42] For the teen years, I like *The Primal Teen* and *Secrets of the Teenage Brain*.[43]

In measuring the effectiveness of any program, there are intuitions about a program, then there's the hard science. The highest quality, the "gold standards" for these types of programs, are simple:

1. Longitudinal (multiyear) studies with identical twins, raised separately, in highly contrasting environments (from their siblings). Ask, "How much of a difference did the environment make?"
2. Longitudinal studies, using randomized and matched experimental group and control groups. Design well-controlled, comprehensively measured interventions or educational programs and ask, "What's the difference between our experimental sample and our control sample?"

Three well-designed projects (The Abecedarian, Project CARE, and the Infant Health and Development Program [IHDP]) featured early interventions and randomized, controlled trials (scientifically supportable). The first two programs (n = 111 and n = 63) enrolled children at birth who were biologically healthy but who came from very poor and undereducated families (contrast used to maximize the gains). The third, IHDP, used eight sites and low birth weight children. Each population was at risk for health, behavioral, and cognitive delays. Almost three quarters of the mothers were unmarried, and most had a tenth-grade education in these high poverty samples. You may recall from the earlier chapter dealing with poverty that its effects are not just in the bank account; they go wide and deep.

A well-designed experiment needs both a group to test differences, known as the "experimental" group (they get the actual intervention or program being tested), and a separate control group (presumably they get what they were already getting). In these studies, the enhanced (in hopes of an "enrichment response") group received pediatric care; nutritional supplements; social services; and a customized, developmentally appropriate learning program. But in these studies, the control group was not a completely untreated group. Group members received not just their "status quo" but, for ethical reasons, got pediatric follow-up services, social services, home visits, and unlimited iron-fortified formula. It should be obvious that the two groups were not as highly contrasted as is preferred to get "the enrichment response." This more ethical treatment of the control families was likely to make the eventual contrast between the two groups much less apparent.

What did these early childhood programs, that were aiming strongly for the "enrichment response," actually do? Enrichment pioneers Craig Ramey and Sharon Ramey of Georgetown University researched the critical program characteristics. They determined that they (1) had a well-designed and customized curriculum, (2) had programs of a half-day or longer, (3) began early in the child's life, (4) established a strong communication pattern between adults and children, and (5) targeted a broad-based approach; developing emotional, physical, cognitive, linguistic, and social competences.[44] These factors were all designed to maximize human potential and to be in contrast to what the child might be getting. Now, let's examine the results of these well-designed studies.

Research Results

The overall results from all three studies were no less than astonishing. In seventeen of the eighteen comparisons, at the three-year period across the Abecedarian, CARE, and IHDP projects, the statistical measures showed that intensive and enhanced early intervention improved cognitive function compared with those in the randomized control groups. At thirty-six months the mean IQ scores were as follows:

Improvements in Mean IQ (Experimental Group versus Controls)

Abecedarian Project	seventeen points higher
Project CARE	twelve points higher
IHDP	thirteen points higher

The positive improvements in IQ are statistically significant. Naturally, there are other important measures besides IQ. And while some would argue that these numbers mean that the children were merely getting up to where they should be, there are alternative possibilities. They include the following:

- We don't know what the "true mean" is for humans since we have only limited funding to test alternative hypotheses.
- Maybe all children have a "natural IQ" of 90, and we are *already* artificially inducing a higher mean up to 100.
- Possibly *all* humans, even the so-called healthy ones, may actually be below a "base potential" of 120 IQ or more.

I am not offering proof for any of these hypotheses, but we should not be so quick to dismiss the positive, enhancing effects of effective programs as merely "catch-up" programs. What we do know is that the outcomes were measurably better. The children in the experimental groups showed across-the-board improvements. Their home environments were rated as developmentally more supportive, their mothers interacted with them more in developmentally appropriate ways, and their mothers were better at solving everyday problems concerning childrearing. Thus, a comprehensive early childhood and family support program produced broad and positive developmental outcomes for every one of the following indicators:

- Fewer behavior problems
- Larger vocabularies
- Better receptive language

- Better reasoning skills
- Greater learning and cognitive performance
- More language development
- Greater resilience to nonoptimal conditions
- Higher social responsiveness
- Academic locus of control
- Higher maternal education
- Fewer encounters with the police
- Better maternal employment

There's no doubt that an "enrichment response" occurred. Even at age twenty-one, sixteen years after the end of phase I of the Abecedarian Project, there were measurable positive effects in the young adults' lives.[45] The cognitive benefits produced by these programs better prepared these high-risk children to succeed in nearly every type of measure available. The children mastered social, emotional, and other life skills that helped them do better throughout school and into young adulthood. The poor outlook at birth was fundamentally altered; the high-quality preschool education that focused on cognitive development, conversational skills, and social competence offset most all negative predictive scenarios.

Research Summary

These principles have been found valid by countless studies and are considered standards by psychologists, neurobiologists, and pediatricians. It's quite clear to many child care experts, such as Craig and Sharon Ramey, that we must change our thinking and act differently. Both experts recommend these critical policy steps:

1. Provide appropriate levels and types of early childhood programs to those children in greatest need.
2. Review and revamp existing program standards to become consistent with scientific evidence for program effectiveness. Increase high-quality teacher training and technical assistance to improve teacher knowledge and skills.

3. Create a nationwide network of model demonstration programs that have been certified as exemplary.
4. Create and distribute practical and scientific public information that shows the importance of parents and teacher actions
in the development of young children.[46]

These steps may seem like socialized medicine or education. But the
Rameys' research (and that of many others) shows very clearly, succinctly,
and persuasively that we must look at the science. It supports early childhood interventions done right, done often, and started now. For those
looking at the costs, many have calculated that for every dollar we invest
in early childhood care services, the value to our society will be returned
from two to four times over the life of the child, depending on the analysis you read.[47] How? These are children who, as they grow up, will need
fewer special education services and will have fewer encounters with the
police, the welfare system, child protective services, and the criminal justice system. They're more likely to get a better education, to graduate,
to have fewer children, take better care of their children, and pay more
taxes.

Prevention always sounds good to some in hindsight. When the
problems pile up, it's worth asking, "Could any of them have been pre-
vented?" Many parents make the time to deal with adolescent problems
of oppositional personalities, attention deficits, depression, anxiety disorders, drug abuse, poor choices in activities and friends, and other
growing-up issues. But the evidence suggests we might have far fewer of
those problems if we invest better in the first five years. The brain is
developing faster and more critically in these years than at any other
time. Why not do the prevention early on when the child is far more
cooperative?

Some argue against the early investment in child care, saying, "Why
not wait and deal only with the ones that become a problem?" Can later
problems get fixed? For the most part, yes. But the amount of time,
headache, and resources it takes to fix a teenager's problem usually far
outweighs the prevention investment. Part of the benefit of early enrich-

ment is that by doing things smarter and earlier and better in a child's life, you'll be able to enjoy the benefits for a lifetime.

Summary

A pioneer in the early childhood enrichment field, Dr. Craig Ramey, says, "What is needed from the research community is a shift in the central question being asked in contemporary early childhood education research. We need to realize that the old question of whether the development of high-risk children *can* be positively changed has been answered with a resounding '*yes.*' We must now move on to more refined questions concerning the relative influence of different types of programs including practical questions concerning age of onset, intensity, and duration of treatment as well as the effects of various specific educational curricula."[48] He's right; early smart programs that invest in human potential have the capacity to pay off for a lifetime. Are you on board?

Enriching the Future

OUR FINAL CHAPTER BEGINS WITH A QUOTE FROM A RENOWNED NEUROSCIENTIST and pediatric psychiatrist, Dr. Bruce Perry, chief of psychiatry at Texas Children's Hospital and a neuroscientist at the Baylor College of Medicine in Houston, Texas. Perry says, "There's so much more we can do. . . . Our current living systems are disrespectful of the brain's potential."[1] This chapter pulls together what we've learned about creating the enrichment response. We, as parents, teachers, child care providers, and policymakers, have to say, "We have the research; it's time for action." Here I'll tie together what parents can do, what educational policymakers can do, and what classroom teachers can do. In addition, I'll suggest what individuals can do for themselves. Enrichment is for everyone who wants a richer, fuller life.

Are We Short-Changing Ourselves?

Unless schools are purposeful about creating a consistent enrichment response, they're shortchanging our students. Enrichment is not a bonus, not a treat or a reward. Enrichment is the whole point of school. I believe that many of us have shortchanged the upcoming generation and ourselves. Yet there's good reason why that might have happened. We all grew up hearing cautionary slogans and reminders of our limitations. You might remember hearing things such as

"We are who we are; you can't argue with genes or our destiny."
"Keep your feet firmly on the ground."
"Well, look at who his parents were; there's the story."
"You can't change who you are; accept it."
"Don't get any wild or crazy ideas."
"The apple doesn't fall far from the tree."

All of those, at one time or another, had some good reason for being said. Years ago the science wasn't there to support a model of enrichment as a possibility. It was only two generations ago that scientists even began to understand that brains could be regulated and changed by our environments. But the limiting thoughts remain for many. It's time to start with some new thoughts:

"The brain is constantly changing; anything's possible."
"Genes and environment are both powerful forces to harness."
"We can become nearly anything that we imagine and act upon."
"Brain enhancements will become commonplace in our lifetimes."
"Our past is far from our real potential."

Today, enrichment is full of more possibilities than ever. But let's remember, enrichment is a response; it's the resulting effect and not the cause. Enrichment is what happens in the brain (and body) of someone who enters an environment substantially richer in opportunities than his or her accustomed one to explore and grow. It must be sufficiently secure and supportive to make the experience welcome rather than impossibly stressful. The strategy "to get there" is to enhance the environment through the seven maximizers. No given situation will be equally enriching for every child (or adult)—but I hope that a case has been made that it is worthwhile to try to make every situation as rich as feasible.

Earlier we looked at the original animal studies that foreshadowed the whole enrichment movement. Pioneers such as Mark Rosenzweig, Marian Diamond, and Bill Greenough were all doing the groundbreaking studies in the 1960s, 1970s, and 1980s. What they discovered is that there is, indeed, a wide variety of "enrichment responses." In the past several decades there has been an explosion of new studies, with new heroes uncovering the brain's secrets faster than we can keep up with. Over time, the details of an enrichment response have emerged to mean positive changes in the following:

- *Metabolic allostasis:* Changes in blood flow, baseline chemical levels, and metabolic functioning
- *Enhanced anatomical structures:* Larger neurons and more developed cell structures
- *Increased connectivity:* Increased circuitry and branching from one neuron to another
- *Responsiveness and learning efficiency:* Enhanced electrical signaling, cell efficiency, and neural processing
- *Increased neurogenesis and growth factors:* Production of new brain cells as well as special proteins important for the brain's survival
- *Recovery from trauma and system disorders:* Protection from stress and greater capacity to heal when damaged

It was not the scope of this book to explore the neural mechanisms that cause these changes, but multiple systems and pathways are suspected. We looked at one of many of these pathways: gene expression. New evidence reveals that genes are not just dormant blueprints, activated by changes in our body's calendars. We discovered that environmental events can and do alter the expression of many types of genes. This is just as important as the findings in the earlier list. Why? Each of these suggests that the human brain can and does change in an increasing (not decreasing) number of ways. There is greater malleability and plasticity and more opportunities to enhance the brain than most anyone envisioned two generations ago. This suggests that enrichment is not a strategy for the pushy parent; it's a lifelong program. Enrichment changes the brain in each of us. Remember what it is:

Enrichment is a positive biological response to a contrasting environment, in which measurable, global, and synergistic changes have occurred.

Later chapters explored more extreme brains: those in poverty and those labeled as gifted. The evidence suggests that both of those are strong candidates for the enrichment response. Brains in poverty often have much further to go than a healthy brain. Poverty exerts a wide-ranging effect on brains, and the effects are often synergistic in a negative way. But that should create even more excitement over the opportunity and the eventual value. The brains of those who would qualify as gifted, those in the top 2 percent of the population, might seem as if they would not need enrichment, but they do! Their brains crave new learning, novelty, and challenge just as much or more than the rest of us. When they don't get those enhancing factors, it's just as boring, frustrating, or annoying as it is for average students who get a dumbed-down curriculum or one that is way over their heads. There's got to be a match between skill level and the challenge offered. Enrichment fits like a custom-made glove for these two populations.

Other populations can benefit from enrichment. The evidence is that effective early childhood education can enrich children's lives. The experiments with early childhood sample populations of high-risk infants showed tremendous results, especially when examined over time. While there were some short-term IQ differences among those that received enrichment protocols (from 12 to 17 points higher), the more amazing differences were the ones over time. The Abecedarian project showed results lasting sixteen years, suggesting the effects may even last a lifetime. That's a huge payback not just to those subjects but also to society. The studies on deprived children told us that it's a prudent investment in that population.

Finally, we explored the school issues with enrichment. We cannot and should not buy into the "same ol', same ol'" attitude that we don't have the time, money, or mandate to provide enrichment to all kids. The fact is, it works. I have given example after example of programs, schools, or situations that make it work. If policymakers are concerned about test scores and they narrow their curriculums too much, we'll only get a narrowed, "negative enrichment" effect (impoverished by shortsightedness) in children. These kids will have learned to do just what's on the tests, but not much more. They'll be missing the broader life skills in social-emotional skills as well as the broad range of knowledge and skill sets needed for tomorrow's world.

Enrichment is worthwhile for all school-age kids, and not just the ones at the bottom or the top. Why? Old measures that suggested that enrichment might help only certain populations were using too narrow a range of data. If all you measure is a traditional IQ, you might find some temporary limitations. But if you're measuring *a wider range of positive human change,* you're likely to find that the human brain can and does change in many wondrous ways—if you know how to change it. Mounting evidence suggests that K–12 education can be better organized around the core principle of enrichment: contrast. I suggested that all schools adopt the policy that some have: individualized education plans for all students.

Enrichment, after all, requires the provision of stimuli that are over, above, and beyond what would be typical and characteristic for each individual child. There's significant upside for students in school, but you won't get the perceptible jumps of enrichment unless you can make a clear improvement in conditions. That takes purposefulness and execution of clear policies designed to maximize the growing brain. Every single student should be learning in ways that are contrasting, challenging, and novel. I think we'd see fewer dropouts and much more excitement about learning. Why? In the programs that already apply this important understanding about the brain, we see exactly those student characteristics.

Why Is Enrichment for Everyone?

While traditional researchers have long asserted that enrichment is only possible for those who are neglected, abused, deprived, or have otherwise suboptimal lives, I believe the likelihood is that *we can all become enriched* if we use a broader measure of enrichment. Today's evidence, so far, may still suggest some kind of upper limit on rat brains, but again if one measures using very narrow indices of rat intelligence, one comes up with very narrow conclusions. Rats are typically tested for spatial memory in locating food sources or a hidden platform in a water maze. Although behaviorally relevant, these are hardly a wide range of possibilities with which to compare with humans. Clearly, we're not asking rats to write computer code, run a day care center, invent new products, direct a customer service team, or volunteer for church programs. Humans have more capacity for enrichment because their lives are wider and deeper.

I hope that by now you've lost any temptation to pooh-pooh as crazy the idea of enrichment for everybody. Many believed that you can't provide enrichment to the average person, but earlier chapters showed that it is being done every day. Remember, enrichment is a global effect, not narrow. If it were merely skills learning, then the effects would be limited to just the skills learned. But there is evidence of far broader changes in those who have achieved enrichment. That's why enrichment is for everybody.

Broad-Based Human Potential

In humans, there are greater possibilities than many of us have ever envisioned. The musical genius can develop better social-emotional skills. The athlete can develop writing skills. The homebound spouse can develop leadership skills. The overworked executive can learn yoga or massage therapy. The student can develop greater empathy and listening skills. The junk-food eating teenager can begin to eat healthy. The fact is, none of those "additions" to our lives would show up on a traditional IQ test. You might say that those are narrow skill sets. But the new science is suggesting otherwise.

We know that our brains and body are complex, nonlinear, pattern-forming, self-organizing systems. If anything, we are each a synchrony of multiple systems. Change one thing in ourselves and usually other things change. If we learn to play music, it may affect our self-confidence and social life. If we get a doctorate, it may affect our income level and exposure to travel. Something as simple as a change in the foods we eat can influence gene expression and potentially induce cognitive deficits or enhancements.[2] There are very few localized, minor changes we make; changes typically become widespread. That's the essence of the enrichment response.

This reminds us that we rarely induce or receive minor changes to ourselves. As an example, I had corrective surgery two decades ago. Usually, the reassuring doctor reminds patients to relax and that everything will be just fine. But I remember hearing this insightful physician tell me, "There is no such thing as minor surgery." He's right; you can't pretend that getting operated on is a localized trauma. It should have been a minor operation. However, all surgery (even minor) can and has caused in some patients everything from phobias to personality changes to death. This time, the surgery went bad and I almost died. What's the relevance of this? If a localized procedure can have a global negative effect (sometimes), why wouldn't the reverse be possible? Could a localized skill, emotion, or amazing insight make wholesale changes also? It seems that they can.

We can either become enriched "wide" (with a broader range of life skills) or "deeper" (more in-depth cognitive factors). It's very likely that although today's enhancements involve alterations in lifestyle, nutrition, social conditions, and exercise (which change our brains and bodies and affect gene expression), there may be more going on than we think. What we do have is evidence that we can enhance a wide range of human performance. For example, Don Campbell in *The Mozart Effect* relates dozens of real-world stories and research that suggest that the right kind of music can be healing and highly transformative.[3] In Goleman's *Emotional Intelligence,* we see not just the risks of poor emotional skill sets but how strong emotional intelligence can enrich social capital, longevity, cognition, and both mental and physical health.[4] We now know that nearly everything, from nutrition to exercise, can influence gene expression and make changes in our brains and bodies.[5] Enrichment means that a good deal of our potential is *not* set. Our past is not our future. Our future is now truly "up for grabs."

How Far Can We Take the "Enrichment Response"?

Only one generation ago no one believed that a change in lifestyle, health, or emotions could change the expression of genes, but we now know that's true.[6] This suggests that there is much more we have to learn about changing and improving the human brain. The ability to make changes in gene expression means that a far greater range of options is now on the table. That's good news for those who want to get the enrichment response. As an example of changes on the horizon, the new role of enhanced nutrition and super-brain supplements for already healthy users is moving quickly. There exists a large underground market of high-performance users of performance-enhancing mind drugs. They include the following:

- Performing artists who take propranolol, a hypertension and angina medication, to ease preperformance jitters
- Busy executives who take choline supplements to improve memory
- College students who take modafinal (Provigil), a sleep apnea medication, for powerful, enduring, jitter-free stimulation

Neuroscientist Gary Lynch at the University of California at Irvine, made unique discoveries about how our memories form and later cofounded a biotech company called Cortex Pharmaceuticals. It's now in the second (of three) stage trial with 160 patients testing memory-enhancing drugs. Memory Pharmaceuticals is doing the same; it was cofounded by Nobel Prize–winning neuroscientist Eric Kandel. Another neuroscientist, Tim Tully, founded Helicon Therapeutics to do the same. These and over one hundred other companies are chasing practical applications for drugs that improve cognition and memory. Using smarter nutrients and better nutritional programs, we are already learning how we can improve alertness, concentration, and memory. Right now over forty such brain-enriching drugs are in trials or production. The possibilities for enrichment are endless.

Another example of how our brains can change through purposeful enrichment is found in cognitive scientist Elkhonon Goldberg's insightful book *The Wisdom Paradox: How Your Mind Can Grow Stronger as Your Brain Grows Old.*[7] Goldberg's thesis is that by understanding how we change, we can continually change the type of intelligence that we develop and enjoy. We can shift it from a typical IQ to a far more valuable wisdom. Neuroscientist Nancy Andreasen suggests, in *The Creating Brain,* that we develop the cognitive equivalent of physical fitness centers.[8] This is powerful; top scientists are urging our understanding of the brain's plasticity to suggest new possibilities for creating enrichment in our brains. It's no different from a fitness expert reminding us to get exercise and use our muscles.

Is the "Enrichment Response" Cheating?

No one seems to begrudge the fact that some people have a higher starting intelligence than others. But what if the playing field has been set artificially low for nearly everyone else? What if we are all, in some way, below our potential? What if the standard for the playing field has been set 20 percent or 50 percent below our actual capacity?

I'm sold on enrichment for a reason. I've seen it work miracles on babies, children, students, and adults. My wife and I think about enrichment often. We could have waited until retirement to travel, but we try to make the time to travel while we are young enough to really enjoy it. We have taken short car trips and even trips overseas, but the main thing is that we find a way to explore our world. We've read the actuary tables and know that we're supposed to live until eighty or so, but what if we don't? We could wait until we retire to take the time to read our favorite books, but we don't wait—we read every day. Between the two of us, we maybe read twenty-five books a year. That's not a record, but it keeps our brains active. We could wait until we're older to spend more time with our parents, but instead we try to spend it with them now. My idea of retirement is *to do anything except* sit on a rocking chair on the front porch. There's always a way to learn something new or something challenging.

The Future of the "Enrichment Response"

The future of enrichment doesn't mean we have to become bionic to be better; but it could happen. For an insight into the future, you might want to meet Ray Kurzweil. He's been a renowned futurist and leading-edge scientist for forty years, having received the National Medal of Technology, the nation's highest honor in technology, and scores of other national and international awards. He has founded multiple technology companies, and his recent book, *The Singularity Is Near*, dispels any notion that humans can only improve up until they reach a statistical, healthy average.[9] Kurzweil believes human intelligence is artificially low when you put *all* available options on the table.

Kurzweil actually shows how technology can support the creation of smarter-than-human intelligence. He is gung-ho on direct brain-computer interfaces, biological augmentation of the brain, and smart-brain genetic engineering. Does this sound ridiculous? Do not count him out; he was the principal developer of the first omnifont optical character recognition, the first print-to-speech reading machine for the blind, the first CCD flat-bed scanner, the first text-to-speech synthesizer, the first music synthesizer capable of recreating the grand piano and other orchestral instruments, and the first commercially marketed large-vocabulary speech recognition.

Kurzweil was inducted in 2002 into the National Inventors Hall of Fame, established by the U.S. Patent Office, invited to the White House for a commendation award, and voted Engineer of the Year by the more than one million readers of *Design News* magazine. He doesn't just predict the future—he creates it! If super-enriched brains sound far out to you, answer this question: "Could fifteenth-century citizens have predicted twentieth-century technology?" There's *no way* we should base the likelihood of potential technology on past predictions. In 1950, it's likely that not one person on planet earth could have predicted the worldwide Internet, which was just a few short years away! We live in truly amazing times.

Enrich Your Life!

This whole book has pushed the "enrichment response" as not just something for a select few, but for all of us. There's a good reason for that. It's all about not settling for status quo. Life is not to be watched from the sidelines or only read about on your favorite Website. Life is to be sipped, gulped, chewed, digested, and enjoyed. Make enrichment a priority because there's really no point to life except to live it well. That does not mean "living large" with toys, cars, and bills beyond your financial means. It means living wider, deeper, with more passion, and with more challenge. Whether you're in a wheelchair, a penthouse, a nursery, an assisted-living arrangement, a classroom, or a trailer park, there's room for enrichment. Remember the seven golden maximizers that can be your sources for specific life-enhancing strategies. These are a must to use every day because without them, there is no enrichment response. There is, however, one additional factor that can also fuel an enrichment response.

For most of our lives we've been brought up to believe that it's some elusive ingredient that fuels success. Some think a family history of successful relatives can help. Others believe money helps success while others think it's talent, not money. If I were to add anything to the list of seven brain maximizers, I might add "passion." That's right; there's a considerable body of anecdotal evidence that it fuels success as much or more than genes, money, or talent.[10] This is not just an on-off perseverance. Passion fuels a nearly endless supply of grit that allows you to push through disappointment, pain, heartbreaks, failure, setbacks, and even humiliation. When you embrace, recycle, and foster your passion, you have just increased your odds of success dramatically. I suspect passion may even spark changes in gene expression, but we'll let scientists discover that in the near future.

Enrichment pioneer and award-winning neuroanatomist Marian Diamond says, "The typical American child does not experience an enriched environment."[11] She's right; there's *always* room for *something* to be *more enriched*—more physical activity and exploration, better nutrition, learning new complex things, or even managing stress better. Just assume that whatever the baseline, there's always an action we can all do to enrich our lives and the lives of the children we look after every day. It may be something small or something large. It could be cognitive, emotional, physical, or social changes, but any of them might do it.

I'm hoping you've enjoyed this journey into the world of enrichment. Would today be a good day to start?

NOTES

PREFACE

1. M. H. Johnson, "Functional Brain Development in Humans," *Nature Reviews Neuroscience*, 2001, 2(7), 475-483.
2. W. T. Greenough, *Neural Mechanisms of Learning and Memory*, eds. M. R. Rosenzweig and E. L. Bennett (Cambridge: MIT Press, 1976), pp. 255-278.
3. P. S. Eriksson, E. Perfilieva, T. Bjork-Eriksson, A. M. Alborn, C. Nordborg, D. A. Peterson, and F. H. Gage, "Neurogenesis in the Adult Human Hippocampus," *Nature Medicine*, 1998, 4(11), 1313-1317; H. van Praag, G. Kempermann, and F. H. Gage, "Running Increases Cell Proliferation and Neurogenesis in the Adult Mouse Dentate Gyrus," *Nature Neuroscience*, 1999, 2(3), 266-270.
4. F. A. Campbell and C. T. Ramey, "Effects of Early Intervention on Intellectual and Academic Achievement: A Follow-Up Study of Children from Low-Income Families," *Child Development*, 1994, 65, 684-698.
5. W. Overman and J. Bachevalier, "Inferences About the Functional Development of Neural Systems in Children via the Application of Animal Tests in Cognition," in *Handbook of Developmental Cognitive Neuroscience*, ed. C. Nelson and M. Luciana (Cambridge: MIT Press, 2001).

CHAPTER ONE

1. T. Attwood, "The Babel of Bioinformatics," *Science*, 2000, 290, 471.
2. F. G. Giancotti and E. Ruoslahti, "Integrin Signaling," *Science*, 1999, 285, 1028-1032.
3. M. Hagmann, "How Chromatin Changes Its Shape," *Science*, 1999, 285, 1201-1203.
4. E. Kandel, "A New Intellectual Framework for Psychiatry?" *American Journal of Psychiatry*, 1998, 155, 461.
5. V. A. Berezovskii, T. M. Zelenskaia, T. V. Serebrovskaia, A. S. Zverkova, and N. V. Il'chevich, "Degree of Concordance of the Adaptive Reactions in Twins Under Mountain Climate Conditions and Their Relationship to the Reactivity of the Physiological Connective Tissue System," *Fiziol Cheloveka*, 1986 Nov.-Dec. 12(6), 992-998.

6. J. Cairns, J. Overbaugh, and S. Miller, "The Origin of Mutants," *Nature*, 1988, *335*, 142–145.

7. V. Morell, "How the Malarial Parasite Manipulates Its Hosts," *Science*, 1997, *278*, 223.

8. M. Balter, "Was Lamarck Just a Little Bit Right?" *Science*, 2000, *288*, 39.

9. R. Dawkins, *The Selfish Gene* (Oxford, UK: Oxford University Press, 1976); M. Ridley, *The Cooperative Gene: How Mendel's Demon Explains the Evolution of Complex Beings* (New York: Free Press, 2001).

10. W. Reik, W. Dean, and J. Walter, "Epigenetic Reprogramming in Mammalian Development," *Science*, 2001, *293*, 1089–1093.

11. A. P. Wolffe and M. A. Matzke, "Epigenetics: Regulation Through Repression," *Science*, 1999, *286*(5439), 481–486.

12. C. Mann, "Behavioral Genetics in Transition," *Science*, 1994, *264*, 1686–1689.

13. M. Rosenzweig, E. Bennett, and M. Diamond, "Brain Changes in Response to Experience," *Scientific American*, 1972, *226*(2), 22–29.

14. D. Normile, "Habitat Seen Playing Larger Role in Shaping Behavior," *Science*, 1998, *279*, 1454–1455.

15. B. Jacobs, M. Schall, and A. Scheibel, "A Quantitative Dendritic Analysis of Bernice's Area in Humans. II. Gender, Hemispheric and Environmental Factor," *The Journal of Comparative Neurology*, 1993, *327*, 97–111.

16. N. B. Farber and J. W. Olney, "Drugs of Abuse That Cause Developing Neurons to Commit Suicide," *Brain Research, Developmental Brain Research*, 2003, *147*(1–2), 37–45.

17. K. C. Koenen, T. E. Moffitt, A. Caspi, A. Taylor, and S. Purcell, "Domestic Violence Is Associated with Environmental Suppression of IQ in Young Children," *Development and Psychopathology*, 2003, *15*(2), 297–311.

18. G. O'Kane, E. A. Kensinger, and S. Corkin, "Evidence for Semantic Learning in Profound Amnesia: An Investigation with Patient H.M.," *Hippocampus*, 2004, *14*(4), 417–425.

19. See the exhibit on Gage at www.deakin.edu.au/hbs/GAGEPAGE/.

20. H. Damasio, T. Grabowski, F. Randall, A. M. Galaburda, and A. R. Damasio, "The Return of Phineas Gage: Clues About the Brain from the Skull of a Famous Patient," *Science*, 1994, *264*, 1102–1105.

21. F. A. Champagne, and J. P. Curley, "How Social Experiences Influence the Brain," *Current Opinions in Neurobiology*, 2005 Dec., *15*(6), 704–709.

CHAPTER TWO

1. R. K. Wagner and R. J. Sternberg, "Practical Intelligence in Real-World Pursuits: The Role of Tacit Knowledge," *Journal of Personality and Social Psychology*, 1985, *52*, 1236–1247.

2. T. Carraher, D. Carraher, and A. Schliemann, "Mathematics in the Streets and in the Schools," *British Journal of Developmental Psychology*, 1985, *3*, 21–29.

3. B. Leshowitz, "It Is Time We Did Something About Scientific Illiteracy," *American Psychologist*, 1989, *44*, 1159–1160.

4. S. J. Ceci and A. Roazzi, "The Effects of Context on Cognition: Postcards from Brazil," in *Mind in Context: Interactionist Perspectives on Human Intelligence*, ed. R. J. Sternberg and R. K. Wagner (New York: Cambridge University Press, 1994), pp. 74–101.

5. Carraher and others, "Mathematics in the Streets," 98.

6. Leshowitz, "It Is Time We Did Something."

7. Leshowitz, "It Is Time We Did Something," p. 1160.

8. C. Murray and R. J. Herrnstein, *The Bell Curve: Intelligence and Class Structure in American Life* (New York: Free Press, 1994).

9. T. Schmader and M. Johns, "Converging Evidence That Stereotype Threat Reduces Working Memory Capacity," *Journal of Personality and Social Psychology*, 2003, *85*(3), 440–452.

10. A. Huizink, E. Mulder, and J. Buitelaar, "Prenatal Stress and Risk for Psychopathology: Specific Effects or Induction of General Susceptibility?" *Psychology Bulletin*, 2004, *130*(1), 115–142.

11. J. T. DeCuir and A. D. Dixson, "'So When It Comes Out, They Aren't That Surprised That It Is There': Using Critical Race Theory as a Tool of Analysis of Race and Racism in Education," *Educational Research, 33*(5), 2004, 26–31.

12. G. Evans, S. Hygge, and M. Bullinger, "Chronic Noise and Psychological Stress," *Psychological Science*, 1995, *6*(6), 333–338; G. Evans, "Noise Impairs Long-Term Memory and Reading Ability," *Psychological Science*, 2002 Sept., *13*(5); G. W. Evans, P. Lercher, M. Meis, H. Ising, and W. W. Kofler, "Community Noise Exposure and Stress in Children," *Journal of Acoustical Society of America*, 2001, *109*(3), 1023–1027.

13. I. Blanchette and A. Richards, "Anxiety and the Interpretation of Ambiguous Information: Beyond the Emotion-Congruent Effect," *Journal of Experimental Psychology: General*, 2003, *132*(2), 294–309.

14. J. Brooks-Gunn, P. K. Klebanov, and G. J. Duncan, "Ethnic Differences in Children's Intelligence Test Scores: Role of Economic Deprivation, Home Environment, and Maternal Characteristics," *Child Development*, 1996, *67*(2), 396–408.

15. R. B. Johnson and A. J. Onwuegbuzie, "Mixed Methods Research: A Research Paradigm Whose Time Has Come," *Educational Researcher*, 2004, *33*(7), 14–26.

16. H. Gardner, *The Theory of Multiple Intelligences* (New York: Basic Books, 1983).

17. P. Carter, *The Complete Book of Intelligence Tests: 500 Exercises to Improve, Upgrade and Enhance Your Mind Strength* (Hoboken, NJ: Wiley, 2005).

18. A. R. Jensen, *The g Factor: The Science of Mental Ability* (Westport, CT: Praeger, 1998).

19. J. R. Flynn, "Massive IQ Gains in 14 Nations: What IQ Tests Really Measure," *Psychological Bulletin*, 1987, *101*, 171–191.

20. Flynn, "Massive IQ Gains in 14 Nations."

21. D. Bowman, P. Markham, and R. Roberts, "Expanding the Frontier of Human Cognitive Abilities: So Much More Than (Plain) g!" *Learning and Individual Differences*, 2001, *13*(2), 127–158.

22. L. M. Terman, *Genetic Studies of Genius: Mental and Physical Traits of a Thousand Gifted Children* (Stanford, CA: Stanford University Press, 1925).

23. S. A. Rose, L. R. Futterweit, and J. J. Jankowski, "The Relation of Affect to Attention and Learning in Infancy," *Child Development*, 1999, *70*(3), 549–559.

24. R. B. McCall, "Environmental Effects on Intelligence: The Forgotten Realm of Discontinuous Nonshared Within-Family Factors," *Child Development*, 1983 Apr., *54*(2), 408–415.

25. R. B. McCall and M. S. Garriger, "A Meta-Analysis of Infant Habituation and Recognition Memory Performance as Predictors of Later IQ," *Child Development*, 1993, *64*, 57–79.

26. H. Gardner, *Frames of Mind: The Theory of Multiple Intelligences* (New York: Basic Books, 1983).

27. R. J. Sternberg, *The Triarchic Mind: A New Theory of Human Intelligence* (New York: Viking, 1988).

28. D. Goleman, *Emotional Intelligence* (New York: Bantam, 1995).

29. Y. Shoda, W. Mischel, and P. K. Peake, "Predicting Adolescent Cognitive and Social Competence from Preschool Delay of Gratification: Identifying Diagnostic Conditions," *Developmental Psychology*, 1990, *26*, 978–986.

30. J. G. Maree and L. Ebersohn, "Emotional Intelligence and Achievement: Redefining Giftedness?" *Gifted Education International*, 2002, *16*(3), 261–273.

31. J. D. Mayer, P. Salovey, D. R. Caruso, and G. Sitarenios, "Emotional Intelligence as a Standard Intelligence," *Emotion*, 2001, *1*(3), 232–242.

32. K. van der Zee, K. Thijs, and L. Schakel, "The Relationship of Emotional Intelligence with Academic Intelligence and the Big Five," *European Journal of Personality*, 2002, *16*(2), 103–125.

33. M. Zeidner, G. Matthews, and R. D. Roberts, "Slow Down, You Move Too Fast: Emotional Intelligence Remains an 'Elusive' Intelligence," *Emotion*, 2001, *1*(3), 265–275.

34. R. M. Carrothers, S. W. Gregory Jr., and T. J. Gallagher, "Measuring Emotional Intelligence of Medical School Applicants," *Academic Medicine: Journal of the Association of American Medical Colleges*, 2000 May, *75*(5), 456–463.

35. J. A. Parker, L. Summerfeldt, M. Hogan, and S. Majeski, "Emotional Intelligence and Academic Success: Examining the Transition from High School to University," *Personality & Individual Differences*, 2004, *36*(1), 163–172.

36. M. Brackett, J. Mayer, and R. Warner, "Emotional Intelligence and Its Relation to Everyday Behaviour," *Personality & Individual Differences*, 2004, *36*(6), 1387–1402.

37. C. E. Izard, "Emotional Intelligence or Adaptive Emotions?" *Emotion*, 2001, *1*(3), 249–257.

38. J. Lave, *Cognition in Practice* (Cambridge, UK: Cambridge University Press, 1988).

39. H. Sujan, "Optimism and Street-Smarts: Identifying and Improving Salesperson Intelligence," *Journal of Personal Selling & Sales Management*, 1999, *19*(3), 17–33.

40. S. J. Ceci and J. Liker, "A Day at the Races: A Study of IQ, Expertise, and Cognitive Complexity," *Journal of Experimental Psychology: General*, 1986, *115*, 255–266.

41. A. Duckworth and M. Seligman, "Self-Discipline Outdoes IQ in Predicting Academic Performance of Adolescents," *Psychological Science*, December 2005, *16*(12), 939–944.

42. K. A. Ericsson, "The Acquisition of Expert Performance," in *The Road to Excellence: The Acquisition of Expert Performance in the Arts, Science and Games*, ed. K. A. Ericsson (Mahwah, NJ: Lawrence Erlbaum Associates, 1996).

43. A. Mehrabian, "Beyond IQ: Broad-Based Measurement of Individual Success Potential or 'Emotional Intelligence'," *Genetic, Social, & General Psychology Monographs*, 2002, *126*(2), 133–239.

44. S. J. Gould, *The Mismeasure of Man* (New York: W.W. Norton, 1996); R. Sternberg, *Encyclopedia of Human Intelligence* (New York: Macmillan Reference Books, 1994); S. Ceci, *On Intelligence: More or Less* (Boston: Harvard University Press, 1996); Goleman, *Emotional Intelligence;* and Gardner, *Frames of Mind*.

45. R. Kurzweil, *The Singularity Is Near: When Humans Transcend Biology* (New York: Viking Press, 2005).

46. D. N. Perkins, *Outsmarting IQ: The Emerging Science of Learnable Intelligence* (New York: Free Press, 1995).

47. A. R. Jensen, "Cumulative Deficit in IQ of Blacks in the Rural South," *Developmental Psychology,* 1977, *13*, 184–191.

48. E. S. Lee, "Negro Intelligence and Selective Migration: A Philadelphia Test of the Klineberg Hypothesis," *American Sociological Review,* 1951, *16*, 227–232.

49. R. L. Green, L. T. Hoffman, R. Morse, M. E. Hayes, and R. F. Morgan, *The Educational Status of Children in a District Without Public Schools* (Cooperative Research Project No. 23211) (Washington, D.C.: Office of Education, U.S. Department of Health, Education, and Welfare, 1964).

50. J. Richeson, S. Richeson, and J. Nicole, "When Prejudice Does Not Pay: Effects of Interracial Contact on Executive Function," *Psychological Science,* 2003, *14*(3), 287–290.

51. K. C. Koenen, T. E. Moffitt, A. Caspi, A. Taylor, and S. Purcell, "Domestic Violence Is Associated with Environmental Suppression of IQ in Young Children," *Development and Psychopathology,* 2003, *15*(2), 297–311.

52. T. W. Frazier, H. A. Demaree, and E. A. Youngstrom, "Meta-Analysis of Intellectual and Neuropsychological Test Performance in Attention-Deficit/Hyperactivity Disorder," *Neuropsychology,* 2004, *18*(3), 543–555.

53. L. Ewing-Cobbs, J. M. Fletcher, H. S. Levin, D. J. Francis, K. Davidson, and M. E. Miner, "Longitudinal Neuropsychological Outcome in Infants and Preschoolers with Traumatic Brain Injury," *Journal of the International Neuropsychological Society,* 1997, *3*(6), 581–591.

54. V. Delaney-Black, C. Covington, S. J. Ondersma, B. Nordstrom-Klee, T. Templin, J. Ager, J. Janisse, and R. J. Sokol, "Violence Exposure, Trauma, and IQ and/or Reading Deficits Among Urban Children," *Archives of Pediatrics and Adolescent Medicine,* 2002, *156*(3), 280–285.

55. M. Diamond and J. Hopson, *Magic Trees of the Mind* (New York: Penguin-Dutton, 1998).

56. M. Duyme, A. C. Dumaret, and S. Tomkiewicz, "How Can We Boost IQs of 'Dull Children'?: A Late Adoption Study," *Proceedings of the National Academy of Sciences of the United States of America,* 1999, *96*(15), 8790–8794.

57. A. Lewis, "The Payoff from a Quality Preschool," *Phi Delta Kappan,* 1993 June, 746–749.

58. C. T. Ramey and F. A. Campbell, "Poverty, Early Childhood Education, and Academic Competence: The Abecedarian Experiment," in *Children Reared in Poverty,* ed. A. Huston (New York: Cambridge University Press, 1991), pp. 190–221; C. T. Ramey, F. A. Campbell, M. Burchinal, M. L. Skinner, D. M. Gardner, and S. L. Ramey, "Persistent Effects of Early Childhood Education on High-Risk Children and Their Mothers," *Applied Developmental Science,* 2000, *4*, 2–14.

59. R. Feuerstein, Y. Rand, M. Hoffman, M. Hoffman, and R. Miller, "Cognitive Modifiability in Retarded Adolescents: Effects of Instrumental Enrichment," *Pediatric Rehabilitation,* 2004, *7*(1), 20–29.

60. F. A. Campbell and C. T. Ramey, "Cognitive and School Outcomes for High-Risk African-American Students at Middle Adolescence: Positive Effects of Early Intervention," *American Educational Research Journal,* 1995, *32*, 743–772.

61. A. Tekian and L. Hruska, "A Review of Medical School Records to Investigate the Effectiveness of Enrichment Programs for 'At Risk' Students," *Teaching and Learning in Medicine,* 2004, *16*(1), 28–33.

62. T. Gravely, A. McCann, E. Brooks, W. Harman, and E. J. Schneiderman, "Enrichment and Recruitment Programs at Dental Schools: Impact on Enrollment of Underrepresented Minority Students," *Dental Education*, 2004, *68*(5), 542–552.

63. A. Raine, K. Mellingen, J. Liu, P. Venables, and S. A. Mednick, "Effects of Environmental Enrichment at Ages 3–5 Years on Schizotypal Personality and Antisocial Behavior at Ages 17 and 23 Years," *The American Journal of Psychiatry*, 2003, *160*(9), 1627–1635.

Chapter Three

1. A. Barnea and F. Nottebohm, "Recruitment and Replacement of Hippocampal Neurons in Young and Adult Chickadees: An Addition to the Theory of Hippocampal Learning," *Proceedings of the National Academy of Sciences of the United States of America*, 1996, *93*, 714–718.

2. M. J. Renner and M. R. Rosenzweig, *Enriched and Impoverished Environments: Effects on Brain and Behavior* (New York: Springer, 1987).

3. B. E. Will, M. R. Rosenzweig, E. L. Bennett, M. Hebert, and H. A. Morimoto, "Relatively Brief Environmental Enrichment Aids Recovery of Learning Capacity and Alters Brain Measures After Postweaning Brain Lesions in Rats," *Journal of Comparative Physiological Psychology*, 1977, *91*, 33–50.

4. W. Overman and J. Bachevalier, "Inferences About the Functional Development of Neural Systems in Children via the Application of Animal Tests in Cognition," in *Handbook of Developmental Cognitive Neuroscience*, ed. C. Nelson and M. Luciana (Cambridge: MIT Press, 2001).

5. D. O. Hebb, *Organization of Behavior* (Mahwah, N.J.: Lawrence Erlbaum Associates, 1947).

6. D. Krech, M. R. Rosenzweig, and E. L. Bennett, "Effects of Environmental Complexity and Training on Brain Chemistry," *Journal of Comparative Physiological Psychology*, 1960, *53*, 509–515.

7. M. R. Rosenzweig, D. Krech, E. L. Bennett, and M. C. Diamond, "Effects of Environmental Complexity and Training on Brain Chemistry and Anatomy," *The Journal of Comparative Physiological Psychology*, 1962, *55*, 429–437.

8. J. Altman, "Are New Neurons Formed in the Brains of Adult Mammals?" *Science*, 1962, *135*, 1127–1128.

9. P. S. Eriksson, E. Perfilieva, T. Bjork-Eriksson, A. M. Alborn, C. Nordborg, D. A. Peterson, and F. H. Gage, "Neurogenesis in the Adult Human Hippocampus," *Nature Medicine*, 1998, *4*(11), 1313–1317.

10. H. van Praag, B. R. Christie, T. J. Sejnowski, and F. H. Gage, "Running Enhances Neurogenesis, Learning and Long-term Potentiation in Mice," *Proceedings of the National Academy of Sciences of the United States of America*, 1999, *96*, 13427–13431.

11. J. Brown, C. M. Cooper-Kuhn, G. Kempermann, H. van Praag, J. Winkler, F. H. Gage, and H. G. Kuhn, "Enriched Environment and Physical Activity Stimulate Hippocampal but Not Olfactory Bulb Neurogenesis," *European Journal of Neuroscience*, May 2003, *17*(10), 2042–2046.

12. H. van Praag, G. Kemperman, and F. Gage, "Neural Consequences of Environmental Enrichment," *Nature Review Neuroscience*, 2000, *1*(3), 191–198.

13. van Praag and others, "Neural Consequences of Environmental Enrichment."

14. J. N. Nobrega, M. J. Saari, J. N. Armstrong, and T. Reed, "Neonatal 6-OHDA Lesions and Rearing in Complex Environments: Regional Effects on Adult Brain 14C-2-Deoxyglucose Uptake Revealed by Exposure to Novel Stimulation," *Developmental Psychobiology,* April 1992, *25*(3), 183-198.

15. D. R. Westhead, T. W. Slidel, T. P. Flores, and J. M. Thornton, "Protein Structural Topology: Automated Analysis and Diagrammatic Representation," *Protein Science,* April 1999 *8*(4), 897-904.

16. M. R. Rosenzweig and E. L. Bennett, "Effects of Differential Environments on Brain Weights and Enzyme Activities in Gerbils, Rats, and Mice," *Developmental Psychobiology,* 1969, *2,* 87-95; M. R. Rosenzweig, E. L. Bennett, and M. C. Diamond, "Effects of Differential Environments on Brain Anatomy and Brain Chemistry," in *Psychopathology of Mental Development,* ed. J. Zubin and G. Jervis (New York: Grune & Stratton, 1967).

17. G. A. Sforzo, T. F. Seeger, C. B. Pert, A. Pert, and C. O. Dotson, "*In Vivo* Opioid Receptor Occupation in the Rat Brain Following Exercise," *Medicine and Science in Sports and Exercise,* 1986, *18,* 380-384.

18. S. Rasmuson, T. Olsson, B. G. Henriksson, P. A. Kelly, M. C. Holmes, J. R. Seckl, and A. H. Mohammed, "Environmental Enrichment Selectively Increases 5-HT1A Receptor mRNA Expression and Binding in the Rat Hippocampus," *Brain Research, Molecular Brain Research,* 1998, *53*(1-2), 285-290; H. F. Clarke, J. W. Dalley, H. S. Crofts, T. W. Robbins, and A. C. Roberts, "Cognitive Inflexibility After Prefrontal Serotonin Depletion," *Science,* 2004, *304*(5672), 878-80.

19. F. Moncek, R. Duncko, B. B. Johansson, and D. Jezova, "Effect of Environmental Enrichment on Stress-Related Systems in Rats," *Journal of Neuroendocrinology,* 2004, *16*(5), 423-31; A. Fernández-Teruel, R. Escorihuela, B. Castellano, B. González, and A. Tobeña, "Neonatal Handling and Environmental Enrichment Effects on Emotionality, Novelty/Reward Seeking, and Age-Related Cognitive and Hippocampal Impairments: Focus on the Roman Rat Lines," *Behavior Genetics,* 1997, *27*(6), 513-526.

20. E. Belz, J. Kennell, R. Czambel, R. Rubin, and M. Rhodes, "Environmental Enrichment Lowers Stress-Responsive Hormones in Singly Housed Male and Female Rats," *Pharmacology, Biochemistry, and Behavior,* 2003, *76*(3-4), 481-486.

21. K. G. Hellemans, L. C. Benge, and M. C. Olmstead, "Adolescent Enrichment Partially Reverses the Social Isolation Syndrome," *Brain Research, Developmental Brain Research,* 2004, *150*(2), 103-115.

22. P. E. Honess and C. M. Marin, "Enrichment and Aggression in Primates," *Neuroscience Biobehavioral Review,* 2005, *30*(3), 413-436.

23. J. E. Black, K. R. Isaacs, B. J. Anderson, A. A. Alcantara, and W. T. Greenough, "Learning Causes Synaptogenesis, Whereas Motor Activity Causes Angiogenesis, in Cerebellar Cortex of Adult Rats," *Proceedings of the National Academy of Sciences of the United States of America,* 1990, *87,* 5568-5572.

24. A. M. Sirevaag and W. T. Greenough, "Plasticity of GFAP-Immunoreactive Astrocyte Size and Number in Visual Cortex of Rats Reared in Complex Environments," *Brain Research,* 1991, *540*(1-2), 273-278.

25. M. C. Diamond, D. Krech, and M. R. Rosenzweig, "The Effects of an Enriched Environment on the Histology of the Rat Cerebral Cortex," *The Journal of Comparative Neurology,* 1964, *123,* 111-120; M. C. Diamond, B. Lindner, and

A. Raymond, "Extensive Cortical Depth Measurements and Neuron Size Increases in the Cortex of Environmentally Enriched Rats," *The Journal of Comparative Neurology,* 1967, *131,* 357–364.

26. E. J. Green, W. T. Greenough, and B. E. Schlumph, "Effects of Complex or Isolated Environments on Cortical Dendrites of Middle-Aged Rats," *Brain Research,* 1983, *264,* 233–240; J. M. Juraska, J. M. Fitch, C. Henderson, and N. Rivers, "Sex Differences in the Dendritic Branching of Dentate Granule Cells Following Differential Experience," *Brain Research,* 1985, *333,* 73–80; F. R. Volkmar and W. T. Greenough, "Rearing Complexity Affects Branching of Dendrites in the Visual Cortex of the Rat," *Science,* 1972, *176,* 1445–1447.

27. E. L. Bennett, M. R. Rosenzweig, and M. C. Diamond, "Rat Brain: Effects of Environmental Enrichment on Wet and Dry Weights," *Science,* 1969, *164,* 825–826; J. Altman, R. B. Wallace, W. J. Anderson, and G. D. Das, "Behaviorally Induced Changes in Length of Cerebrum in Rat," *Developmental Psychobiology,* 1968, *1,* 112–117.

28. B. Kolb, *Brain Plasticity and Behavior* (Mahwah, NJ: Lawrence Earlbaum Associates, 1995).

29. M. C. Diamond, C. C. Ingham, R. E. Johnson, E. L. Bennett, and M. R. Rosenzweig, "Effects of Environment on Morphology of Rat Cerebral Cortex and Hippocampus," *Journal of Neurobiology,* 1976, *7,* 75–85; W. T. Greenough and F. R. Volkmar, "Pattern of Dendritic Branching in Occipital Cortex of Rats Reared in Complex Environments," *Experimental Neurology,* 1973, *40,* 491–504.

30. A. Globus, M. R. Rosenzweig, E. L. Bennett, and M. C. Diamond, "Effects of Differential Environments on Dendritic Spine Counts," *Journal of Comparative Physiological Psychology,* 1973, *84,* 598–604.

31. A. Turner and W. T. Greenough, "Differential Rearing Effects on Rat Visual Cortex Synapses. I. Synaptic and Neuronal Density and Synapses per Neuron," *Brain Research,* 1985, *329,* 195–203.

32. Black and others, "Learning Causes Synaptogenesis"; W. Greenough and A. Alcantara, "The Roles of Experience in Different Developmental Information Stage Processes," in *Developmental Neurocognition,* ed. B. Boyyson-Bardies, S. de Schonen, P. Jusczyk, P. McNeilage, and J. Morton (Dordrecht: Kluwer Academic, 1993), pp. 3–16.

33. Y. Geinisman, J. Disterhoft, H. Gundersen, M. McEchron, I. Persina, J. Power, E. van der Zee, and M. West, "Remodeling of Hippocampal Synapses After Hippocampus-Dependent Associative Learning," *The Journal* of *Comparative Neurology,* 2000, *417,* 49–59.

34. E. J. Green and W. T. Greenough, "Altered Synaptic Transmission in Dentate Gyrus of Rats Reared in Complex Environments: Evidence from Hippocampal Slices Maintained *in vitro,*" *Journal of Neurophysiology,* 1986, *55,* 739–750.

35. P. E. Sharp, B. L. McNaughton and C. A. Barnes, "Enhancement of Hippocampal Field Potentials in Rats Exposed to a Novel, Complex Environment," *Brain Research,* 1985, *339,* 361–365.

36. S. Wang, B. W. Scott and J. M. Wojtowicz, "Heterogeneous Properties of Dentate Granule Neurons in Adult Rats," *Journal of Neurobiology,* 2000, *42,* 248–257.

37. N. D. Engineer, C. R. Percaccio, P. K. Pandya, R. Moucha, D. L. Rathbun, and M. P. Kilgard, "Environmental Enrichment Improves Response Strength, Threshold, Selectivity, and Latency of Auditory Cortex Neurons," *Journal of Neurophysiology,*

2004, *92*(1), 73–82; L. Cancedda, E. Putignano, A. Sale, A. Viegi, N. Berardi, and L. Maffei, "Acceleration of Visual System Development by Environmental Enrichment," *Journal of Neuroscience*, 2004, *24*(20), 4840–4848.

38. C. Wallace, G. Withers, I. Weiler, J. George, D. Clayton, and W. Greenough, "Correspondence Between Sites of NGFI-A Induction and Sites of Morphological Plasticity Following Exposure to Environmental Complexity," *Molecular Brain Research*, 1995, *32*, 211–220.

39. S. Duffy, K. Craddock, T. Abel, and P. V. Nguyen, "Environmental Enrichment Modifies the PKA-Dependence of Hippocampal LTP and Improves Hippocampus-Dependent Memory," *Learning and Memory*, 2001, *8*(1), 26–34.

40. E. H. Lee, W. L. Hsu, Y. L. Ma, P. J. Lee, and C. C. Chao, "Enrichment Enhances the Expression of SGK, a Glucocorticoid-Induced Gene, and Facilitates Spatial Learning Through Glutamate AMPA Receptor Mediation," *The European Journal of Neuroscience*, 2003, *18*(10), 2842–2852; K. M. Frick, N. A. Stearns, J. Y. Pan, and J. Berger-Sweeney, "Effects of Environmental Enrichment on Spatial Memory and Neurochemistry in Middle-Aged Mice," *Learning Memory*, 2003, *10*(3), 187–198.

41. G. Kempermann, D. Gast, and F. Gage, "Neuroplasticity in Old Age: Sustained Fivefold Induction of Hippocampal Neurogenesis by Long-Term Environmental Enrichment," *Annals of Neurology*, 2002, *52*(2), 135–143.

42. G. Kempermann, E. P. Brandon, and F. H. Gage, "Environmental Stimulation of 129/SvJ Mice Results in Increased Cell Proliferation and Neurogenesis in the Adult Dentate Gyrus," *Current Biology*. 1998, *8*, 939–942.

43. Eriksson and others, "Neurogenesis in the Adult Human Hippocampus."

44. F. Gomez-Pinilla, V. So, and J. P. Kesslak, "Spatial Learning and Physical Activity Contribute to the Induction of Fibroblast Growth Factor: Neural Substrates for Increased Cognition Associated with Exercise," *Neuroscience*, 1998, *85*, 53–61.

45. S. Rasika, A. Alvarez-Buylla, and F. Nottebohm, "BDNF Mediates the Effects of Testosterone on the Survival of New Neurons in an Adult Brain," *Neuron*, 1999, *22*, 53–62; M. A. Aberg, N. D. Aberg, H. Hedbacker, J. Oscarsson, and P. S. Eriksson, "Peripheral Infusion of IGF-1 Selectively Induces Neurogenesis in the Adult Rat Hippocampus," *Journal of Neuroscience*, 2000, *20*(8), 2896–2903.

46. H. van Praag, G. Kempermann, and F. H. Gage, "Running Increases Cell Proliferation and Neurogenesis in the Adult Mouse Dentate Gyrus," *Nature Neuroscience*, 1999, *2*(3), 266–270.

47. R. Gerlai, "Gene-Targeting Studies of Mammalian Behavior: Is It the Mutation or the Background Genotype?" *Trends in Neuroscience*, 1996, *19*, 177–181.

48. G. Kempermann, E. P. Brandon, and F. H. Gage, "Environmental Stimulation of 129/SvJ Mice Results in Increased Cell Proliferation and Neurogenesis in the Adult Dentate Gyrus," *Current Biology*, 1998, *8*, 939–942.

49. A. Y. Klintsova, R. M. Cowell, R. A. Swain, R. M. Napper, C. R. Goodlett, and W. T. Greenough, "Therapeutic Effects of Complex Motor Training on Motor Performance Deficits Induced by Neonatal Binge-Like Alcohol Exposure in Rats," *Brain Research*, 1998, *800*(1), 48–61.

50. Hellemans and others, "Adolescent Enrichment Partially Reverses the Social Isolation Syndrome."

51. D. D. Francis, J. Diorio, P. M. Plotsky, and M. Meaney, "Environmental Enrichment Reverses the Effects of Maternal Separation on Stress Reactivity," *The Journal of Neuroscience*, 2002, *22*(18), 7840–7843.

52. R. Waterland and R. Jirtle, "Transposable Elements: Targets for Early Nutritional Effects on Epigenetic Gene Regulation," *Molecular and Cellular Biology*, 2003, *23*(15), 5293-5300.

53. M. D. Dobrossy and S. B. Dunnett, "Environmental Enrichment Affects Striatal Graft Morphology and Functional Recovery," *The European Journal of Neuroscience*, 2004, *19*(1), 159-168; B. Will, R. Galani, C. Kelche, and M. R. Rosenzweig, "Recovery from Brain Injury in Animals: Relative Efficacy of Environmental Enrichment, Physical Exercise or Formal Training, 1990-2002," *Progress in Neurobiology*, February 2004, *72*(3), 167-182.

    P. Dahlqvist, A. Ronnback, S. A. Bergstrom, I. Soderstrom, and T. Olsson, "Environmental Enrichment Reverses Learning Impairment in the Morris Water Maze After Focal Cerebral Ischemia in Rats," *The European Journal of Neuroscience*, 2004 April, *19*(8), 2288-2298.

54. T. R. Guilarte, C. D. Toscano, J. L. McGlothan, and S. A. Weaver, "Environmental Enrichment Reverses Cognitive and Molecular Deficits Induced by Developmental Lead Exposure," *Annals of Neurology*, 2003, *53*(1), 50-6.

55. P. A. Ferchmin and E. L. Bennett, "Direct Contact with Enriched Environment Is Required to Alter Cerebral Weights in Rats," *Journal of Comparative and Physiological Psychology*, 1975, *88*, 360-367.

56. D. E. Fordyce and J. M. Wehner, "Physical Activity Enhances Spatial Learning Performance with an Associated Alteration in Hippocampal Protein Kinase C Activity in C57BL/6 and DBA/2 Mice," *Brain Research*, 1993, *619*, 111-119; van Praag and others, "Running Enhances Neurogenesis, Learning, and Long-Term Potentiation in Mice."

57. van Praag and others, "Neural Consequences of Environmental Enrichment."

58. van Praag and others, "Running Increases Cell Proliferation and Neurogenesis in the Adult Mouse Dentate Gyrus."

59. S. A. Neeper, F. Gomez-Pinilla, J. Choi, and C. Cotman, "Exercise and Brain Neurotrophins," *Nature*, 1995, *373*, 109.

60. Volkmar and Greenough, "Rearing Complexity Affects Branching of Dendrites"; Turner and Greenough, "Differential Rearing Effects on Rat Visual Cortex Synapses"; Black and others, "Learning Causes Synaptogenesis."

61. Engineer and others, "Environmental Enrichment Improves Response Strength."

62. E. Gould, P. Tanapat, T. Rydel, and N. Hastings, "Regulation of Hippocampal Neurogenesis in Adulthood," *Biological Psychiatry*, 2000, *48*, 715-720; G. Kempermann, "Why New Neurons? Possible Functions for Adult Hippocampal Neurogenesis," *Journal of Neuroscience*, 2002, *22*(3), 635-638.

63. M. Kilgard and M. Merzenich, "Cortical Map Reorganization Enabled by Nucleus Basalis Activity," *Science*, 1998, *279*, 1714-1718.

64. E. Ahissar, E. Vaadia, M. Ahissar, H. Bergman, A. Arielli, and M. Abeles, "Dependence of Cortical Plasticity on Correlated Activity of Single Neurons and on Behavioral Context," *Science*, 1992, *257*, 1412-1415.

65. L. Stewart, R. Henson, K. Kampe, V. Walsh, R. Turner, and U. Frith, "Brain Changes After Learning to Read and Play Music," *Neuroimage*, 2003, *20*(1), 71-83.

66. M. R. Rosenzweig, "Environmental Complexity, Cerebral Change, and Behavior," *The American Psychologist*, 1966, *21*, 321-332.

67. Wallace and others, "Correspondence Between Sites of NGFI-A Induction."

68. M. Diamond and J. Hopson, *Magic Trees of the Mind* (New York: Penguin-Dutton, 1998).

69. B. Jacobs, M. Schall, and A. Scheibel, "A Quantitative Dendritic Analysis of Bernice's Area in Humans. II. Gender, Hemispheric and Environmental Factor," *The Journal of Comparative Neurology*, 1993, *327*, 97-111.

70. R. J. Hamm, M. D. Temple, D. M. O'Dell, B. R. Pike, and B. G. Lyeth, "Exposure to Environmental Complexity Promotes Recovery of Cognitive Function After Traumatic Brain Injury," *Journal of Neurotrauma*, 1996, *13*, 41-47.

71. Wallace and others, "Correspondence Between Sites of NGFI-A Induction."

72. Diamond and Hopson, *Magic Trees of the Mind*.

73. S. C. Cook and C. L. Wellman, "Chronic Stress Alters Dendritic Morphology in Rat Medial Prefrontal Cortex," *Journal of Neurobiology*, 2004, *60*(2), 236-248.

74. J. F. Sheridan, D. A. Padgett, R. Avitsur, and P. T. Marucha, "Experimental Models of Stress and Wound Healing," *World Journal of Surgery*, 2004 March, (3), 327-330. R. Avitsur, D. A. Padgett, F. S. Dhabhar, J. L. Stark, K. A. Kramer, H. Engler, and J. F. Sheridan, "Expression of Glucocorticoid Resistance Following Social Stress Requires a Second Signal," *Journal of Leukocyte Biology*, 2003, *74*(4), 507-513.

75. J. C. Wommack, A. Salinas, R. H. Melloni Jr., and Y. Delville, "Behavioral and Neuroendocrine Adaptations to Repeated Stress During Puberty in Male Golden Hamsters," *Journal of Neuroendocrinology*, 2004, *16*(9), 767-775.

76. P. Tanapat, L. Galea, and E. Gould, "Stress Inhibits the Proliferation of Granule Cell Precursors in the Development of the Dentate Gyrus," *The International Journal of Developmental Neuroscience*, 1998, *16*, 235-239.

77. E. Epel, E. Blackburn, J. Lin, F. Dhabhar, N. Adler, J. Morrow, and R. Cawthon, "Accelerated Telomere Shortening in Response to Life Stress," *Proceedings of the National Academy of Sciences of the United States of America*, 2004, *101*(49), 17312-17315.

78. G. Evans and L. Maxwell, "Chronic Noise Exposure and Reading Deficits: The Mediating Effects of Language Acquisition," *Environment & Behavior*, 1997, *29*(5), 638-656.

79. Engineer and others, "Environmental Enrichment Improves Response Strength."

80. E. Pekkarinen and V. Wiljanen, "Effect of Sound-Absorbing Treatment on Speech Discrimination in Rooms," *Audiology*, 1990, *29*(4), 219-227.

81. L. Heschong and Heschong Mahone Consulting Group, *Daylighting in Schools: An Investigation into the Relationship Between Daylighting and Human Performance*, 1999. A study performed on behalf of the California Board for Energy Efficiency for the Third Party Program administered by Pacific Gas & Electric, as part of the PG & E contract 460-000. Available online at www.h-m-g.com/daylighting/main.htm unpublished data; Heschong Mahone Group, *Windows and Classrooms: A Study of Student Performance and the Indoor Environment*, 2003. A study performed on behalf of the California Energy Commission administered by Pacific Gas & Electric, October, contract P500-03-082-A-7. Available online at www.h-m-g.com/daylighting/main.htm unpublished data.

82. Heschong and Heschong Mahone Consulting Group, *Daylighting in Schools*.

83. J. Connor and M. Diamond, "A Comparison of Dendritic Spine Number and Type on Pyramidal Neurons of the Visual Cortex of Old Rats from Social or Isolated Environments," *The Journal of Comparative Neurology*, 1982, *210*, 99-106; B. B. Johansson and A. Ohlsson, "Environment, Social Interaction, and Physical

Activity as Determinants of Functional Outcome After Cerebral Infarction in the Rat," *Experimental Neurology*, 1996, *139*, 322–327.

84. Hellemans and others, "Adolescent Enrichment Partially Reverses the Social Isolation Syndrome."

85. Dobrossy and Dunnett, "Environmental Enrichment Affects Striatal Graft Morphology and Functional Recovery."

86. Frick and others, "Effects of Environmental Enrichment on Spatial Memory."

87. S. Pietropaolo, I. Branchi, F. Cirulli, F. Chiarotti, L. Aloe, and E. Alleva, "Long-Term Effects of the Periadolescent Environment on Exploratory Activity and Aggressive Behavior in Mice: Social Versus Physical Enrichment," *Physiology & Behavior*, 2004, *81*(3), 443–453.

88. S. Suomi, "Attachment in Rhesus Monkeys," in *Handbook of Attachment*, eds. J. Cassidy and P. Shaver (New York: Guilford Press, 1999), pp. 181–197; T. Wilson and C. Grim, "Biohistory of Slavery and Blood Pressure Differences in Blacks Today," *Hypertension*, 1991, *17*(Suppl I), 1122–1128.

89. E. Kandel, "A New Intellectual Framework for Psychiatry?" *American Journal of Psychiatry*, 1998, *155*, 460.

90. M. Alamy, M. Errami, K. Taghzouti, F. Saddiki-Traki, and W. A. Bengelloun, "Effects of Postweaning Undernutrition on Exploratory Behavior, Memory and Sensory Reactivity in Rats: Implication of the Dopaminergic System," *Physiological Behavior*, 2005 Sept.; *86*(1–2), 195–202.

91. S. Y. Lim, J. Hoshiba, T. Moriguchi, and N. Salem Jr., "N-3 Fatty Acid Deficiency Induced by a Modified Artificial Rearing Method Leads to Poorer Performance in Spatial Learning Tasks," *Pediatric Research*, 2005 Oct., *58*(4), 741–748.

92. Y. Tanabe, M. Hashimoto, K. Sugioka, M. Maruyama, Y. Fujii, R. Hagiwara, T. Hara, S. M. Hossain, and O. Shido, "Improvement of Spatial Cognition with Dietary Docosahexaenoic Acid Is Associated with an Increase in Fos Expression in Rat CA1 Hippocampus," *Clinical Experiments in Pharmacology and Physiology*, 2005 Oct., *31*(10), 700–703.

93. S. H. Zeisel, "Choline: Needed for Normal Development of Memory," *Journal of American College of Nutrition*, 2000 Oct., *19*(5 Suppl), 528S–531S.

94. M. Georgieff and R. Rao, "The Role of Nutrition in Cognitive Development," in *Handbook of Developmental Cognitive Neuroscience*, eds. C. Nelson and M. Luciana (Cambridge: MIT Press, 2001).

95. E. Pollitt and K. Gorman, "Nutritional Deficiencies as Developmental Risk Factors," in *Threats to Optimal Development*, ed. C. Nelson (Mahwah, NJ: Lawrence Erlbaum Associates, 1994), pp. 121–144; E. Pollitt, K. Gorman, P. Engle, J. Rivera, and R. Martorelli, "Nutrition in Early Life and the Fulfillment of Intellectual Potential," *Journal of Nutrition*, 1995, *125*, S1111–S1118; E. Pollitt, W. Watkins, and M. Husaini, "Three-Month Nutritional Supplementation in Indonesian and Toddlers Benefits Memory Function Eight Years Later," *American Journal of Clinical Nutrition*, 1997, *66*, 1357–1363.

96. A. Raine, K. Mellingen, J. Liu, P. Venables, and S. A. Mednick, "Effects of Environmental Enrichment at Ages 3–5 Years on Schizotypal Personality and Antisocial Behavior at Ages 17 and 23 Years," *The American Journal of Psychiatry*, 2003, *160*(9), 1627–1635.

97. J. Lee, W. Duan, J. M. Long, D. K. Ingram, and M. P. Mattson, "Dietary Restriction Increases the Number of Newly Generated Neural Cells, and Induces BDNF

Expression, in the Dentate Gyrus of Rats," *Journal of Molecular Neuroscience*, 2000, *15*(2), 99–108.

98. J. A. Kleim, K. Vij, K. Ballard, and W. T. Greenough, "Learning-Dependent Synaptic Modifications in the Cerebellar Cortex of the Adult Rat Persist for at Least Four Weeks," *Journal of Neuroscience*, 1997, *17*, 717–721.

99. E. L. Bennett, M. R. Rosenzweig, M. C. Diamond, H. Morimoto, and M. Hebert, "Effects of Successive Environments on Brain Measures," *Physiological Behavior*, April 1974, *12*, 621–631.

100. B. Bower, "Brain Clues to Energy-Efficient Learning," *Science News*, 1992, *141*, 215.

101. B. Schoner and S. Kelso, "A Synergetic Theory of Environmentally Specified and Learned Patterns of Movement Coordination: Relative Phase Dynamics," *Biological Cybernetics*, 1988, *58*, 71–80.

102. F. A. Campbell and C. T. Ramey, "Effects of Early Intervention on Intellectual and Academic Achievement: A Follow-Up Study of Children from Low-Income Families," *Child Development*, 1994, *65*, 684–698.

103. Diamond and Hopson, *Magic Trees of the Mind.*

104. G. Kempermann, H. G. Kuhn, and F. H. Gage, "Experience-Induced Neurogenesis in the Senescent Dentate Gyrus," *Journal of Neuroscience*, 1998, *18*, 3206–3212; G. Kempermann and F. H. Gage, "Experience-Dependent Regulation of Adult Hippocampal Neurogenesis: Effects of Long-Term Stimulation and Stimulus Withdrawal," *Hippocampus*, 1999, *9*, 321–332.

105. J. Bruer, *The Myth of the First Three Years* (New York: Free Press, 1999).

106. Green and others, "Effects of Complex or Isolated Environments."

107. Kempermann and others, "Environmental Stimulation of 129/SvJ Mice Results."

108. C. Rampon, Y. P. Tang, J. Goodhouse, E. Shimizu, M. Kyin, and J. Z. Tsien, "Enrichment Induces Structural Changes and Recovery from Nonspatial Memory Deficits in CA1 NMDAR1-Knockout Mice," *Nature Neuroscience*, 2000, *3*(3), 238–244.

109. Campbell and Ramey, "Effects of Early Intervention on Intellectual and Academic Achievement."

110. T. F. Munte, E. Altenmuller, and L. Jancke, "The Musician's Brain as a Model of Neuroplasticity," *Nature Reviews Neuroscience*, 2002, *3*(6), 473–478.

111. Ahissar and others, "Dependence of Cortical Plasticity on Correlated Activity of Single Neurons."

112. Kempermann, "Why New Neurons?"

113. H. A. Cameron, C. S. Wolley, B. S. McEwen, and E. Gould, "Differentiation of Newly Born Neurons and Glia in the Dentate Gyrus of the Adult Rat," *Neuroscience*, 1993, *56*, 337–344; van Praag and others, "Running Enhances Neurogenesis."

CHAPTER FOUR

1. B. D. Perry, "Neurobiological Sequelae of Childhood Trauma: Post-Traumatic Stress Disorders in Children," in *Catecholamine Function in Post-Traumatic Stress Disorder: Emerging Concepts,* ed. M. Murburg (Washington, DC: American Psychiatric Press, 1994).

2. S. Greenspan, *The Growth of the Mind* (New York: Basic Books, 1997).

3. D. Amen, *Change Your Brain, Change Your Life* (New York: Random House, 1998).

4. W. T. Greenough and F. R. Volkmar, "Pattern of Dendritic Branching in Occipital Cortex of Rats Reared in Complex Environments," *Experimental Neurology*, 1973, *40*,

491–504; W. T. Greenough, J. E. Black, and C. S. Wallace, "Experience and Brain Development," *Child Development*, 1987, *58*(3), 539–559.

5. A. Schore, *Affect Regulation and the Origin of the Self: The Neurobiology of Emotional Development* (Mahwah, NJ: Lawrence Erlbaum Associates, 1994).

6. M. H. Johnson, "Functional Brain Development in Humans," *Nature Reviews Neuroscience*, 2001, *2*(7), 475–483.

7. H. Chugani, "A Critical Period of Brain Development: Studies of Cerebral Glucose Utilization with PET," *Preventive Medicine*, 1998, *27*, 184–188.

8. M. Pines, "The Civilizing of Genie," in *Teaching English Through the Disciplines: Psychology*, ed. L. F. Kasper (New York: Whittier, 1997).

9. B. Carson, *The Big Picture* (Grand Rapids, MI: Zondervan, 2000).

10. P. Huttenlocher, *Neural Plasticity* (Cambridge, MA: Harvard University Press, 2002).

11. M. A. Tansey, J. A. Tansey, and K. H. Tachiki, "Electroencephalographic Cartography of Conscious States," *International Journal of Neuroscience*, 1994, *77* (1–2), 89–98.

12. V. Rideout and E. Vandewater, *Zero to Six: Electronic Media in the Lives of Infants and Toddlers and Preschoolers*, Fall, 2003. A Kaiser Foundation Report at www.kff.org/entmedia/entmedia102803nr.cfm.

13. R. S. Lichter and D. Amundson, *A Day of TV Violence: 1992 vs. 1994* (Washington, DC: Center for Media and Public Affairs, 1994).

14. L. A. Joy, M. Kimball, and M. L. Zabrack, "Television Exposure and Children's Aggressive Behavior," in *The Impact of Television: A Natural Experiment Involving Three Towns*, ed. T. M. Williams (New York: Academic Press, 1986).

15. B. Perry, "Incubated in Terror: Neurodevelopmental Factors in the 'Cycle of Violence'," in *Children in a Violent Society*, ed. J. Osofsky (New York: Guilford Press, 1997).

16. D. Anderson, B. Jennings, A. Wilder, and others, "Researching Blue's Clues: Viewing Behavior and Impact," *Media Psychology*, 2000, *2*(2), 179–194; S. Fisch, R. Truglio, and C. Cole, "The Impact of Sesame Street on Preschool Children: A Review and Synthesis of 30 Years' Research," *Media Psychology*, 1999, *1*(2), 156–190; G. Gerbner and N. Signorielli, *Violence Profile, 1967 Through 1988–89: Enduring Patterns*, unpublished manuscript, on file at the Annenberg School of Communications of the University of Pennsylvania, 1990; A. Sanson and C. Di Muccio, "The Influence of Aggressive and Neutral Cartoons and Toys on the Behaviour of Preschool Children," *Australian Psychologist*, 1993, *28*, 93–99.

17. E. Bates and K. Roe, "Language Development in Children with Unilateral Brain Injury," in *Handbook of Developmental Cognitive Neuroscience*, eds. C. Nelson and M. Luciana (Cambridge: MIT Press, 2001).

18. R. Aslin and R. Hunt, "Development, Plasticity and Learning in the Auditory System," in *Handbook of Developmental Cognitive Neuroscience*, eds. C. Nelson and M. Luciana (Cambridge: MIT Press, 2001), pp. 205–220.

19. P. Huttenlocher, *Neural Plasticity*.

20. J. Huttenlocher, W. Haight, A. Bruk, M. Seltzer, and T. Lyons, "Early Vocabulary Growth: Relation to Language Input and Gender," *Developmental Psychology*, March 1991, *27*(2), 236–248.

21. P. Huttenlocher, *Neural Plasticity*.

22. Chugani, "A Critical Period of Brain Development."

23. P. Huttenlocher and A. Dabholkar, "Regional Differences in Synaptogenesis in

Human Cerebral Cortex," *The Journal of Comparative Neurology,* 1997, *387*(2), 167–178.

24. J. P. Bourgeois, "Synaptogenesis, Heterochrony and Epigenesis in the Mammalian Neocortex," *Acta Pediatric Supplement,* 1997, *422,* 27–33.

25. K. C. Koenen, T. E. Moffitt, A. Caspi, A. Taylor, and S. Purcell, "Domestic Violence Is Associated with Environmental Suppression of IQ in Young Children," *Development and Psychopathology,* 2003, *15*(2), 297–311.

26. B. McEwen and H. Schmeck, *The Hostage Brain* (New York: Rockefeller University Press, 1994).

27. L. X. Zhang, S. Levine, G. Dent, Y. Zhan, G. Xing, D. Okimoto, M. K. Gordon, R. M. Post, and M. A. Smith, "Maternal Deprivation Increases Cell Death in the Infant Rat Brain," *Brain Research, Developmental Brain Research,* 2002, *133*(1), 1–11.

28. P. M. Thompson, J. N. Giedd, R. P. Woods, D. MacDonald, A. C. Evans, and A. W. Toga, "Growth Patterns in the Developing Brain Detected by Using Continuum Mechanical Tensor Maps," *Nature,* 2000, *404*(6774), 190–193.

29. B. J. Casey, J. N. Giedd, and K. M. Thomas, "Structural and Functional Brain Development and Its Relation to Cognitive Development," *Child Development,* 1998, *69*(1), 154–163.

30. W. D. Gaillard, L. Hertz-Pannier, S. H. Mott, A. S. Barnett, D. LeBihan, and W. H. Theodore, "Functional Anatomy of Cognitive Development: fMRI of Verbal Fluency in Children and Adults," *Neurology,* 2000 Jan., *54*(1), 180–185.

31. S. A. Bunge, N. M. Dudukovic, M. E. Thomason, C. J. Vaidya, and J. D. Gabrieli, "Immature Frontal Lobe Contributions to Cognitive Control in Children: Evidence from fMRI," *Neuron,* 2002 Jan., *33*(2), 301–311.

32. K. Ueda, Y. Okamoto, G. Okada, H. Yamashita, T. Hori, and S. Yamawaki, "Brain Activity During Expectancy of Emotional Stimuli: An fMRI Study," *Neuroreport,* 2003, *14*(1), 51–55.

33. V. Vuontela, M. R. Steenari, S. Carlson, J. Koivisto, M. Fjallberg, and E. T. Aronen, "Audiospatial and Visuospatial Working Memory in 6-13-Year-Old School Children," *Learning and Memory,* 2003 Jan.–Feb., *10*(1), 74–81.

34. T. Paus, A. Zijdenbos, K. Worsley, D. L. Collins, J. Blumenthal, J. N. Giedd, and others, "Structural Maturation of Neural Pathways in Children and Adolescents: In Vivo Study," *Science,* 1999, *283,* 1908–1911.

35. S. Durston, H. E. Hulshoff-Pol, and B. J. Casey, "Anatomical MRI of the Developing Human Brain: What Have We Learned?" *Journal of the American Academy of Child and Adolescent Psychiatry,* 2001, *40,* 1012–1020.

36. E. R. Sowell, P. M. Thompson, C. J. Holmes, T. L. Jernigan, and A. W. Toga, "In Vivo Evidence for Post-Adolescent Brain Maturation in Frontal and Striatal Regions," *Nature Neuroscience,* 1999, *2*(10), 859–861.

37. A. R. Wolfson and M. A. Carskadon, "Sleep Schedules and Daytime Functioning in Adolescents," *Child Development,* 1998, *69*(4), 875–887.

38. R. W. Larson, G. L. Clore, and G. A. Wood, "The Emotions of Romantic Relationships: Do They Wreak Havoc on Adolescents?" in *The Development of Romantic Relationships in Adolescence,* eds. W. Furman, B. B. Brown, and C. Feiring (New York: Cambridge University Press, 1999), pp. 19–49.

39. J. Hawkins, *On Intelligence* (New York: Henry Holt, 2004).

40. J. Johnson, P. Cohen, E. Smailes, S. Kasen, and J. Brook, "Television Viewing and Aggressive Behavior During Adolescence and Adulthood," *Science,* 2002, *295*(5564),

2468-2471; V. C. Strasburger and E. Donnerstein, "Children, Adolescents, and the Media in the 21st Century," *Adolescent Medicine,* 2000, *11*(1), 51-68.

41. J. West, K. Denton, and E. Germino-Hausken, *America's Kindergartners* (Washington, D.C.: National Center for Education Statistics, 2000).

42. National Institute of Child Health and Human Development (NICHD), "Does Amount of Time Spent in Child Care Predict Socioemotional Adjustment During the Transition to Kindergarten?" *Child Development,* 2003, *74*(4), 976-1005.

43. J. Kaufman, P. M. Plotsky, C. B. Nemeroff, and D. S. Charney, "Effects of Early Adverse Experiences on Brain Structure and Function: Clinical Implications," *Biological Psychiatry,* 2000, *48*(8), 778-790.

44. S. Luthar, "The Culture of Affluence: Psychological Costs of Material Wealth," *Child Development,* 2003, *74*(6), 1581-1593.

45. NICHD, "Does Amount of Time Spent."

46. U.S. General Accounting Office, *Elementary School Children: Many Change Schools Frequently, Harming Their Education* (Washington, D.C.: U.S. General Accounting Office, 1994).

47. B. Perry and I. Azad, "Post Traumatic Stress Disorders in Children and Adolescents," *Current Opinions in Pediatrics,* 1999, *11*(4).

48. B. Bender, "Learning Disorders Associated with Asthma and Allergies," *School Psychology Review,* 1999, *28*(2), 204-214.

49. I. Weaver, F. Champagne, S. Brown, S. Dymov, S. Sharma, M. Meaney, and M. Szy, "Reversal of Maternal Programming of Stress Responses in Adult Offspring Through Methyl Supplementation: Altering Epigenetic Marking Later in Life," *The Journal of Neuroscience,* 2005, *25*(47), 11045-11054.

Chapter Five

1. C. DeNavas-Walt, B. D. Proctor, and R. J. Mills, "Income, Poverty, and Health Insurance Coverage in the United States," in *U.S. Census Bureau, Current Population Reports, P60-226* (Washington, D.C.: U.S. Government Printing Office, 2004); J. Dalaker, *Poverty in the United States: 1998,* U.S. Census Bureau Current Population Reports, Series P, 60-207, (Washington, DC: U.S. Government Printing Office, 1999). (ERIC document ED 446 208).

2. D. Brody, J. Pirkle, R. Kramer, K. Flegal, T. Matte, E. Gunter, R. Bullard, and B. Wright, "Environmental Justice for All: Current Perspectives on Health and Research Needs," *Toxicology and Industrial Health,* 1993, *9,* 821-841.

3. Environmental Protection Agency, *Indoor Air Quality and Student Performance.* EPA report number: EPA 402-F-00-009 (Washington, D.C.: Environmental Protection Agency, 2000). Retrieved June 10, 2002, from www.epa.gov/iaq/schools/perform-ance.html.

4. M. Moses, E. Johnson, W. Anger, V. Burse, S. Horstman, and R. Jackson, "Environmental Equity and Pesticide Exposure," *Toxicology and Industrial Health,* 1993, *9,* 913-959 (pesticides); Brody and others, "Environmental Justice for All" (lead).

5. Childstats, Federal Interagency Forum on Child and Family Statistics, *Federal Agencies Report on Nation's Children: Teen Smoking, Birth Rates Down, Children's and Youth's Diets Need Improvement,* taken from www.childstats.gov/ac1999/pressrel.asp.

6. G. T. Fujiura and K. Yamaki, "Trends in Demography of Childhood Poverty and Disability," *Exceptional Children,* 2000, *66,* 187-199.

7. D. Frank, N. Roos, A. Meyers, M. Napoleone, K. Peterson, A. Cather, and L. Cupples, "Seasonal Variation in Weight for Age in a Pediatric Emergency Room," *Public Health Reports*, 1995, *111*, 366–371.

8. B. Hart and T. Risley, *Meaningful Differences in the Everyday Experiences of Young American Children* (Baltimore: Brookes Publishing, 1995).

9. R. Coley, *An Uneven Start: Indicators of Inequality in School Readiness* (Princeton, NJ: Educational Testing Service, 2002).

10. E. Hoff, "The Specificity of Environmental Influence: Socioeconomic Status Affects Early Vocabulary Development via Maternal Speech," *Child Development*, 2003, *74*(5), 1368–1378.

11. "The Health of America's Middle Childhood Population," Policy Center fact sheets, available at http://youth.ucsf.edu/policycenter/publications.html. Hard copies can be requested at (415) 502-4856, or by e-mail at policy@itsa.ucsf.edu; Public Policy Analysis and Education Center for Middle Childhood and Adolescent Health, *Fact Sheet on Census Demographics: Middle Childhood* (San Francisco: Author, 2003).

12. U.S. Census Bureau, *Marital Status and Living Arrangements: March 1998* (Update). (Unpublished Tables—P20-514) (Washington, D.C.: U.S. Bureau of the Census, 1998). Retrieved December 2002 from www.census.gov/prod/99pubs/p20-514u.pdf.

13. G. R. Weitoft, A. Hjern, B. Haglund, and M. Rosen, "Mortality, Severe Morbidity, and Injury in Children Living with Single Parents in Sweden: A Population-Based Study," *Lancet*, 2003, *361*(9354), 289–295.

14. J. D. McLeod and M. J. Shanahan, "Poverty, Parenting, and Children's Mental Health," *American Sociological Review*, 1993, *58*, 351–366.

15. J. M. Fields and L. M. Casper, *America's Families and Living Arrangements: March 2000*. U.S. Census Bureau Current Population Reports, P20-537, (Washington, D.C.: U.S. Government Printing Office, 2001).

16. M. Federman, T. Garner, K. Short, W. Cutter, D. Levine, D. McGough, and M. McMillin, "What Does It Mean to Be Poor in America?" *Monthly Labor Review*, 1996, 3–17; E. Jensen, S. James, T. Boyce, and S. Hartnett, "The Family Routine Inventory: Development and Validation," *Social Science and Medicine*, 1983, *17*, 201–211.

17. B. Attar, N. Guerra, and P. Tolan, "Neighborhood Disadvantage, Stressful Life Events, and Adjustment in Urban Elementary School Children," *Journal of Clinical Child Psychology*, 1994, *23*, 391–400.

18. A. Macpherson, I. Roberts, and I. B. Pless, "Children's Exposure to Traffic and Pedestrian Injuries," *American Journal of Public Health*, 1998, *88*, 1840–1843.

19. J. Sinclair, G. Pettit, A. Harrist, K. Dodge, and J. Bates, "Encounters with Aggressive Peers in Early Childhood: Frequency, Age Differences and Correlates of Risk for Behavior Problems," *International Journal of Behavioral Development*, 1994, *17*, 675–696.

20. R. W. Larson and S. Verma, "How Children and Adolescents Spend Time Across the World: Work, Play, and Developmental Opportunities," *Psychological Bulletin*, 1999, *125*(6), 701–736; U.S. Department of Health and Human Services, *Trends in the Well-Being of America's Children and Youth* (Washington D.C.: U.S. Government Printing Office, 2000).

21. K. Moreland, S. Wing, A. Diez-Rioux, and C. Poole, "Neighborhood Characteristics Associated with the Location of Food Stores and Food Service Places,"

American Journal of Preventative Medicine, 2002, *22,* 23–29; K. Glantz, M. Basil, E. Maibach, J. Goldberg, and D. Snyder, "Why Americans Eat What They Do: Taste, Nutrition, Cost, Convenience, and Weight Control Concerns as Influences on Food Consumption," *Journal of American Dietetic Association,* 1998, *98,* 1118–1126; K. Alaimo, C. Olsen, and E. Frongillo, "Food Insufficiency, Family Income and Health in the U.S. Preschool and School-Aged Children," *American Journal of Public Health,* 2001, *91,* 781–786.

22. J. Miller and S. Korenman, "Poverty and Children's Nutritional Status in the United States," *American Journal of Epidemiology,* 1994, *140,* 233–243.

23. R. Molteni, R. J. Barnard, Z. Ying, C. K. Roberts, and F. Gomez-Pinilla, "A High-Fat, Refined Sugar Diet Reduces Hippocampal Brain-Derived Neurotrophic Factor, Neuronal Plasticity, and Learning," *Neuroscience,* 2002, *112*(4), 803–814.

24. N. Atzaba-Poria, A. Pike, and K. Deater-Deckard, "Do Risk Factors for Problem Behaviour Act in a Cumulative Manner? An Examination of Ethnic Minority and Majority Children Through an Ecological Perspective," *Journal of Child Psychology and Psychiatry, and Allied Disciplines,* 2004, *45*(4), 707–718.

25. R. Payne, *Poverty: A Framework for Understanding and Working with Students and Adults from Poverty,* rev. ed. (Highlands, Texas: Aha Process, 1995).

26. K. Bolger, D. Patterson, W. Thompson, and J. Kupersmidt, "Psychosocial Adjustment Among Children Experiencing Persistent and Intermittent Family Economic Hardship," *Child Development,* 1995, *66,* 1107–1129.

27. R. H. Bradley and R. F. Corwyn, "Socioeconomic Status and Child Development," *Annual Review of Psychology,* 2002, *53,* 371–399.

28. T. Leventhal and J. Brooks-Gunn, "A Randomized Study of Neighborhood Effects on Low-Income Children's Educational Outcomes," *Developmental Psychology,* 2004, *40*(4), 488–507.

29. L. Benveniste, M. Carnoy, and R. Rothstein, *All Else Equal* (New York: Routledge-Farmer, 2003).

30. Coley, *An Uneven Start.*

31. U.S. Department of Health and Human Services, *Trends in the Well-Being of America's Children and Youth.*

32. K. E. Smith, L. E. Bass, and J. M. Fields, *Child Well-Being: Indicators From the SIPP (Survey of Income and Program Participation),* Population Division working paper no. 24 (Washington, D.C.: U.S. Bureau of the Census, April 1998).

33. R. Ingersoll, "The Problem of Underqualified Teachers in American Secondary Schools," *Educational Researcher,* 1999, *28,* 26–37.

34. G. Gallup, *America's Youth in the 1990s* (Princeton, NJ: Gallup Institute, 1993).

35. K. C. Koenen, T. E. Moffitt, A. Caspi, A. Taylor, and S. Purcell, "Domestic Violence Is Associated with Environmental Suppression of IQ in Young Children," *Development and Psychopathology,* 2003, *15*(2), 297–311.

36. G. J. Duncan and J. Brooks-Gunn, *Consequences of Growing Up Poor* (New York: Russell Sage Foundation, 1997); E. M. Lewit, D. L. Terman, and R. E. Behrman, "Children and Poverty: Analysis and Recommendations," *The Future of Children,* 1997, *7,* 4–24.

37. C. Marder and R. Cox, "More Than a Label: Characteristics of Youth with Disabilities," in *Youth with Disabilities: How Are They Doing?* eds. M. Wagner, L. Newman, R. D'Amico, E. D. Jay, P. Butler-Nalin, C. Marder, and R. Cox (Menlo Park, CA: SRI International, 1991).

38. U.S. Census Bureau, *Income 1999,* 2001. Available at www.census.gov/hhes/income/income99/99tablea.html.

39. M. Duyme, A. C. Dumaret, and S. Tomkiewicz, "How Can We Boost IQs of 'Dull Children'?: A Late Adoption Study," *Proceedings of the National Academy of Sciences of the United States of America,* 1999, *96*(15), 8790–8794.

40. C. Jiaxu and Y. Weiyi, "Influence of Acute and Chronic Treadmill Exercise on Rat Brain Pomc Gene Expression," *Medicine & Science in Sports & Exercise,* 2000, *32*(5), 954–957; E. Rossi, *Psychobiology of Gene Expression* (New York: W. W. Norton, 2002).

41. B. Nankova and E. Sabban, "Multiple Signalling Pathways Exist in the Stress-Triggered Regulation of Gene Expression for Catecholamine Biosynthetic Enzymes and Several Neuropeptides in the Rat Adrenal Medulla," *Acta Physiologica Scandinavica,* 1999, *167*(1), 1–9; K. Anokhin, A. Ryabinin, and K. Sudakov, "Expression of the c-fos Gene in the Mouse Brain During the Acquisition of Defensive Behavior Habits," *Neuroscience and Behavioral Physiology,* 2001, *31*(2), 139–143.

42. Rossi, *The Psychobiology of Gene Expression,* p. 4.

43. S. Oden, L. Schweinhart, and D. Weikart, *Into Adulthood: A Study of the Effects of Head Start* (Ypsilanti, MI: High/Scope Press, 2000).

44. U.S. Department of Health and Human Services, Administration for Children and Families, Head Start Bureau, *Head Start Program Fact Sheet-Fiscal Year 2002,* 2003. Retrieved August 15, 2005, from www.acf.hhs.gov/programs/hsb/research/2003.htm.

45. L. J. Schweinhart, H. V. Barnes, and D. P. Weikart, *Significant Benefits: The High/Scope Perry Preschool Study Through Age 27* (Monographs of the High/Scope Educational Research Foundation) (Ypsilanti, MI: High/Scope Press, 1993).

46. W. S. Barnett, "Long-Term Effects on Cognitive Development and School Success," in *Early Care and Education for Children in Poverty,* eds. W. S. Barnett and S. S. Boocock (Albany: State University of New York Press, 1998).

47. S. P. Schinke, K. C. Cole, and S. R. Poulin, "Enhancing the Educational Achievement of At-Risk Youth," *Prevention Science: The Official Journal of the Society for Prevention Research,* 2000, *1*(1), 51–60.

48. J. Mahoney, H. Lord, and E. Carryl, "An Ecological Analysis of After-School Program Participation and the Development of Academic Performance and Motivational Attributes for Disadvantaged Children," *Child Development,* 2005, *76*(4), 811–825.

49. P. A. Lauer, M. Akiba, S. Wilkerson, H. S. Apthorp, D. Snow, and M. Martin-Glenn, *The Effectiveness of Out-of-School-Time Strategies in Assisting Low-Achieving Students in Reading and Mathematics: A Research Synthesis,* Updated ed. (Aurora, CO: Mid-continent Research for Education and Learning, 2004). Posted December 11, 2003, retrieved December 5, 2005, from www.mcrel.org/newsroom/OSTsynthesis.asp.

50. K. M. Riggins-Caspers, R. J. Cadoret, J. F. Knutson, and D. Langbehn, "Biology-Environment Interaction and Evocative Biology-Environment Correlation: Contributions of Harsh Discipline and Parental Psychopathology to Problem Adolescent Behaviors," *Behavior Genetics,* 2003, *33*(3), 205–220.

51. Special Education Elementary Longitudinal Study (SEELS), *The Children We Serve: The Demographic Characteristics of Elementary and Middle School Students with Disabilities and Their Households* (Menlo Park, CA: SRI International, 2002). Prepared by Mary Wagner, Camille Marder, and Jose Blackorby, with Denise Cardoso, for

the Office of Special Education Programs, U.S. Department of Education, September, SRI Project P10656.

52. SEELS, *The Children We Serve.*

53. U.S. Department of Health and Human Services, *Mental Health: A Report of the Surgeon General-Executive Summary* (Rockville, MD: U.S. Department of Health and Human Services, National Institute of Mental Health, 1999).

54. Fujiura and Yamaki, "Trends in Demography of Childhood Poverty and Disability."

55. SEELS, *The Children We Serve.*

56. W. Schneider, E. Roth, and M. Ennemoser, "Training Phonological Skills and Letter Knowledge in Children at Risk for Dyslexia: A Comparison of Three Kindergarten Intervention Programs," *Journal of Educational Psychology,* 2000, 92(2), 284–295.

57. E. Temple, G. Deutsch, R. Poldrack, S. Miller, P. Tallal, M. Merzenich, and J. Gabrieli, "Neural Deficits in Children with Dyslexia Ameliorated by Behavioral Remediation: Evidence from Functional MRI," *Proceedings of the National Academy of Sciences of the United States of America,* 2003, 100(5), 2860–2865.

58. L. Robison, T. Skaer, D. Sclar, and R. Galin, "Is Attention Deficit Hyperactivity Disorder Increasing Among Girls in the U.S.?: Trends in Diagnosis and the Prescribing of Stimulants," *CNS Drugs,* 2002, 16(2), 129–137.

59. G. August, G. Realmuto, A. MacDonald, S. Nugent, and R. Crosby, "Prevalence of ADHD and Comorbid Disorders Among Elementary School Children Screened for Disruptive Behavior," *Journal of Abnormal Child Psychology,* 1966, 24(5), 571–595.

60. B. Lipton, *The Biology of Belief* (Santa Rosa, CA: Mountain of Love, 2005).

61. E. Chang, *Optimism & Pessimism: Implications for Theory, Research and Practice* (Washington D.C.: American Psychological Association, 2001).

CHAPTER SIX

1. M. Kalbfleisch, "Functional Neural Anatomy of Talent," *The Anatomical Record,* 2004, 277B(1), 21–36.

2. R. Plomin and J. DeFries, "The Genetics of Cognitive Abilities and Disabilities," *Scientific American,* 1998, 278(5), 62–69.

3. E. Winner, "The Origins and Ends of Giftedness," *American Psychology,* 2000, 55(1), 159–169.

4. N. Andreasen, *The Creating Brain: The Neuroscience of Genius* (New York: Dana Press, 2005).

5. J. S. Renzulli, "What Makes Giftedness? Reexamining a Definition," *Phi Delta Kappan,* 1978, 60, 180–184, 261.

6. T. Leventhal and J. Brooks-Gunn, "A Randomized Study of Neighborhood Effects on Low-Income Children's Educational Outcomes," *Developmental Psychology,* 2004, 40(4), 488–507.

7. K. S. Chan and M. K. Kitano, "Demographic Characteristics of Exceptional Asian Students," in *Exceptional Asian Children and Youth,* eds. M. K. Kitano and P. C. Chinn (Reston, VA: The Council for Exceptional Children, 1986).

8. J. R. Flynn, *Asian-Americans: Achievement Beyond IQ* (Mahwah, NJ: Lawrence Erlbaum Associates, 1991).

9. U. Neisser, G. Boodoo, T. J. Bouchard, A. W. Boykin, N. Brody, S. J. Ceci, D. F.

Halpern, J. C. Loehlin, R. Perloff, R. J. Sternberg, and S. Urbina, "Intelligence: Knowns and Unknowns," *American Psychologist,* 1996, *51,* 77–101.

10. J. Brooks-Gunn, P. K. Klebanov, and G. J. Duncan, "Ethnic Differences in Children's Intelligence Test Scores: Role of Economic Deprivation, Home Environment, and Maternal Characteristics," *Child Development,* 1996, *67*(2), 396–408.

11. J. C. Stanley, "Boys and Girls Who Reason Well Mathematically," *Ciba Foundation Symposium,* 1993, *178,* 119–134; discussion 134–138.

12. S. M. Reis, "Obstacles, Challenges and Choices Faced by Smart Girls," *Proceedings: The National Association of Principals of Schools for Girls,* 2000, 51–101.

13. K. A. Ericsson and P. F. Delaney, "Working Memory and Expert Performance," in *Working Memory and Thinking,* eds. R. H. Logie and K. J. Gilhooly (Mahwah, NJ: Lawrence Erlbaum Associates, 1998).

14. K. A. Ericsson, "Attaining Excellence Through Deliberate Practice: Insights from the Study of Expert Performance," in *The Pursuit of Excellence in Education,* ed. M. Ferrari (Mahwah, NJ: Lawrence Erlbaum Associates, 2000), 21–55.

15. R. Hyllegard, "Parental Attribution of Artistic Ability in Talented Children," *Perceptual and Motor Skills,* 2000, *91*(3, pt. 2), 1134–1144.

16. M.J.A. Howe, "The Childhood and Early Lives of Geniuses: Combining Psychological and Biographical Evidence," in *The Road to Excellence: The Acquisition of Expert Performance in the Arts and Sciences, Sports and Games,* ed. K. A. Ericsson (Mahwah, NJ: Lawrence Erlbaum Associates, 1996).

17. R. J. Haier, R. E. Jung, R. A. Yeo, K. Head, and M. T. Alkire, "Structural Brain Variation and General Intelligence," *Neuroimage,* 2004, *23*(1), 425–433.

18. D. M. Ivanovic, B. P. Leiva, H. T. Perez, M. G. Olivares, N. S. Diaz, M. S. Urrutia, A. F. Almagia, T. D. Toro, P. T. Miller, E. O. Bosch, and C. G. Larrain, "Head Size and Intelligence, Learning, Nutritional Status and Brain Development," *Neuropsychologia,* 2004, *42*(8), 1118–1131.

19. F. Castellanos and M. Acosta, "The Neuroanatomy of Attention Deficit/ Hyperactivity Disorder," *Revista de neurologia,* 2002, *38*(1), S131–S136.

20. N. S. Orzhekhovskaia, "The Cytoarchitectonic Characteristics of the Frontal Fields of the Brain in Gifted People," *Morfologiia,* 1996, *109*(3), 7–9; M. Soffie, K. Hahn, E. Terao, and F. Eclancher, "Behavioural and Glial Changes in Old Rats Following Environmental Enrichment," *Behavioral Brain Research,* 1999, *101,* 37–49.

21. M. Diamond, A. Schiebel, G. Murphy, and T. Harvey, "On the Brain of a Scientist: Albert Einstein," *Experimental Neurology,* 1985, *88*(1), 198–204.

22. C. Abraham, *Possessing Genius: The Bizarre Odyssey of Einstein's Brain* (New York: St. Martin's Press, 2001).

23. Orzhekhovskaia, "The Cytoarchitectonic Characteristics,"; Soffie and others, "Behavioural and Glial Changes in Old Rats."

24. I. Bogolepova and L. Malofeeva, "Variability in the Structure of Field 39 of the Lower Parietal Area of the Cortex in the Left and Right Hemispheres of Adult Human Brains," *Neuroscience and Behavioral Physiology,* 2004, *34*(4), 363–367.

25. I. Bogolepova, "The Cytoarchitectonic Characteristics of the Speech Center of the Brain in Gifted People in the Plan to Study Individual Variability of Human Brain Structure," *Morfologiia,* 1994, *106*(4–6), 31–38.

26. D. J. Felleman and D. C. Van Essen, "Distributed Hierarchical Processing in the Primate Cerebral Cortex," *Cerebral Cortex,* 1991, *1*(1), 1–47.

27. J. D. Churchill, A. W. Grossman, S. A. Irwin, R. Galvez, A. Y. Klintsova, I. J. Weiler, and W. T. Greenough, "A Converging-Methods Approach to Fragile X Syndrome," *Developmental Psychobiology*, 2002, *40*(3), 323-338.

28. K. J. Friston, "Testing for Anatomically Specified Regional Effects," *Human Brain Mapping*, 1997, *5*(2), 133-136; G. Tononi, O. Sporns, and G. M. Edelman, "Reentry and the Problem of Integrating Multiple Cortical Areas: Simulation of Dynamic Integration in the Visual System," *Cerebral Cortex*, 1992, *2*(4), 310-335.

29. R. J. Haier, B. V. Siegel Jr., A. MacLachlan, E. Soderling, S. Lottenberg, and M. S. Buchsbaum, "Regional Glucose Metabolic Changes After Learning a Complex Visuospatial/Motor Task: A Positron Emission Tomographic Study," *Brain Research*, 1992, *570*(1-2), 134-143.

30. L. A. Baker, P. A. Vernon, and H. Z. Ho, "The Genetic Correlation Between Intelligence and Speed of Information Processing," *Behavior Genetics*, 1991, *21*(4), 351-367.

31. F. V. Rijsdijk, D. I. Boomsma, and P. A. Vernon, "Genetic Analysis of Peripheral Nerve Conduction Velocity in Twins," *Behavior Genetics*, 1995, *25*(4), 341-348.

32. M. Houlihan, R. Stelmack, and K. Campbell, "Intelligence and the Effects of Perceptual Processing Demands, Task Difficulty and Processing Speed on P300, Reaction Time and Movement Time," *Intelligence*, 1998, *26*(1), 9-25.

33. C. R. Brumback, K. A. Low, G. Gratton, and M. Fabiani, "Sensory ERPs Predict Differences in Working Memory Span and Fluid Intelligence," *Neuroreport*, 2004, *15*(2), 373-376.

34. W. Gruhn, N. Galley, and C. Kluth, "Do Mental Speed and Musical Abilities Interact?" *Annals of the New York Academy of Sciences*, 2003, *999*, 485-496.

35. M. M. Mesulam, "From Sensation to Cognition," *Brain*, 1998, *121*(6), 1013-1052.

36. H. Singh and M. O'Boyle, "Interhemispheric Interaction During Global-Local Processing in Mathematically Gifted Adolescents, Average-Ability Youth, and College Students," *Neuropsychology*, 2004, *18*(2), 371-377.

37. F. G. Ashby, A. M. Isen, and A. U. Turken, "A Neuropsychological Theory of Positive Affect and Its Influence on Cognition," *Psychological Review*, 1999, *106*(3), 529-550.

38. A. C. Neubauer, R. H. Grabner, H. H. Freudenthaler, J. F. Beckmann, and J. Guthke, "Intelligence and Individual Differences in Becoming Neurally Efficient," *Acta Psychologica*, 2004, *116*(1), 55-74.

39. Brumback and others, "Sensory ERPs Predict Differences in Working Memory Span."

40. T. W. Frazier, H. A. Demaree, and E. A. Youngstrom, "Meta-Analysis of Intellectual and Neuropsychological Test Performance in Attention-Deficit/Hyperactivity Disorder," *Neuropsychology*, 2004, *18*(3), 543-555.

41. J. Alexander, M. O'Boyle, and C. Benbow, "Developmentally Advanced EEG Alpha Power in Gifted Male and Female Adolescents," *International Journal of Psychophysiology*, 1966, *23*(1-2), 25-31.

42. N. Jausovec and K. Jausovec, "Differences in Induced Brain Activity During the Performance of Learning and Working-Memory Tasks Related to Intelligence," *Brain and Cognition*, 2004, *54*(1), 65-74.

43. A. A. Gonzalez-Garrido, J. L. Ruiz-Sandoval, F. R. Gomez-Velazquez, J. L. de Alba, and T. Villasenor-Cabrera, "Hypercalculia in Savant Syndrome: Central Executive Failure?" *Archives of Medical Research*, 2002, *33*(6), 586-589.

44. M. W. O'Boyle, J. E. Alexander, and C. P. Benbow, "Enhanced Right Hemisphere Activation in the Mathematically Precocious: A Preliminary EEG Investigation," *Brain Cognition*, 1991, *17*(2), 138–153.

45. W. W. O'Boyle, H. S. Gill, C. P. Benbow, and J. E. Alexander, "Concurrent Finger-Tapping in Mathematically Gifted Males: Evidence for Enhanced Right Hemisphere Involvement During Linguistic Processing," *Cortex*, 1994, *30*(3), 519–526.

46. D. G. Fischer, D. Hunt, and B. S. Randhawa, "Spontaneous EEG Correlates of Intellectual Functioning in Talented and Handicapped Adolescents," *Perceptual and Motor Skills*, 1982, *54*(3), 751–762.

47. M. R. Peterson, D. Balzarini, M. Bodner, E. G. Jones, T. Phillips, D. Richardson, and G. L. Shaw, "Innate Spatial-Temporal Reasoning and the Identification of Genius," *Neurological Research*, 2004, *26*(1), 2–8.

48. A. W. Snyder, E. Mulcahy, J. L. Taylor, D. J. Mitchell, P. Sachdev, and S. C. Gandevia, "Savant-Like Skills Exposed in Normal People by Suppressing the Left Fronto-Temporal Lobe," *Journal of Integrated Neuroscience*, 2003, *2*(2), 149–158.

49. Brumback and others, "Sensory ERPs Predict Differences in Working Memory Span."

50. J. F. Lubar, C. A. Mann, D. M. Gross, and M. S. Shively, "Differences in Semantic Event-Related Potentials in Learning-Disabled, Normal, and Gifted Children," *Biofeedback and Self-Regulation*, 1992, *17*(1), 41–57.

51. A. Raine, C. Reynolds, P. Venables, and S. Mednick, "Stimulation Seeking and Intelligence: A Prospective Longitudinal Study," *Journal of Personality & Social Psychology*, 2002, *82*(4), 663–674.

52. D. Ostatnikova, M. Dohnanyiova, A. Mataseje, Z. Putz, J. Laznibatova, and J. Hajek, "Salivary Testosterone and Cognitive Ability in Children," *Bratislavske Lekarske Listy*, 2000, *101*(8), 470–473.

53. T. C. Neylan, "Pathophysiology of Schizophrenia: Dopamine Hypothesis," *The Journal of Neuropsychiatry and Clinical Neurosciences*, 1996, *8*(2), 222.

54. S. Castner, G. Williams, and P. Goldman-Rakic, "Reversal of Antipsychotic-Induced Working Memory Deficits by Short-Term Dopamine D1 Receptor Stimulation," *Science*, 2000, *287*(5460), 2020.

55. S. Bandyopadhyay, C. Gonzalez-Islas, and J. J. Hablitz, "Dopamine Enhances Spatiotemporal Spread of Activity in Rat Prefrontal Cortex," *Journal of Neurophysiology*, February 2004, *93*(2), 864–872; P. R. Montague, S. E. Hyman, and J. D. Cohen, "Computational Roles for Dopamine in Behavioural Control," *Nature*, 2004, *431*(7010), 760–767.

56. H. F. Clarke, J. W. Dalley, H. S. Crofts, T. W. Robbins, and A. C. Roberts, "Cognitive Inflexibility After Prefrontal Serotonin Depletion," *Science*, 2004, *304*(5672), 878–880.

57. L. K. Silverman and L. P. Leviton, "Advice to Parents in Search of the Perfect Program," *The Gifted Child Today*, 1991, *14*(6), 31–34.

58. S. Winebrenner, *Teaching Gifted Kids in the Regular Classroom* (Minneapolis: Free Spirit Press, 2001).

59. J. Davidson and B. Davidson, *Genius Denied: How to Stop Wasting Our Brightest Young Minds* (New York: Simon & Schuster, 2004).

60. C. Jencks, *Who Gets Ahead? The Determinants of Economic Success in America* (New York: Basic Books, 1979).

CHAPTER SEVEN

1. M. Diamond and J. Hopson, *Magic Trees of the Mind* (New York: Penguin-Dutton, 1998).

2. L. Miller and R. Bizzell, "Long-Term Effects of Four Pre-School Programs: Sixth, Seventh, and Eighth Grades," *Child Development,* 1983, *54,* 727–741.

3. F. Gomez-Pinilla, L. Dao, and V. So, "Physical Exercise Induces FGF-2 and Its mRNA in the Hippocampus," *Brain Research,* 1997, *764*(1–2), 1–8.

4. H. van Praag, B. R. Christie, T. J. Sejnowski, and F. H. Gage, "Running Enhances Neurogenesis, Learning, and Long-Term Potentiation in Mice," *Proceedings of the National Academy of Science,* November 1999, *96*(23), 13427–13431; K. Fabel, K. Fabel, B. Tam, D. Kaufer, A. Baiker, N. Simmons, C. J. Kuo, and T. D. Palmer, "VEGF Is Necessary for Exercise-Induced Adult Hippocampal Neurogenesis," *The European Journal of Neuroscience,* 2003, *18*(10), 2803–2812.

5. D. Sutoo and K. Akiyama, "Regulation of Brain Function by Exercise," *Neurobiology of Disease,* 2003, *13*(1), 1–14.

6. T. Harada, S. Okagawa, and K. Kubota, "Jogging Improved Performance of a Behavioral Branching Task: Implications for Prefrontal Activation," *Neuroscience Research,* 2004, *49*(3), 325–337.

7. M. S. Tremblay, J. W. Inman, and J. D. Williams, "The Relationship Between Physical Activity, Self-Esteem, and Academic Achievement in 12-Year-Old Children," *Pediatric Exercise Science,* 2000, *12,* 312–324; M. Wagner, *The Effects of Isotonic Resistance Exercise on Aggression Variable in Adult Male Inmates in the Texas Department of Criminal Justice,* Texas A & M University: UMI Order Number AAM9701731, Dissertation Abstracts International Section A: Humanities and Social Sciences: February 1997, p. 57 (8A): 3442.

8. J. F. Sallis, T. L. McKenzie, J. E. Alcaraz, B. Kolody, N. Faucette, and M. F. Hovell, "The Effects of a Two-Year Physical Education Program (SPARK) on Physical Activity and Fitness in Elementary School Students," *American Journal of Public Health,* 1997, *87,* 1328–1334; T. Dwyer, J. F. Sallis, L. Blizzard, R. Lazarus, and K. Dean, "Relation of Academic Performance to Physical Activity and Fitness in Children," *Pediatric Exercise Science,* 2001, *13,* 225–238.

9. S. G. Stella, A. P. Vilar, C. Lacroix, M. Fisberg, R. F. Santos, M. T. Mello, and S. Tufik, "Effects of Type of Physical Exercise and Leisure Activities on the Depression Scores of Obese Brazilian Adolescent Girls," *Brazilian Journal of Medical Biology Resources,* November 2005, *38*(11), 1683–1689; C. Nabkasorn, N. Miyai, A. Sootmongkol, S. Junprasert, H. Yamamoto, M. Arita, and K. Miyashita, "Effects of Physical Exercise on Depression, Neuroendocrine Stress Hormones and Physiological Fitness in Adolescent Females with Depressive Symptoms," *European Journal of Public Health,* August 2005.

10. California Department of Education, *California Physical Fitness Testing 2002,* California Department of Education, Standards and Assessment Division, prepared January 2003. Retrieved March 13, 2006, from www.cde.ca.gov/ta/tg/pf/documents/rptgov2002.pdf.

11. J. A. Grunbaum, L. Kann, S. A. Kinchen, B. Williams, J. G. Ross, R. Lowry, L. Kolbe, "Youth Risk Behavior Surveillance (in U.S. of A.)," *Journal of School Health,* 2002 Oct., *72*(8), 313–328.

12. B. Sibley and J. Etnier, "The Effects of Physical Activity on Cognition in Children:

A Meta-Analysis," *Medicine & Science in Sports & Exercise,* 2002, *34*(5) Supplement 1, S214; A. Pelligrini and C. Bohn, "The Role of Recess in Children's Cognitive Performance," *Educational Researcher,* 2003, *34*(1) 13–19.

13. E. Gould, P. Tanapat, T. Rydel, and N. Hastings, "Regulation of Hippocampal Neurogenesis in Adulthood," *Biological Psychiatry,* 2000, *48,* 715–720; G. Kempermann, "Why New Neurons? Possible Functions for Adult Hippocampal Neurogenesis," *Journal of Neuroscience,* 2002, *22*(3), 635–638.

14. C. Dufouil, A. Alperovitch, and C. Tzourio, "Influence of Education on the Relationship Between White Matter Lesions and Cognition," *Neurology,* March 2003, *60*(5), 831–836.

15. M. Kilgard and M. Merzenich, "Cortical Map Reorganization Enabled by Nucleus Basalis Activity," *Science,* 1998, *279,* 1714–1718.

16. E. Ahissar, E. Vaadia, M. Ahissar, H. Bergman, A. Arielli, and M. Abeles, "Dependence of Cortical Plasticity on Correlated Activity of Single Neurons and on Behavioral Context," *Science,* 1992, *257,* 1412–1415.

17. C. A. Tomlinson, *The Differentiated Classroom: Responding to the Needs of All Learners* (Alexandria, VA: Association for Supervision and Curriculum Development, 1999).

18. S. C. Cook and C. L. Wellman, "Chronic Stress Alters Dendritic Morphology in Rat Medial Prefrontal Cortex," *Journal of Neurobiology,* 2004, *60*(2), 236–248.

19. E. Jensen, *Arts with the Brain in Mind* (Alexandria, VA: Association for Supervision and Curriculum Development, 2001).

20. National Association of Music Educators, *Scores of Students in the Arts,* SAT scores compiled and contrasted from the College Board, 2004. Available at www.menc.org/information/advocate/sat.html.

21. C. Yang, C. Huang, and K. Hsui, "Behavioral Stress Modifies Hippocampal Synaptic Plasticity Through Corticosterone-Induced Sustained Extracellular Signal-Regulated Kinase/Mitogen-Activated Protein Kinase Activation," *The Journal of Neuroscience,* 2004, *24*(49), 11029–11034.

22. Cook and Wellman, "Chronic Stress Alters Dendritic Morphology."

23. A. Hoffman, *Schools, Violence, and Society* (Westport, CT: Praeger Publishers/Greenwood Publishing Group, 1996).

24. D. Schwartz and A. Gorman, "Community Violence Exposure and Children's Academic Functioning," *Journal of Educational Psychology,* 2003, *95*(1), 163–173.

25. P. Pratt, F. Tallis, and M. Eysenck, "Information-Processing, Storage Characteristics and Worry," *Behaviour Research and Therapy,* 1997, *35*(11), 1015–1033.

26. T. Schmader and M. Johns, "Converging Evidence That Stereotype Threat Reduces Working Memory Capacity," *Journal of Personality and Social Psychology,* 2003, *85*(3), 440–452.

27. B. J. Kaplan, J. E. Fisher, S. G. Crawford, C. J. Field, and B. Kolb, "Improved Mood and Behavior During Treatment with a Mineral-Vitamin Supplement: An Open-Label Case Series of Children," *Journal of Child and Adolescent Psychopharmacology,* 2004, *14*(1), 115–122; F. Bellisle, "Effects of Diet on Behaviour and Cognition in Children," *The British Journal of Nutrition,* 2004, *92*(2), S227–S232.

28. S. J. Schoenthaler, I. D. Bier, K. Young, D. Nichols, and S. Jansenns, "The Effect of Vitamin-Mineral Supplementation on the Intelligence of American Schoolchildren: A Randomized, Double-Blind Placebo-Controlled Trial," *Journal of Alternative and Complementary Medicine,* 2000 Feb., *6*(1), 19–29.

29. National Center for Educational Statistics, *Digest of Education Statistics.* U.S.

Department of Education, 2004. Retrieved on September 2, 2005, from http://nces.ed.gov/programs/digest/do4/tables/dt04_002.asp

30. S. M. Reis and J. S. Renzulli, "Using Curriculum Compacting to Challenge the Above Average," *Educational Leadership,* 1992, *50*(2), 51-57.

31. R. G. Hacker and M. J. Rowe, "A Study of the Effects of an Organization Change from Streamlined to Mixed-Ability Classes Upon Science Classroom Instruction," *Journal of Research in Science Teaching,* 1993, *30*(3), 223-231.

32. J. S. Renzulli, "What Is This Thing Called Giftedness, and How Do We Develop It? A Twenty-Five-Year Perspective," *Journal for the Education of the Gifted,* 1999, *23*(1), 3-54.

33. B. DePorter and M. Hernacki, *Quantum Learning* (New York: Dell Paperbacks, 1992), p. 19.

34. W. Benn, *New Evaluation Study of Quantum Learning's Impact on Achievement in Multiple Settings.* An independent assessment by William Benn and Associates, Laguna Hills, California, July, 2003. Contact wbenngrants@aol.com.

35. T. Jernigan, *Imaging the Functioning Human Brain,* speaker address at the Brain Expo conference in San Diego, California, January 19, 2003.

CHAPTER EIGHT

1. J. Zull, *The Art of Changing the Brain* (Sterling, UT: Stylus Publishing, 2002); E. Jensen, *Teaching with the Brain in Mind* (Alexandria, VA: Association for Supervision and Curriculum Development, 2005.

2. K. Rogers, "Grouping the Gifted and Talented," *Roeper Review,* 2002, *24*(4), 103-107.

3. J. S. Renzulli, *Five Dimensions of Differentiation,* keynote presentation at the 20th Annual Confratute Conference, Storrs, Connecticut, July 1997.

4. C. A. Tomlinson, *The Differentiated Classroom: Responding to the Needs of All Learners* (Alexandria, VA: Association for Supervision and Curriculum Development, 1999).

5. C. A. Tomlinson, "Differentiatied Instruction in the Regular Classroom: What Does It Mean? How Does It Look?" *Understanding our Gifted,* 2001, *14*(1), 3-6.

6. T. Schmader and M. Johns, "Converging Evidence That Stereotype Threat Reduces Working Memory Capacity," *Journal of Personality and Social Psychology,* 2003, *85*(3), 440-452.

7. C. Gooda, J. Aronson, and M. Inzlicht, "Improving Adolescents' Standardized Test Performance: An Intervention to Reduce the Effects of Stereotype Threat," *Journal of Applied Developmental Psychology,* 2003, *24*(6), 645-662.

8. L. Oczkus, *Reciprocal Teaching at Work: Strategies for Improving Reading Comprehension* (Newark, DE: International Reading Association, 2003).

9. A. S. Palincsar and A. Brown, "Reciprocal Teaching of Comprehension-Fostering and Comprehension Monitoring Activities," *Cognition and Instruction,* 1984, *1*(2), 117-175.

10. Oczkus, *Reciprocal Teaching at Work.*

11. W. Glasser, *The Quality School* (New York: HarperCollins, 1998).

12. S. M. Reis, D. E. Burns, and J. S. Renzulli, *Curriculum Compacting: The Complete Guide to Modifying the Regular Curriculum for High Ability Students* (Mansfield Center, CT: Creative Learning Press, 1992); S. M. Reis, K. L. Westberg, J. Kulikowich, F. Calliard, T. Hébert, J. H. Purcell, J. Rogers, J. Smist, and J. Plucker, *Why Not Let High Ability Students Start School in January? The Curriculum Compacting Study,* Research monograph 93106 (Storrs, CT: The National Research Center on the Gifted and Talented, University of Connecticut, 1992).

13. S. J. Lynch, "Fast-Paced High School Science for Academically Talented: A 6-Year Perspective," *Gifted Child Quarterly*, 1992, *36*, 147–154; C. J. Mills, K. E. Ablard, and S. J. Lynch, "Academically Talented Students' Preparation for Advanced-Level Coursework After Individually-Paced Precalculus Class," *Journal for the Education of the Gifted*, 1992, *16*, 2–17.

14. C. Shields, "A Comparison Study of Student Attitudes and Perceptions in Homogeneous and Heterogeneous Classrooms," *Roeper Review*, 2002, *24*(3), 115–119.

15. J. S. Renzulli, *How to Develop an Authentic Enrichment Cluster* (Storrs, CT: National Research Center on the Gifted and Talented, University of Connecticut, 1997).

16. V. Vaughn, J. Feldhusen, J. Asher, "Meta-Analysis and Review of Research on Pull-Out Programs in Gifted Education," *Gifted Child Quarterly*, 1991, *35*(2), 92–98.

17. L. E. Brody and C. P. Benbow, "Accelerative Strategies: How Effective Are They for the Gifted? *Gifted Child Quarterly*, 1987 Summer, *31*(3), 105–110.

18. For example, see Vaughn and others, "Meta-Analysis and Review of Research on Pull-Out Programs"; D. Viadero, "Report Urges Acceleration for Gifted Students," *Education Week*, 2004 September, *24*(5), 5.

19. J. VanTassel-Baska and E. E. Brown, *An Analysis of Gifted Education Curriculum Models*, in *Methods and Materials for Teaching the Gifted*, ed. F. A. Karnes and S. M. Bean (Waco, TX: Prufrock Press, 2001).

20. J. A. Kulik and C. C. Kulik, "Meta-Analytic Findings on Grouping Programs," *Gifted Child Quarterly*, 1992, *36*, 73–77.

21. C. P. Benbow and D. Lubinski, *Intellectual Talent* (Baltimore: Johns Hopkins Press, 1996).

22. M. R. Coleman, "Exploring Options: Developing a Comprehensive Array of High School Services," *Gifted Child Today Magazine*, 1997 May–June, *20*(3), 32, 48.

23. E. Fiske (ed.), *Champions of Change: The Impact of Arts on Learning*, The Arts Education Partnership, 1999. Available at www.artsedge.kennedy-center.org/champions.

24. E. Jensen, *Arts with the Brain in Mind* (Alexandria, VA: Association for Supervision and Curriculum Development, 2001).

25. Quote from the Boston Arts Academy Website: www.boston-arts-academy.org/curriculum/curriculum.html.

26. M. Silverberg, E. Warner, M. Fong, and D. Goodwin, *National Assessment of Vocational Education: Final Report to Congress Executive Summary*. Available at www.ed.gov/rschstat/eval/sectech/nave/naveexesum.pdf.

27. M. R. Bulls and T. L. Riley, "Weaving Qualitatively Differentiated Units with the World Wide Web," *Gifted Child Today Magazine*, 1997 Jan.–Feb., *20*(1), 20–27,50.

28. R. Stiggins, *Student-Involved Assessment for Learning* (Upper Saddle River, NJ: Prentice-Hall, 2004).

29. I. Kirsch, *How Expectancies Shape Experiences* (Washington, D.C.: American Psychological Association, 1999).

30. J. F. Smutny, *Stand Up for Your Gifted Child* (Minneapolis: Free Spirit, 2001).

CHAPTER NINE

1. J. P. Shonkoff and D. A. Phillips, *From Neurons to Neighborhoods: The Science of Early Childhood Development* (Washington, D.C.: National Academy Press, 2000).

2. C. Ramey and S. Ramey, *Right from Birth* (New York: Goddard Press, 1999).

3. C. T. Ramey and S. L. Ramey, "Early Intervention and Early Experience," *American Psychologist*, 1998, *53*, 109–120.

4. A. Raine, C. Reynolds, P. Venables, and S. Mednick, "Stimulation Seeking and Intelligence: A Prospective Longitudinal Study," *Journal of Personality & Social Psychology*, 2002, 82(4), 663–674.

5. P. Hu and J. Young, *Summary of Travel Trends: 1995 Nationwide Personal Transportation Survey*, U.S. Department of Transportation, 1999. Retrieved November 2, 2005, from www.cta.ornl.gov/npts/1995/Doc/trends_report.pdf.

6. Bureau of Transportation Statistics, *National Household Travel Survey, 2001–2002*, National Transportation Library, 1999. Retrieved November 4, 2005 from www.bts.gov/publications/the_changing_face_of_transportation; H. Carter, "Couch Potato Culture Starts in the Cradle," *Newswise*, April 1999. Retrieved November 4, 2005 from www.dialogueworks.co.uk/newswise/months/april99/cojun.html.

7. Minnesota Learning Resource Center, MLRC Report: "A Chance to Grow," MLRC, 1800 Second Street NE, Minneapolis, Minnesota 55418, 2002, pp. 9–62. Access through www.actg.org or e-mail at mlrc@mail.actg.org.

8. P. Ekman, *Emotions Revealed* (New York: Henry Holt, 2003).

9. D. Siegel, *The Developing Mind* (New York: Guilford Press, 1999).

10. S. L. Ramey and C. T. Ramey, "Early Childhood Experiences and Developmental Competence," in *Securing the Future: Investing in Children from Birth to College*, eds. J. Waldfogel and S. Danziger (New York: Russell Sage Foundation, 2000), pp. 122–150).

11. A. N. Schore, "Attachment and the Regulation of the Right Brain," *Attachment and Human Development*, 2000, 2(1), 23–47.

12. J. Hodges and B. Tizard, "Social and Family Relationships of Ex-Institutional Adolescents," *Journal of Child Psychology and Psychiatry*, 1989, 30, 77–97.

13. M. Gunnar, "Early Adversity and the Development of Stress Reactivity and Regulation," in *The Minnesota Symposium on Child Psychology, vol. 31: The Effects of Early Adversity on Neurobehavioral Development*, ed. C. Nelson (Mahwah, NJ: Lawrence Erlbaum Associates, 2000).

14. S. Greenspan, *The Growth of the Mind* (New York: Basic Books, 1997).

15. J. Kim-Cohen, T. E. Moffitt, A. Caspi, and A. Taylor, "Genetic and Environmental Processes in Young Children's Resilience and Vulnerability to Socioeconomic Deprivation," *Child Development*, 2004, 75(3), 651–668.

16. S. Kastner, P. De Weerd, R. Desimone, and L. G. Ungerleider, "Mechanisms of Directed Attention in the Human Extrastriate Cortex as Revealed by Functional MRI," *Science*, 1998, 282(5386), 108–111.

17. J. Healy, *Failure to Connect* (New York: Simon & Schuster, 1999).

18. B. Hart and T. Risley, "American Parenting of Language-Learning Children: Persisting Differences in Family-Child Interactions Observed in Natural Home Environments," *Developmental Psychology*, 1992, 28(6), 1096–1105.

19. J. R. Katz and C. E. Snow, "Language Development in Early Childhood: The Role of Social Interaction," in *Infants and Toddlers in Out-of-Home Care*, eds. D. Cryer and T. Harms (Baltimore: Brookes Publishing, 2000).

20. M. H. Goldstein, A. P. King, and M. J. West, "Social Interaction Shapes Babbling: Testing Parallels Between Birdsong and Speech," *Proceedings of the National Academy of Sciences*, 2003 June, 100(13), 8030–8035.

21. M. H. Bornstein, M. O. Haynes, and K. M. Painter, "Sources of Child Vocabulary Competence: A Multivariate Model," *Journal of Child Language*, 1998, 25(2), 367–393.

22. V. Rideout and E. Vandewater, *Zero to Six: Electronic Media in the Lives of Infants and Toddlers and Preschoolers.* A Kaiser Foundation Report, 2003 Fall. Available at www.kff.org/entmedia/entmedia102803nr.cfm.

23. Rideout and Vandewater, *Zero to Six.*

24. V. C. Strasburger and E. Donnerstein, "Children, Adolescents, and the Media in the 21st Century," *Adolescent Medicine,* 2000, *11*(1), 51–68.

25. J. Murray, "The Impact of Televised Violence," *Hofstra Law Review,* 1994, *22,* 809–825.

26. J. Johnson, P. Cohen, E. Smailes, S. Kasen, and J. Brook, "Television Viewing and Aggressive Behavior During Adolescence and Adulthood," *Science,* 2002, *295*(5564), 2468–2471.

27. D. A. Christakis, F. J. Zimmerman, D. L. DiGiuseppe, and C. A. McCarty, "Early Television Exposure and Subsequent Attentional Problems in Children," *Pediatrics,* 2004, *113*(4), 708–713.

28. C. A. Anderson and B. J. Bushman, "Effects of Violent Video Games on Aggressive Behavior, Aggressive Cognition, Aggressive Affect, Physiological Arousal, and Prosocial Behavior: A Meta-Analytic Review of the Scientific Literature," *Psychological Science: A Journal of the American Psychological Society,* 2001, *12*(5), 353–359.

29. F. Rauscher, K. Robinson, and J. Jason, "Improved Maze Learning Through Early Music Exposure to Music in Rats," *Neurological Research,* 1998, *20,* 427–432.

30. T. Malyrenko, G. Kureav, E. Yu, and M. Khatova, "The Development of Brain Electrical Activity in 4-Year-Old Children by Long-Term Stimulation with Music," *Human Physiology,* 1996, *22,* 76–81.

31. C. Heim, P. M. Plotsky, and C. B. Nemeroff, "Importance of Studying the Contributions of Early Adverse Experience to Neurobiological Findings in Depression," *Neuropsychopharmacology,* 2004, *29*(4), 641–648.

32. J. M. Detemple, "Book Reading Styles of Low-Income Mothers with Preschoolers and Children's Later Literacy Skills," *Dissertation Abstracts International,* 1995 Jan., *55*(7-A), 1817.

33. L. M. Justice, "An Experimental Evaluation of an Intervention to Stimulate Written Language Awareness in Preschool Children from Low-Income Households," *Dissertation Abstracts International,* 2001 Feb., *61*(7-A), 2587.

34. M. Fox, S. Pac, B. Devaney, and L. Jankowski, "Feeding Infants and Toddlers Study: What Foods Are Infants and Toddlers Eating?" *Journal of the American Dietetic Association,* 2004, *104*(1), 22–30.

35. M. Georgieff and R. Rao, "The Role of Nutrition in Cognitive Development," in *Handbook of Developmental Cognitive Neuroscience,* eds. C. Nelson and M. Luciana (Cambridge: MIT Press, 2001).

36. M. Hermanussen and J. A. Tresguerres, "Does High Glutamate Intake Cause Obesity?" *Journal of Pediatrical Endocrinology Metabolism,* 2003 September, *16*(7), 965–968; J. A. Fernandez-Tresguerres Hernandez, "Effect of Monosodium Glutamate Given Orally on Appetite Control (A New Theory for the Obesity Epidemic)," *An R Acad Nac Medicine,* 2005, *122*(2), 341–355.

37. E. Pollitt, K. Gorman, P. Engle, J. Rivera, and R. Martorelli, "Nutrition in Early Life and the Fulfillment of Intellectual Potential," *Journal of Nutrition,* 1995, *125,* S1111–S1118.

38. P. Huttenlocher, *Neural Plasticity* (Cambridge, MA: Harvard University Press, 2002).

39. K. Hirsch-Pasek, D. Eyer, and R. M. Golinkoff, *Einstein Never Used Flash Cards: How Our Children Really Learn—And Why They Need to Play More and Memorize Less* (Emmaus, PA: Rodale Press, 2003).

40. Carnegie Report, *Years of Promise: A Comprehensive Learning Strategy for America's Children* (New York: Carnegie Corporation of New York, 1995).
41. Ramey and Ramey, *Right from Birth*.
42. J. Healy, *Your Child's Growing Mind* (New York: Broadway Books, Random House, 2004).
43. B. Strauch, *The Primal Teen* (New York: Doubleday, 2003); S. Feinstein, *Secrets of the Teenage Brain* (Thousand Oaks, CA: Sage/Corwin, 2003).
44. C. T. Ramey and S. L. Ramey, "Early Intervention and Early Experience," *American Psychologist*, 1998, *53*, 109–120.
45. C. T. Ramey and F. A. Campbell, "Poverty, Early Childhood Education, and Academic Competence: The Abecedarian Experiment," in *Children Reared in Poverty*, ed. A. Huston (New York: Cambridge University Press, 1991), 190–221.
46. C. Ramey and S. Ramey, *Early Childhood Education: The Journey from Efficacy Research to Effective, Everyday Practice*. Paper presented at Summit on Early Childhood Cognitive Development, Boise, Idaho, June 10, 2002.
47. L. Masse and S. Barnett, *A Benefit-Cost Analysis of the Abecedarian Early Childhood Intervention* (New Brunswick, NJ: National Institute for Early Education Research, 2002). Retrieved October 5, 2005, from http://nieer.org/resources/research/AbecedarianStudy.pdf.
48. Ramey and Ramey, *Early Childhood Education*, p. 3.

Chapter Ten

1. D. Blum, "More Work, More Play," *Mother Jones*, 1999, *2*, p. 31.
2. M. S. Kilberg, Y. X. Pan, H. Chen, and V. Leung-Pineda, "Nutritional Control of Gene Expression: How Mammalian Cells Respond to Amino Acid Limitation," *Annual Review of Nutrition*, 2005, *25*, 59–85; J. Mahoney, H. Lord, and E. Carryl, "An Ecological Analysis of After-School Program Participation and the Development of Academic Performance and Motivational Attributes for Disadvantaged Children," *Child Development*, 2005, *76*(4), 811–825.
3. D. Campbell, *The Mozart Effect* (New York: Avon Books, 1997).
4. D. Goleman, *Emotional Intelligence* (New York: Bantam, 1995).
5. D. Zieker, E. Fehrenbach, J. Dietzsch, J. Fliegner, M. Waidmann, K. Nieselt, P. Gebicke-Haerter, R. Spanagel, P. Simon, A. M. Niess, and H. Northoff, "cDNA Microarray Analysis Reveals Novel Candidate Genes Expressed in Human Peripheral Blood Following Exhaustive Exercise," *Physiological Genomics*, 2005, *23*(3), 287–294.
6. E. Rossi, *The Psychobiology of Gene Expression* (New York: W. W. Norton, 2002).
7. E. Goldberg, *The Wisdom Paradox: How Your Mind Can Grow Stronger as Your Brain Grows Older* (New York: Gotham Press, 2005).
8. N. Andreasen, *The Creating Brain: The Neuroscience of Genius* (New York: Dana Press, 2005).
9. R. Kurzweil, *The Singularity Is Near: When Humans Transcend Biology* (New York: Viking Press, 2005).
10. P. Doskoch, "The Winning Edge," *Psychology Today*, 2005, *38*(6), 42–52.
11. M. Diamond and J. Hopson, *Magic Trees of the Mind* (New York: Penguin-Dutton, 1998), p. 5.

THE AUTHOR

Eric Jensen is a former teacher with a real love of learning. He has taught at all levels, from elementary through university, and is currently completing his Ph.D. degree in psychology. In 1981, Jensen cofounded Super-Camp, the nation's first and largest brain-compatible learning program, now with over fifty thousand graduates. He has since written *Teaching with the Brain in Mind, Brain-Based Learning, SuperTeaching, Arts with the Brain in Mind,* and twenty-one other books on learning and the brain. A leader in the brain-based movement, Jensen has made over sixty-five visits to neuroscience labs and interacts with countless neuroscientists. He's currently a member of the Society for Neuroscience and New York Academy of Sciences. He was the founder of the Learning Brain EXPO and has trained educators and trainers for twenty-five years worldwide in this field. He is deeply committed to making a positive, significant, lasting difference in the way we learn.

Currently, Jensen does conference speaking, staff development, and in-depth trainings. Go to www.jensenlearning.com, call (858) 642-0400, or e-mail diane@jlcbrain.com.

INDEX